Teaching Chinese as a Foreign Language

Theories and Applications

Edited by

Michael E. Everson and Yun Xiao

Cheng & Tsui Company

Boston

16 15 14 13 12 11 10 09 08   1 2 3 4 5 6 7 8 9 10

Published by
Cheng & Tsui Company, Inc.
25 West Street
Boston, MA 02111-1213 USA
Fax (617) 426-3669
www.cheng-tsui.com
"Bringing Asia to the World"™

Library of Congress Cataloging-in-Publication Data

Teaching Chinese as a foreign language : theories and applications / edited by Michael Everson and Yun Xiao.
    p. cm.
  ISBN 978-0-88727-668-2
  1. Chinese language—Textbooks for foreign speakers—English. I. Everson, Michael Erwin, 1947- II. Xiao, Yun. III. title.

  PL1129.E5T43 2008
  495.1'82421—dc22

                                                                    2008015274

Printed in the United States of America

Publisher's Note

The Cheng & Tsui Professional Development Series is designed to support teachers of Asian languages as they strive for excellence in the classroom. In this first volume of essays written specifically for teachers of Chinese in North America, we have collected essays written and edited by distinguished Chinese instructors in the Chinese teaching community. In depth and breadth, this book will serve as an excellent course textbook for teacher training and certification programs in Chinese. It is also recommended for all instructors of Chinese, whether they are new to the field or veteran teachers.

We are honored to have the opportunity to publish such a diverse collection of essays that not only brings together a broad range of expert opinion and class-tested experience to deal with the challenges facing Chinese instructors today, but also represents the future of a field that is at a crossroads. As Chinese language enrollments continue to rise in schools nationwide, teachers have an unprecedented opportunity to foster meaningful East-West cultural exchange. We salute teachers who step up to the task, and thank the editors of this volume for the opportunity to be involved in this project.

Most of the essays in this volume are written primarily in English, but teaching examples are given in Chinese characters (and pinyin) throughout, and Chinese text is occasionally used for longer passages when necessary to explain pedagogical principles for which exact English terms may not be available. Whether to use simplified or traditional characters was determined by the author of each essay. In most cases, the author chose to use simplified characters, although some authors provided both simplified and traditional characters. Occasionally, traditional characters alone are used, especially where the author(s) felt it was important to demonstrate the traditional forms for the purpose of teaching character writing.

We welcome readers' comments and suggestions concerning the publications in this series. Please contact series editors Michael E. Everson or Yun Xiao, in care of our Editorial Department (e-mail: **editor@cheng-tsui.com**).

To
Thomas N. Tegge
My High School Far Eastern History Teacher who Set the Compass

—Mike

To
My Mother
Who Adamantly Insisted that I Should Be a Teacher

—Yun

Contents

Introduction

As China continues its rise on the world stage, demand for Chinese as a foreign language (CFL) is growing in the United States. Yet schools are facing an acute shortage of trained teachers that threatens to impede the creation and establishment of strong Chinese language programs. The consequences of this shortage were highlighted in a 2004 College Board survey, which found that 2,400 American high schools were interested in offering the AP® program in Chinese language and culture, but could not because of a lack of certified Chinese teachers.[1]

A discipline that has achieved modest success in American education, Chinese language study has traditionally been confined to select university programs, Chinatowns, or weekend Chinese community heritage schools. In fact, data from the 2005 Asia Society Report show that the Chinese enrollment in community schools is six times that of mainstream American schools (i.e.,150,000 students for the former and 24,000 for the latter in 2003). Recent studies on Chinese as a heritage language reveal, however, that the Chinese community schools are not as yet full-fledged educational entities, but transient learning centers between home and mainstream schools where learners typically start Chinese learning at a very young age, but drop out once they begin kindergarten or grade school.[2]

With the increasing need to institute longer sequences of language instruction starting in kindergarten and continuing through college, the Chinese language field is now faced with the challenge of training teachers at all levels for a language that has been represented only marginally in American education and only fleetingly in the collective imagination of the American people. With recent initiatives such as Chinese AP programs, Chinese Flagship Programs, and the U.S. government's Startalk program designed to increase the number of Chinese language high school programs as well as Chinese language teacher development initiatives, the dream of making Chinese language programs available to American students at a variety of levels in every state of the union is gaining momentum among students, educators,

---

[1] See the Asia Society report "Expanding Chinese Language Capacity in the United States," by Vivien Stewart and Shuhan Wang, 2005, available at http://www.internationaled.org/expandingchinese.htm.
[2] See Xiao, Yun. 2008. Home literacy environment in Chinese as a heritage language. In Weiyun He and Yun Xiao (Eds.). *Chinese as a Heritage Language: Fostering Rooted World Citizenry* (2008), Honolulu, HI: University of Hawaii, National Foreign Language Resource Center, pp. 151–166.

policymakers, and parents. Yet, for such an ambitious enterprise to succeed, it will be crucial that programs at all levels be staffed with highly qualified teachers.

Who May Become a Chinese Language Teacher in the United States?

Needless to say, the task of finding and training qualified teachers is not an easy one. First, many of the candidates who are coming forward to answer the call for more teachers are native speakers of Chinese who may not necessarily have formal training in teaching their own language, and who may instead have professional qualifications in disciplines other than language teaching. Consequently, they do not have the needed subject matter expertise, or an understanding of the common themes and trends that join all foreign language teachers, regardless of the languages they teach. In short, they are not participants in the ongoing conversation that unites members of the foreign language profession, nor are they participants in the specialized conversation that goes on regularly between teachers of Chinese. Secondly, many of these native speakers are coming from Chinese-speaking countries that have educational systems which differ greatly from that of America, thus creating a wide disparity as to how education is viewed, valued, and carried out. Without an understanding of one's teaching context, environment, and particular school culture, Chinese language programs run the risk of failing because they are not matched to the goals, needs, and desires of a particular setting, or because they have not taken into account the makeup of the various students whom they are trying to serve. Thirdly, some of the teacher candidates come from a group that has been important in filling the ranks of teachers in the more commonly taught languages. As non-native speakers of Chinese, they typically major in Chinese as a foreign language in American universities and, upon their graduation, join in the Chinese teaching profession without going through formal Chinese teacher training. Because of the special characteristics of the Chinese language that make it so different from English and from the leading foreign languages typically taught in American schools, these students are challenged in attaining the requisite amount of Chinese proficiency for actually teaching the language. They have, however, advantages over Chinese native speakers in that they have been enculturated from a very early age in the U.S. school system, and also have fresh memories of the challenges of learning Chinese as a foreign language. Lastly, we have a source of prospective teachers that has long been overlooked — heritage language learners, or those who have learned Chinese while growing up in a Chinese family. These learners have traditionally "not fit" into Chinese language programs designed to educate students who are starting their study of the language from square one, and have presented unique pedagogical challenges for programs that wish to serve them, despite the diverse proficiency profiles that characterize them in both speaking and reading the Chinese language.

How This Book Addresses the Needs of CFL Teachers

Given this widely diverse profile of students who wish to become Chinese language teachers, a volume dealing with teacher development that will help them in their quest towards teacher competence and professionalization is sorely needed. This volume, then, is designed to serve as a resource guide for teachers-in-development who will confront a host of important issues in their everyday teaching, and can be used for both mentors and students involved in both pre-service and in-service teacher education programs. Although its pages contain a variety of hands-on suggestions and recommendations for the practicing teacher, its purpose is not only to be a pedagogical guide, but also a volume that introduces foundational issues and theories of foreign language acquisition that all language educators will encounter on a daily basis. As well, the volume will discuss topics that unite all foreign language teachers, while also probing those issues that are specific to the teaching of Chinese. The book is state-of-the-art in terms of the research that is discussed, and every one of the authors has been a leader in the creation, management, teaching, and/or directing of Chinese language programs or Chinese language teacher development programs.

About the Essays in This Volume

Michael Everson's piece, **The Importance of Standards**, begins the volume and our first section exploring the context of Chinese. It is presented here because the standards represent a general consensus among a variety of stakeholders to articulate a common educational framework in foreign language education, regardless of the foreign language that is being taught. His article traces some of the theoretical and methodological foundations that have led to the creation of the national standards. Since some of the teacher candidates who will be using this volume have learned English or other foreign languages through antiquated methodologies, Everson's essay provides an important foundation as it requires new teachers to look at language learning and teaching through a different lens. His article also discusses how the standards will change the way we look at assessment, and sets the stage for other articles in this volume that will also talk about the standards from different perspectives.

While at first blush, the study of Chinese always seems to be about mastering tones in speech or producing characters with the proper stroke order, Matthew Christensen's article on **Bringing Culture into the Chinese Language Classroom** through Contextualized Performance helps us to understand that our ultimate goal in using Chinese is to get things done in culturally appropriate ways. How this is to be achieved is no mean feat, and his article puts forth solid recommendations for how the social and cultural demands of communication can be presented to students so as to enhance their cultural "performance" through the use of language. Cynthia Ning's article, **Focusing on the Learner in the Chinese Language Classroom,** continues this thread, as her experience in teacher development has indicated that while we can explain the principles of proficiency-based Chinese language instruction to students in our teacher development courses, actually developing and conducting proficiency-based language classes can be extremely difficult for new teachers, especially if their own language learning experience was highly teacher-centered and grammatically-based. Explaining and illustrating, then, what communicative language learning "looks like" will go far to help prospective teachers take the logical next step to making their own lessons more communicative in nature. The last chapter in this section, **AP® Chinese Language and Culture** by T. Richard Chi details the recent creation of the Advanced Placement (AP) Chinese course and examination, newly administered in 2006 and 2007, respectively. This extremely comprehensive article presents an ambitious and exciting view into the future of what Chinese language teaching and learning might hold, and what is possible when high school students are given the opportunity to take a Chinese course equivalent to a fourth-semester college course. His article provides initial data taken from the first administration of the course that holds out promise for the success of this program, while pointing out challenges that need to be addressed if this program is to be implemented on a wider scale.

Section 2 gets to the heart of classroom instruction by presenting issues of both a theoretical and practical nature that are always discussed by Chinese language teachers. Michael Everson begins this section with a chapter on the **Literacy Development in Chinese as a Foreign Language**, and organizes his chapter with an "issues" approach, boiling down the topic of literacy into important theoretical principles that teachers need to understand, while giving general guidance for classroom practice based upon these issues. His ideas are especially relevant for dealing with beginning learners of Chinese who are struggling to adjust to a totally different orthographic system, and he preaches caution in how we teach our beginners to read so as not to overwhelm and de-motivate them in our beginning courses. In the next chapter on **Teaching Chinese Orthography and Discourse**, Yun Xiao continues the discussion of how Chinese characters should be taught, giving important guidance as to how they are structured, and how a principled pedagogy must be developed if our learners are to understand this complex orthographic system. She also writes about the importance of teaching our learners how Chinese speakers build and use discourse to convey more complex and varied meaning when they speak and write. All too often, Chinese teachers wonder why their students are not building fluency and discourse competence, when in fact it is because they are not being taught how. As foreign language educators strive to find ways to take learners to the advanced levels of spoken and written proficiency, this chapter provides solid guidance on the steps teachers need to take to facilitate this process.

Continuing in this section, Xiaohong Wen tackles the topic of **Teaching Listening and Speaking.** Drawing from cognitive models that detail the components of listening comprehension and speaking proficiency, she defines these two skills while also showing how they relate to one another. As the integration of these two skills is critical for comprehension to take place, her chapter details both strategies and activities for the classroom practitioner to include in their pedagogical repertoire. This section concludes with a chapter on the use of **Technology in Chinese Language Learning** by Tianwei Xie and Tao-chung Yao. It is no secret that the Chinese language poses its own set of technological challenges — tone marks, presentation of characters in two different forms (i.e., simplified and traditional), and romanization systems such as *pinyin* and *zhuyinfuhao*, and word processing capability are just a few of the basic capabilities technology has given that were just coming into existence twenty years ago. This chapter will be extremely valuable to classroom practitioners, who will find it an endless resource for all aspects of Chinese educational technology, from word processing to web pages, from podcasts to blogs.

Our last section looks at issues of the American classroom that are fundamental for prospective teachers to gain a strategic view of Chinese language education in general with all the complexities and aspirations it entails. Yun Xiao begins this section with her chapter on Teaching Chinese as a Heritage Language, long viewed as curricular oddities in the sense that they came to beginning Chinese classes with different degrees of proficiency in the various language skills, often in dialects different from standard Mandarin. As the profession has begun to view heritage learners as more of a resource and less of a placement nuisance, serious efforts have been put forth in the area of pedagogy, materials development, and thoughtful class placement so as to nurture the language development of these students. This article will be valuable for all teachers who find that their classes are populated more and more by heritage learners. Madeline Spring also deals with the topic of heritage learners in her essay on **Linking Curriculum, Assessment, and Professional Development**, as she details how the K–16 Chinese Pipeline Program in the Portland, OR, schools is attempting to offer Chinese language starting in Kindergarten so that students will be eventually able to enter colleges at a proficiency level high enough to take content courses in Chinese. Perhaps the most ambitious and coordinated Chinese language effort in the United States, this program is one of the Flagship language initiatives, dedicated to bringing language students in a variety of languages to the superior level of language proficiency. As such, its curriculum is based on a plan that totally rethinks language learning across a child's entire educational career and, as such, represents a vision of language learning that is revolutionary in its conception. Our last chapter, **Understanding the Culture of American Schools, and Managing the Successful Chinese Language Classroom** by Leslie Schrier, completes and grounds the volume by explaining the complexities of the American educational system, a system that differs from Chinese education in very fundamental ways. We hope that by understanding these differences, prospective teachers not well versed in the American system will avoid the problems and pitfalls that can potentially bring well intentioned Chinese programs to termination because they have not been able to acclimate to the educational context in which they find themselves. The chapter concludes with a much needed discussion dealing with classroom management, a topic that even American teachers feel they could have used more of in their teacher education programs as they navigate their way through their beginning careers in K–12 American education.

As with any work of this scope, there are many people deserving of thanks for helping to get this volume into the hands of the many stakeholders committed to fostering Chinese language teacher development. We would first like to thank the contributors, who shared our vision of the importance of this volume, and found time in their busy schedules to write compelling and comprehensive articles. We also wish to thank Jill Cheng of Cheng & Tsui Company for her enthusiastic support for this project from its inception, and Kristen Wanner, also of Cheng & Tsui, for her unflagging and thorough editorial support to help make this the book that we wanted it to become.

Michael E. Everson, Iowa City, Iowa

Yun Xiao, Smithfield, Rhode Island

Section 1

Teaching Chinese in Context

Chapter 1

The Importance of Standards

Michael E. Everson

The University of Iowa

Teachers of Chinese always seem to remark that when they enter a new teaching assignment, they are not only *a* Chinese teacher, but usually the *only* Chinese teacher. What this means is that they have no help or mentoring from a senior Chinese teacher and are often responsible not only for teaching Chinese, but also for designing the entire Chinese curriculum in their school. Because they are often starting from scratch, they must put together a curriculum that flows seamlessly between different levels within the school, and between elementary, middle, high school, and even university levels. Often working in isolation, teachers try their best to establish quality programs, but the fact of the matter is that traditionally, there have been few standards or guidelines in place to help teachers achieve this articulation across different levels of the curriculum, a phenomenon documented by teachers of less commonly taught languages[1] in general. (Schrier and Everson 2000). Such has been the fate of Chinese programs, due largely to the fact that historically, they have not been mainstreamed into the American foreign language setting. Given this marginal presence, critical elements such as supporting infrastructure, a rich variety of materials and textbooks, abundant opportunities and settings for teacher preparation and certification, and longstanding experience in curriculum development have not been hallmarks of less commonly taught languages.

---

[1]Walton (1992) has stated that from the viewpoint of U.S. foreign language education, less commonly taught languages can be defined as any language except Spanish, German, and French, though he has put these other languages into three sub-groups: 1) less commonly taught European languages such as Russian, Italian, Portuguese, and Swedish; 2) higher-enrollment non-Indo-European languages, such as Arabic, Chinese, and Japanese; and 3) lower-enrollment non-Indo-European languages such as Burmese, Indonesian, and Swahili.

Much of this state of affairs went undetected until a survey (Moore, Walton, and Lambert 1992) conducted among high schools teaching Chinese revealed the extent of this problem. Published by the National Foreign Language Center in 1992, the survey examined the teaching of Chinese in a select sample of high school programs sponsored by the Geraldine Dodge Foundation. In the larger landscape of foreign language education, this study might be considered to be relatively insignificant, as it dealt with programs from only 55 high schools across the country — indeed, it would be surprising if your colleagues teaching Spanish, French, or German, or even many of your colleagues teaching Chinese, had ever heard about this survey. Yet, in terms of what it tells us about the lack of consistency and standardization among Chinese language programs in high schools nationwide, it is one of the most significant documents to have ever been published in our field. Its executive summary states:

> There is a lack of consensus among teachers on what the ideal curriculum should be; on which skills should be emphasized; on the choice of phonetic transcription systems; on the type and number of characters that students should learn; on the selection and timing of specific linguistic patterns to be taught; and on the proper emphasis on and way of teaching Chinese culture. (p. 119)

Although it would be natural to assign blame for this state of affairs on teachers' lack of experience in teaching Chinese at the high school level, or to the almost nonexistent teacher training that was carried out at this time, this lack of standardization was not atypical of many foreign language teaching endeavors in the United States until recently, though was especially noticeable in Chinese. This chapter will present a brief history of how a movement for standards in American education came about, and how the foreign language community seized an opportunity to become part of the mainstream by adopting standards-based instruction. To help teachers understand and apply foreign language standards in their day-to-day teaching, this paper summarizes both the content standards and proficiency guidelines as defined by the American Council on the Teaching of Foreign Languages (ACTFL). Most importantly, it explains each of the foreign language content standards, and offers suggestions and examples of how you might wish to incorporate standards-based instruction into your Chinese language classroom.

Why Do We Do the Things We Do in Language Classes?

Teacher education research has established that *how we were taught* is one of the primary determinants in *how we teach*. That is, all of the time we have personally spent in classrooms has a significant effect on the way we go about the task of teaching students. In fact, Lortie (1975) has said that the beginning teacher has already completed a "13,000-hour apprenticeship of observation" before entering a teacher education program. It is no small wonder that we enter the teaching profession with ingrained ideas about how we should go about doing our job. This has been especially true in foreign language teaching, where various methods have taken center stage as being "the right" way to teach a foreign language, causing critics to portray foreign language educators as too eager to jump on the latest methodological "bandwagon" (see Smith 2000). Yet, as the theories underpinning methodologies have been accepted or discredited by foreign language researchers, so too have methodologies risen or fallen out of favor with educators. Such has been the case with audiolingualism, a method that has persisted in foreign language classrooms to this day.

Audiolingualism: "Please Repeat Your Half of the Dialogue"

Audiolingualism as a methodology resulted from a "perfect" marriage between linguistics, psychology, and education after World War II due to the success that was attained in teaching languages to U.S. servicemen through intensive methods that concentrated on developing proficiency in the spoken language. The theory of language learning used to support the audiolingual method was behaviorism, which held that one's first language (L1) was learned just as any other behavior was learned, through habit formation shaped by patterns of stimulus and response. Given that this theory was thought to explain L1 acquisition, theorists believed that it also explained second language (L2) acquisition, and classroom pedagogy was arranged accordingly. That is, dialogues and drills became the staple of the audio-lingual classroom, with repetition, pattern practice, memorization, and correct pronunciation not only being stressed, but also reinforced, through relentless error correction. Errors, it was thought, indicated "interference" from the L1, which had to be dealt with through extensive correction to break these "bad habits." With the advent and expansion of technology in the form of the language laboratory, constant pattern practice could be done repetitively with the help of tape recorders. As the foundation of this method was a very teacher-centered approach to oral language teaching, language skills were "taught in the order of listening, speaking, reading, and writing" (Richards and Rodgers 1986, p. 53).

The audiolingual method would run its course during the 1960s, as students found the method boring and ineffective. But more importantly, the very foundation of the audiolingual method was shaken when Noam Chomsky[2] (1959)

---

[2]Chomsky's contributions to the development of L1 and, by extension, L2 acquisition theories are immeasurable. While an explanation of his many theories are beyond the scope of this chapter, it should be noted that his early work attacked the behaviorist theory of language development, stating

launched a scathing attack against behaviorism as a theory that could comprehensively account for language behavior, eventually leaving foreign language educators to question whether audiolingualism could continue as a viable and effective method for classroom teaching. Applied linguists and foreign language educators were now forced to seek new theories about how students learn a foreign language.

Communicative Competence

Although Chomsky's description of competence would revolutionize how theorists would view L1 and eventually L2 acquisition, his description of competence focused on the system that enables native speakers to form grammatically correct utterances. Hymes (1972) would broaden Chomsky's idea by introducing the term "communicative competence," or the knowledge necessary to use language for communication that is culturally, socially, and contextually appropriate. These ideas expanded the theory of language knowledge and use, and led Canale and Swain (1980) to develop a highly influential model which posited that communicative competence is composed of 1) grammatical competence, such as mastery of pronunciation, grammatical structure, word formation, and other areas having to do with the linguistic code of the language; 2) sociolinguistic competence, or how well the language can be used or understood within a variety of social and cultural contexts and over a variety of communicative functions; 3) discourse competence, or the ability of the language user to attain cohesion and coherence in their language use, often through the use of cohesive structures that facilitate a sense of coherence in the discourse; and 4) strategic competence, or the ability to use verbal and non-verbal strategies to compensate for deficiencies in other areas of language use, or to help repair and salvage breakdowns in overall communication. While more traditional theories of language learning that emphasized the importance of grammatical knowledge were still retained in this model, the highlighting of sociolinguistic competence that emphasized the role of speech acts, language functions, the role of speaker and listener, and a host of other variables in language communication gave grist to educators who wanted to explore language as a communicative activity, as well as to learners who wished to communicate meaningfully across cultures. Thus came about a new philosophy to replace the reliance

---

that a theory that viewed language in terms of habit formation did not account for a child's ability to utter innovative and new sentences in a relatively short period of time. His theory of "universal grammar," or innate linguistic knowledge that humans possess to facilitate language development, has also been influential in providing theoretical guidance for researchers interested in exploring whether L1 and L2 acquisition are similar processes. For an excellent discussion of Chomsky's overall influence on L1 and L2 acquisition, see Stern (1983); for an introduction to L1 and L2 acquisition, see Lightbown & Spada (2006).

on individual methods, a philosophy that was known broadly as communicative language teaching.

Communicative Language Teaching

Richards and Rodgers (1986) state that a somewhat eclectic theoretical base underlies communicative language teaching, namely, that it views language

1. as a system for expressing meaning;
2. as a system of interaction and communication;
3. as having a structure that reflects its functional and communicative uses; and
4. as having units that are not merely its grammatical and structural features, but also categories of functional and communicative meaning as exemplified in discourse. (p. 71)

Lightbown and Spada (2006) describe communicative language teaching as being "... based on the premise that successful language learning involves not only a knowledge of the structures and forms of a language, but also the functions and purposes that a language serves in different communicative settings" (p. 196), thus emphasizing the importance of going after meaning in context, and not just grammatical forms in isolation.

As the field of foreign language education struggled with the broadening of its theoretical boundaries to be more inclusive of communication and meaning in language use, President Carter's Commission on Foreign Language and International Studies 1979 report, *Strength Through Wisdom*, decried the nation's incompetence in foreign languages and its deleterious effects on America's standing in the world. One of the several proposals put forward for improving foreign language education was a set of descriptors that could assess language competence, a "common yardstick" that would be based on real-life language use (Watzke 2003). Published first in 1982 by the American Council on the Teaching of Foreign Languages (ACTFL) with subsequent revisions, the *ACTFL Proficiency Guidelines* (1982, 1986) supplied descriptions of appropriate language use from the Novice to Superior levels for the skills of speaking, listening, reading, and writing. The Proficiency Guidelines were put together with the Oral Proficiency Interview (OPI), first used by agencies in United States government language training circles and subsequently developed by ACTFL as a primary assessment for assigning proficiency scores to students. Malone (2003) defines the ACTFL OPI as "... a face-to-face or telephonic interview between a trained interviewer and an examinee that is designed to elicit a profile of the examinee's oral proficiency through a sustained performance" (p. 491). Although the interview has been a widely used measure for assessing oral proficiency, it has triggered a decade of debate over the pros and cons of this method for measuring proficiency.[3]

Standards for Foreign Language Learning

Although foreign language was originally not one of the subject areas designated as needing standards to improve K–12 education for all students as put forth by *America 2000: An Education Strategy* (1991), ACTFL and other foreign language organizations aggressively lobbied for and received funding to develop foreign language standards. In this way, foreign language stakeholders demanded that foreign language be viewed as worthy as any of the other core subject areas in the school curriculum, thus raising the stakes of foreign language as not only an important subject in school, but also one with intrinsic value for helping students grow intellectually in an interdisciplinary way. That is, the design of the standards is intent on achieving a "curricular weave" whereby content (language systems, cultural knowledge, and content from other school disciplines), processes (communication and learning strategies, critical thinking skills), and technology (for communication, language materials, and instructional delivery) undergird the standards and their goals (Phillips 1999). At the heart of the foreign language standards are the content standards, or what students should know and be able to do in the foreign language. In addition to the language-specific content standards themselves (cited below), ACTFL also supplies sample progress indicators that reflect student progress for meeting the standards for Grades 4, 8, and 12. (ACTFL Performance Guidelines for K–12 Learners, 1998).

What Should Students Know? Content Standards

COMMUNICATION GOAL 1: COMMUNICATE IN CHINESE

Standard 1.1: Students engage in conversations, provide and obtain information, express feelings and emotions, and exchange opinions in Chinese.

Standard 1.2: Students understand and interpret written and spoken language on a variety of topics in Chinese.

Standard 1.3: Students present information, concepts, and ideas to an audience of listeners or readers on a variety of topics.

Given the stress on communication that is put forward in communicative language teaching, as well as the goal of proficiency that is tested through the OPI,

---

[3]Although beyond the scope of this chapter, the reliability and validity of the OPI and the ACTFL Guidelines have been called into question. For a concise critique of these issues, as well as more information concerning the OPI, see a special issue of Foreign Language Annals (2003, No. 4), devoted exclusively to this topic.

it should come as no surprise that communication is the first standard. Yet, what is new is the idea of "modes" of communication built into the standards to stress the interpersonal, interpretive, and presentational dimensions of communication. For example, Standard 1.1 above addresses interactive, interpersonal communication among individuals, where clarification, questioning, and negotiation of meaning are possible. Whether this takes the form of actual spoken conversation, or a written chat room exchange, it involves our students learning the varied and complex patterns that go into appropriate interpersonal communication with others. To work towards this standard, a teacher might set up a program with other students studying Chinese across the country, and set up an online chat room where new friendships could be established through the medium of Chinese, with structured assignments whereby students could find out information about one another. Another example of how to achieve the interpersonal communication standard would be for the teacher to invite native speakers into the class who would be interviewed by student "journalists" writing articles for the classroom Chinese newspaper.

Yet, sometimes communication is only one-way, or interpretive, as when one reads the content of a book or novel, listens to a Shanghai weather report on the radio, or views a documentary dealing with the Great Wall of China. Standard 1.2 covers the interpretive mode. To achieve this standard, teachers can use authentic listening and reading materials with tasks that are developmentally appropriate for their students. For instance, students can be given Chinese menus and asked to pick out the dishes that contain pork, beef, or chicken, or indicate the sections of the menu having to do with rice or noodle dishes. They can also be given short segments of listening or reading passages that are highly formatted and predictable in their content, discourse, and vocabulary, such as weather reports, and asked to listen or scan the written text for key words used in weather reports such as sky conditions and temperatures. A student could "adopt a city" in China and each day search the net and be in charge of finding out its weather, then report it to the teacher and the class.

There are also times when we communicate either through writing or through oral language where there are no opportunities for immediate feedback, as when we write a letter or deliver an oral report in class. This presentational mode of communication is reflected in Standard 1.3. Having our students perform these tasks in Chinese is a formidable undertaking. Yet, even beginning-level students can make reports to their class to meet this standard. Early on in their first-year Chinese class, students can, for example, give short reports to their classmates about the times of the day they perform routine activities, such as getting up, coming to school, and what time they attend certain classes. Teachers can also begin having speech competitions in Chinese among their own students, or widen the competition to include other students studying Chinese at neighboring schools. This not only helps the students develop presentational skills, but also gives them important practice in speaking before larger groups of people. Teachers can also help students to develop their letter writing or emailing skills by starting Chinese pen pal programs to introduce their students to others who are studying Chinese, or to students in the Chinese speaking world who wish to make friends with students in America via the internet and email. With online resources and Chinese word-processing capabilities available for students in our schools (see Yao and Xie, this volume), these types of activities have become more possible for our students, and should be exploited to achieve the standards.

CULTURES GOAL 2: GAIN KNOWLEDGE AND UNDERSTANDING OF THE CULTURES OF THE CHINESE-SPEAKING WORLD

Standard 2.1: Students demonstrate an understanding of the relationship between the practices and perspectives of the cultures of the Chinese-speaking world.

Standard 2.2: Students demonstrate an understanding of the relationship between the products and perspectives of the cultures of the Chinese-speaking world.

It has long been recognized that culture is part and parcel of what we do as foreign language teachers, with foreign language teachers knowing intuitively that culture permeates all aspects of language teaching. Yet, we have been less successful as a profession in operationalizing the teaching of culture in our classrooms, often resorting to the teaching of what is known as "achievement culture" or "Big C" culture — a culture's achievements in such fields as architecture, literature, and history. The goal of the culture standard is to establish a framework which enables students to understand the perspectives of Chinese speakers on their cultural practices and cultural products. Another way for teachers to look at the "3 P's" of perspectives, practices, and products, is to help students understand that there is a relationship between what people create (products) and what they think (perspectives); and that there is a relationship between what people do (practices) and what they think (perspectives). When viewed in this light, students will learn that a country's culture must be investigated if it is to be appreciated and enjoyed. Unfortunately, cultural practices and products, while seen every day, are often minimalized or glossed over in the classroom, thus becoming missed opportunities for "teachable moments."

As an example of a way to meet the culture standard, a teacher could develop an interesting unit about how Chinese people respond to praise. Americans, of course, respond to praise and complements by saying "thank you." This, however, is not what Chinese people say. Ross and Ma (2006) state that ". . . Chinese people do not say 謝謝 / 谢谢 (xièxie) 'thank you' in response to a personal compliment of any kind" (p. 364.) In many Chinese classrooms, the lesson would end right here, because the teacher has successfully taught the students about a Chinese cultural PRACTICE that differs from the American practice of receiving praise. But think how much more the students will appreciate this lesson when it is taught with a Chinese PERSPECTIVE about receiving praise. Ross and Ma (2006) continue by saying "In Chinese culture, accepting a personal compliment can be interpreted as showing conceit. Thus, it is customary in China for people to reject rather than to accept compliments" (p. 364). Now we have a PERSPECTIVE about why the actual language (PRACTICE) differs between the two cultures, leading the lesson naturally into the interesting ways Chinese people will respond to praise:

哪里, 哪里 / 哪里, 哪里	"Where, where?"
哪兒的話 / 哪儿的话	"What kind of talk is that?"
沒甚麼 / 沒什么	"It's nothing."
真的嗎 / 真的吗	"Really?"
不好，不好 / 不好，不好	"Not good, not good."

Cultural products are more often apparent to us as educators than cultural practices are, especially when we teach our students about the invention of the compass or gunpowder, and how these inventions changed the course of history. A teacher might consider a lesson on the famous inventions that came out of China. Students would first be introduced to the word for "compass" in Chinese, which is 指南針 / 指南针 or quite literally, "a needle which points south." Students then could be given the task of doing a short research project, in which they locate pictures on the Internet of early compasses in China. They would then learn that the Chinese had developed the compass as early as the third century B.C., using lodestones (composed of iron oxide) which would align themselves north and south. Students would then find pictures of early compasses which looked more like spoons placed on top of square plates for indicating direction. In this example, the compass is a PRODUCT that opens up a PERSPECTIVE for students, as they learn that the Chinese have been curious about science for thousands of years, and that they were among the first civilizations in history to explore and understand the magnetic fields of the earth.

CONNECTIONS GOAL 3: CONNECT WITH OTHER DISCIPLINES AND ACQUIRE INFORMATION

Standard 3.1: Students reinforce and further their knowledge of other disciplines through the study of Chinese.

Standard 3.2: Students acquire information and recognize the distinctive viewpoints that are only available through the Chinese language and culture.

While many teachers are familiar with the idea of inter-disciplinary education whereby courses in related areas are taken to enrich the study of one's primary field of study, this standard not only applauds inter-disciplinary education, but demands it. Learning a foreign language like Chinese, then, is not only considered a discipline in itself, but an opportunity to learn about other subject areas through the medium of Chinese language study. Elementary school students might, for instance, learn the names of the planets in Chinese while studying a unit on the solar system in science class. As the students' proficiency in Chinese develops, they might read about some of the earlier theories of the solar system as put forth by Chinese astronomers that can only be obtained through Chinese sources. As well, high school teachers could take the teaching of the invention of the compass (see above) even further, and ask the students to find out how the compass had "traveled" to other countries so as to be used by other civilizations, or if there were claims by others that they, and not the Chinese, were the inventors of the compass. Advanced learners could be introduced to more complex texts that explain the invention of the compass. Chinese, then, becomes not only a discipline in itself, but a tool with which to explore other disciplines.

COMPARISONS GOAL 4: DEVELOP INSIGHT INTO THE NATURE OF LANGUAGES AND CULTURES

Standard 4.1: Students demonstrate understanding of the nature of language through comparisons of the Chinese language and their own.

Standard 4.2: Students demonstrate understanding of the concept of culture through comparisons of Chinese culture and their own.

A student's first language and home culture are his anchor, a place of reference from which he can grow and develop outwardly into a citizen of the world. With this in mind, it is important that teachers encourage and help students begin to explore their home culture and language by comparing them to those of the Chinese. This is particularly fertile ground for classroom instruction as students begin to see that the language and culture of China are vastly different from their own. As an example, a teacher might design a unit that specifically compares the meaning of New Year's celebrations for Americans and Chinese, and compare and contrast some of the enduring symbols that accompany this event and its accompanying celebrations. New Year's celebrations in America, for instance, are held both on New Year's Eve and New Year's Day, with parties of friends and families staying up until the stroke of midnight on New Year's Eve, counting down the final seconds until the New Year arrives, often while watching the countdown from Times Square in New York City where partygoers gather in often freezing temperatures. Fireworks, traditional toasting of the New Year with glasses filled with champagne, and the making of New Year's resolutions in an attempt to improve the quality of one's life, are all enduring symbols for Americans moving into the New Year. In contrast, the Lunar New Year is more of a major celebration in the Chinese world, with festivities spreading over a period of approximately two weeks, from the first day of the first lunar month on the Chinese calendar to the fifteenth day. Consequently, the time of Chinese New Year is different every year, but usually falls between late January and mid-February. Each New Year is presided over by one of the twelve animals of the zodiac, and is celebrated by activities centering around the family, such as visits and the making and sharing of traditional Chinese dumplings (餃子 / 饺子). Students would learn that red is the color most often associated with the New Year, and is seen traditionally in clothing that people wear, and is the color of the small envelopes (紅包 / 红包) given to children and friends containing money. As the culture standards compel us to look at Chinese culture from the Chinese perspective and investigate products and practices from the Chinese viewpoint, this comparison standard ensures that students are constantly comparing practices and products from their own perspective as well. In this way, students gain an understanding of how people of different cultures view their place in the world.

COMMUNITIES GOAL 5: PARTICIPATE IN MULTILINGUAL COMMUNITIES AT HOME AND AROUND THE WORLD

Standard 5.1: Students use the Chinese language both within and beyond the school setting.

Standard 5.2: Students show evidence of becoming life-long learners by using Chinese for personal enjoyment and enrichment.

Is Chinese something to learn as a subject in school, something to be restricted to the classroom? Is Chinese something to be studied as an academic subject to gain credits, then pushed to the background as language requirements are satisfied and final grades received? The communities standard replies to these questions with a resounding "no," and states that it is our responsibility to see that students begin to move outside the classroom and experience Chinese language and culture within the Chinese speaking communities that reside in their proximity, or thousands of miles away when experienced virtually through technology. This is extremely important to address the issue of Chinese heritage language maintenance where strong ties to the ethnic community can be fostered through use of the heritage language. Many larger cities are fortunate to have vibrant and bustling Chinese communities, while other smaller communities may have Chinese organizations, churches, or weekend schools that serve them. This standard encourages teachers to make every effort to link their students with activities that are ongoing in Chinese communities so as to reinforce language and cultural learning, thus giving students a view of the Chinese language as a living, breathing communicative entity, instead of its being viewed exclusively as an academic subject.

As an example, teachers could develop an ongoing project whereby students could begin to document the history and culture of nearby Chinese speaking communities. If there is no Chinese speaking community nearby, the project could be done "virtually" with students exploring a Chinatown of the largest city nearest to them. I say "ongoing project" because all too often, projects are done on a "one shot" basis, and only give students a very brief introduction to a topic before moving on. With this project, the Chinese community nearby would be used as a sustained resource throughout the year from which the students could learn more about the lives of Chinese-Americans as they maintain their ethnic heritage. Teachers, for example, could arrange visits to these communities during holidays, thus exposing students to the observance of various holidays as celebrated by members of ethnic Chinese communities. At the same time, students could use the Internet or other reference sources to compare and contrast the local observance of these holidays with that of Chinese communities across the world. In order to show how Chinese communities in their local area try to preserve the Chinese language among their members, students could visit "Saturday schools," and make friends with Chinese students their own age who are learning Chinese in these special schools designed to make sure that students maintain their ethnic linguistic heritage. Cultural products such as the community's newspapers could be used in class and contrasted with newspapers used in China, Taiwan, Hong Kong, or Singapore in terms of visual layout and the types of stories that are covered. Students could also chronicle the history of the specific community through websites and visits with local historians.

As we try to instill and regulate the standard of community into our curriculum, it is important to realize that Standard 5.2 often gets lost in the shuffle of designing a program to develop proficient speakers of this challenging language. Standard 5.2 addresses a "bottom line," as it not only serves as an objective of foreign language education, but of general education, as well — laying the groundwork so that our learners will enjoy and wish to study Chinese and Chinese culture in some way and in some form, for the rest of their lives. What is important to understand is that if your curriculum is designed in such a way as to address all of the foreign language standards, then the chances of achieving Standard 5.2 will be greater. This will be so not because you have taught Chinese as an academic subject, but as a living and breathing entity that lives on with a culture and history to support it. As a teacher, you will be able to help your students understand that they can be part of this adventure if they so choose, beginning their own personal journey that is only limited by their imaginations and their effort.

How Do We Know What They Know? — Performance Guidelines

The content standards have achieved a surprisingly wide consensus in defining what our foreign language students should know and be able to do. But defining *how well* students are able to demonstrate these competencies has been the missing part of the puzzle. To remedy this problem, the ACTFL Performance Guidelines for K–12 Learners (1998) were developed to take into account the age of the student, the different tracts of language instruction the student might experience in his/her K–12 career, and the type of language performance that can be expected from a student learning foreign language in a school environment. While it would be wonderful if a student could experience an uninterrupted K–12 experience, this is often not possible, so the guidelines describe language use by students who have experienced any one of the following curricular configurations: K–4; K–8; K–12; 5–8; 5–12; 9–10; 9–12.

Following the content standards for foreign language learning, the ACTFL Performance Guidelines for K–12 Learners (1996) "are organized to describe language use as it is characterized by modes of communication: Interpersonal, Interpretive and Presentational" (p. 4), viewing these modes as more appropriate for describing communication than the traditional "four skills." Language performance descriptors are grouped according to the following criteria for each of the three modes (when applicable):

- Comprehensibility: How well is the student understood?
- Comprehension: How well does the student understand?
- Language Control: How accurate is the student's language?
- Vocabulary: How extensive and applicable is the students' vocabulary?
- Cultural Awareness: How is the student's cultural knowledge reflected in language use?
- Communication Strategies: How does the student maintain communication?

Furthermore, the guidelines present benchmarks labeled Novice Range (K–4 or 5–8 or 9–10 programs), Intermediate Range (K–8 or 7–12 or 9–12 programs), or Pre-Advanced Range (K–12) and present descriptors for the criteria above for each of these benchmarks. A summary of the ACTFL Performance Guidelines for K–12 Learners and samples of performance descriptors are available online (http://www. actfl.org/i4a/pages/index.cfm?pageid=3327). Teachers may also purchase the full guidelines from the ACTFL online store (http://www.actfl.org/i4a/pages/index. cfm?pageid=3327).

Conclusion

Despite the fact that standards-based learning and assessment focuses on the learner and determining what s/he knows and what s/he can do with the language, Phillips (2006) states that "much of classroom assessment (in foreign language) continues to be decades-old testing in the form of quizzes and chapter tests with single written right answers," and that "teacher-made tests tend to be focused on text-covered grammatical items (p. 79)." If this is true of the more commonly taught languages of Spanish, French, and German — languages that have had the benefit of more opportunities to study standards-based curriculum and assessment — one wonders if the tests typically used by Chinese teachers are also of the type described above. This article began by quoting a survey which described the Chinese language high school teaching field mired in confusion, lack of standardization, and uncertainty about how and what to teach. It is hoped that through standards-based instruction, our field will move towards a more common vision of what we think is important for our learners to accomplish with the language.

Questions for Discussion

1. Review the section of this chapter that discusses the various methods and philosophies that have been used to support the teaching of foreign languages in America. Which of these methods/philosophies best describes the way you learned a foreign language?
2. Discuss the ways a standards-based Chinese language classroom will look different from a classroom conducted in the days of audiolingualism.
3. What do you think are the most significant challenges to implementing standards-based instruction? What can we as Chinese language educators do to overcome these challenges?
4. Do you think the implementation of standards-based instruction is something that is ultimately good for Chinese language learning over the long term? Explain your answer.

References

American Council on the Teaching of Foreign Languages. 1982. *ACTFL provisional proficiency guidelines.* Yonkers, NY: ACTFL.

———. 1986. ACTFL *Proficiency guidelines.* Yonkers, NY: ACTFL.

———. 1996. *Standards for foreign language learning in the 21ˢᵗ century.* http://www.actfl. org/i4a/pages/index.cfm?pageid=3324.

———. 1998. *ACTFL performance guidelines for K–12 learners.* Alexandria, VA: ACTFL.

Canale, M., and M. Swain. 1980. Theoretical bases of communicative approaches to second language teaching and testing. *Applied Linguistics* 1: 1–47.

Chomsky, N. 1959. A review of B. F. Skinner's "Verbal Behavior." *Language* 35 (1): 26–58.

Hymes, D. 1971. Competence and performance in linguistic theory. In *Language acquisition: Models and methods,* ed. R. Huxley and E. Ingram. London: Academic Press.

Lightbown, P. M. and N. Spada. 2006. *How languages are learned.* Oxford University Press.

Lortie, D. 1975. *Schoolteacher: A sociological study.* Chicago: University of Chicago Press.

Malone, M. E. 2003. Research on the oral proficiency interview: Analysis, synthesis, and future directions. *Foreign Language Annals* 36 (4): 491–497.

Moore, S. J., A. R. Walton, and R. D. Lambert. 1992. *Introducing Chinese into high schools: The Dodge Initiative.* Washington, D.C.: National Foreign Language Center.

Phillips, J. K. 1999. Introduction: Standards for world languages — On a firm foundation. In *Foreign language standards: Linking research, theories, and practices,* ed. J. K. Phillips, 1–14. Lincolnwood, IL: National Textbook Company.

Phillips, J. K. 2006. Assessment now and into the future. In *2005–2015: Realizing our vision of languages for all,* ed. Audrey L. Heining-Boynton, 75–103. Upper Saddle River, NJ: Pearson / Prentice Hall World Languages.

President's Commission on Foreign Language and International Studies. 1979. *Strength through wisdom: A critique of U.S. capability.* Washington, D.C.: U.S. Government Printing Office.

Richards, J. C. and T. S. Rodgers. 1986. *Approaches and methods in language teaching.* London and New York: Cambridge University Press.

Ross, C. and J. S. Ma. 2006. *Modern Mandarin Chinese grammar: A practical guide.* London and New York: Routledge.

Schrier, L. L. and M. E. Everson. 2000. From the margins to the new millennium: Preparing teachers of critical languages. In *Reflecting on the past to shape the future,* ed. D. W. Birckbichler and R. M. Terry, 125–161. Lincolnwood, IL: National Textbook Company.

Smith, A. N. 2000. Four decades of *bonjour:* The story of one teacher's practice. In *Reflecting on the past to shape the future,* ed. D. W. Birckbichler and R. M. Terry, 19–50. Lincolnwood, IL: National Textbook Company.

Stern, H. H. 1983. *Fundamentals concepts of language teaching.* Oxford University Press.

U.S. Department of Education. 1991. *America 2000: An education strategy.* Washington, D. C.: U.S. Department of Education.

Walton, A. R. 1992. *Expanding the vision of foreign language education: Enter the less commonly taught languages.* Washington, D.C.: The National Foreign Language Center.

Watzke, J. L. 2003. *Lasting change in foreign language education.* Westport, CT: Praeger.

Chapter 2

Bringing Culture into the Chinese Language Classroom through Contextualized Performance

Matthew B. Christensen

Brigham Young University

There is not much argument these days about the importance of culture in the foreign language curriculum. The vast majority of foreign language teachers will agree that gaining cultural skills is an important part of achieving competency in a foreign language. This is reflected in the relatively new Standards for Foreign Language Learning proposed by the American Council on the Teaching of Foreign Languages (www.actfl.org/i4a/pages/index.cfm?pageid=3324). These standards are an attempt to define the key concepts and topics that constitute learning foreign languages in the United States. The National Standards statement of philosophy acknowledges the importance of culture in the teaching of foreign languages. It states, "The United States must educate students who are linguistically and culturally equipped to communicate successfully in a pluralistic American society and abroad." These standards prompt a shift in thinking from traditional, structure-based approaches of learning to more holistic, communicative-based approaches. This chapter describes how to bring culture into the forefront of our classroom instruction.

Omaggio-Hadley (2001, p. 346–47) suggests that there are three reasons why foreign language teachers, though acknowledging the importance of culture, are reluctant to implement a meaningful cultural component in their teaching. These reasons are: one, most teachers feel that there is simply not enough time to bring culture into the language classroom; two, many teachers of foreign languages do not feel comfortable or familiar enough with cultural issues; and three, cultural issues deal with student attitudes and are therefore more difficult to quantify than linguistic knowledge.

Brooks succinctly identifies the problem of bringing culture into foreign language classrooms when he says,

> The desire for a cultural component to language acquisition has long been felt though only vaguely understood by the great majority of language teachers. There is little need to exhort them to teach culture; their willingness is already manifest. But there is a need to help them understand what meaning they should assign to the word *culture* and how it can become significant and fruitful in a sequence of years of language study. (1997, p. 13)

Though we all may agree that culture is important, when we talk about *culture* we may not all be thinking of the same thing. Culture is a loaded term that carries numerous meanings and connotations, some of which are more immediately applicable to foreign language studies than others. Defining culture helps us understand how culture is related to learning a foreign language and how we can best address the issue of culture in the classroom.

Defining Culture

When we hear the word "culture," most people automatically think of the great achievements of a civilization or people, the kinds of things that are usually taught in a "culture" class — things such as art, architecture, literature, religion, history, philosophy, and so on. This kind of culture is what Hammerly (1985, p. 145–46) calls *achievement culture* and *informational culture*. There is no doubt that having an understanding of achievement or informational culture will enhance the learning of students studying the language of a particular society. It is no wonder that we feel we do not have the time to bring these issues into our foreign language classrooms. These kinds of cultural issues are probably best suited to a dedicated course and/or extracurricular activities. However, achievement culture and information culture are not as readily applicable to learning a foreign language as what Hammerly calls *behavioral culture*. Behavioral culture has been defined as "the common daily practices and beliefs that define an individual and *dictate behavior* in a specific society" (Christensen and Warnick 2006, p. 13, italics added). Behavioral culture includes such common things as eating habits and manners, the manner of greet-ing, the protocols of traveling by public transportation, how to conduct a transaction at the bank, how to order a meal in a restaurant, how one treats siblings, parent-child relationships, teacher-student relationships, how emotions are displayed, and how gifts are exchanged. . . . It is the way people behave within their own group (in-group) and interactions with others (out-group)." (ibid, p. 13)

Standard 2.1 of The National Standards for Foreign Language Education states, "students demonstrate an understanding of the relationship between the practices and perspectives of the culture studied." These practices and perspectives can be interpreted as behavioral culture. Perspectives refer to belief systems and how people perceive the world. Practices are how they get things done based on those perceptions. For example, in Chinese culture hierarchy is important (perspective). Where you stand in society in relation to others is essential in determining how you communicate. Interacting with others and using appropriate terms of address based on who you are (hierarchy) is the practice that is informed by this perspective.

Behavioral culture is inextricably connected to language and must be learned alongside the language. Morain states that "being able to read and speak another language does not guarantee that *understanding* will take place" (1986, p. 64). Agar further states, "You can master grammar and the dictionary, but *without* culture you won't communicate. With culture, you can communicate *with* rocky grammar and a limited vocabulary" (1994, p. 29).

It can also be argued that it is *culture* that makes learning Chinese so challeng-ing for native English speakers, thus further emphasizing the importance of bringing culture into the classroom. Jorden and Walton have proposed that some foreign languages are more challenging for English speakers to master than others. They suggest that *truly foreign langauges* are those that are "linguistically unrelated to English — that is, they are non–Indo-European — and spoken within societies that are culturally in marked contrast to our own" (1987, p. 111). They argue that when the base culture is in sharp contrast to the target culture, the learners' native culture attitudes and perceptions "automatically and unconsciously" influence how the target language and culture are perceived. Because Chinese is so culturally and linguistically distant from Western languages, Jorden and Walton consider it to be an ideal example of a truly foreign language. They provide the following linguistic examples to illustrate this point. First, the Chinese sound system requires learners to articulate new and different sounds. The tonal system also proves diffi-cult for many English speaking learners since there is nothing like it in English. Second, the non-alphabetic Chinese orthography presents a considerable challenge for learners. Third, unfamiliar linguistic concepts such as *aspect* require learners to develop new perspectives. Fourth, because the Chinese writing system is non-alphabetic, the written system does not phonologically reflect the spoken language like it does in Western alphabetic languages. In other words, using Chinese characters to represent speech requires learners to be able to read in order to learn the spoken language — two different skills. Jorden and Walton refer to this as skill mix. At higher levels of proficiency this is not as much of a problem, but at lower levels this premature mix of the skills can present considerable problems. This is often reflected in the standard practice of Chinese textbook writers to represent dialogues in both characters and pinyin, only to provide all grammar examples and activities in Chinese characters.

Schumann (1976) also argues that the greater the social distance between two cultures, the more difficult it is to learn the second language. He states, "Congruence or similarity between the culture of the TL (target language) group and that of the 2LL (second language learning) group also affects social distance. If the two cultures are similar, then integration and social distance are reduced (1976, p. 137). Based on these studies and the well-known fact that learning Chinese takes considerably longer than learning cognate languages, (see Christensen & Warnick 2006, p. 2–3 for a discussion of research on this topic), we can surmise that not only is the linguistic code challenging, but perhaps even more so, the complexity of the cultural code presents great difficulties for Western learners of Chinese. Christensen and Warnick state: "The cultural code includes not only the linguistic code (at every level — phonological, morphological, syntactic, discourse, pragmatic) but also many nonlinguistic issues such as body language, gestures, proxemics (distance and space, such as how close you stand to someone), kinesics (movement of the body), and other aspects of behavior. In other words, the cultural code includes a sense of time and space" (2006, p. 6). This sense of time and space may vary considerably between North American English speakers and Chinese speakers in Asia.

The question that must be addressed is, how does one integrate this kind of culture into the foreign language classroom? Contextualization through situated performances provides a way to bring behavioral culture into the Chinese language classroom. Some methodologies in recent years, such as communicative language learning and task-based learning, acknowledge the importance of context in the learning process, but do not fully incorporate a cultural component. The performed culture approach (Christensen and Warnick 2006) puts culture and contextualized performance as the focus of learning East Asian languages.

Culture and Performance

Bringing culture into the Chinese language classroom involves performance. Native-like performance entails speaking, reading, writing, and responding to speech in ways in which Chinese expect people to speak, write, and respond. Walker and Noda (2000, p. 228) suggest that learning to speak an East Asian language involves learning how to behave in the target culture; essentially this means that we learn how to get things done in the foreign language. Getting things done boils down to performance. In other words, if we want our students to be able to *do* things in the target culture, they need to practice doing those things in the classroom. And they need lots of practice.

Walker describes performance as "conscious repetitions of 'situated events'" (2000). In every situation that we encounter, we speak and behave according to the situation at hand. In other words, what we say, how we say it, and what we do, are all determined by the context of the situation. This context can be determined by five factors, derived from Walker (2000, p. 223). How an individual acts (linguistically and culturally) in any communicative situation is determined by

- time of occurrence
- place of occurrence
- roles of the participants
- script (what is said and done)
- audience (those who may be around but are not participants).

The time of day, or the time of year, may influence what we say or how we act. Where we are, whether in public or private places, also influences how we behave and what we say. The role we are playing, whether teacher, student, clerk, business-person, or whatever else, determines what we say, how we say it, and how we interact with others. The script has been defined by Schank as "a set of expectations about what will happen next in a well-understood situation . . . they make clear what is supposed to happen and what various acts on the part of others are supposed to indicate" (1990, p. 7). The script not only gives us the dialogue, but also the appropriate actions that accompany speech, like the script in a theatrical performance. Finally, those around us may also dictate our behavior. For example, students in a class may act and say things differently in the classroom where their peers are present, than one-on-one with a teacher in his or her office.

Communicating successfully, then, involves not only the linguistic code (knowledge of the sound system, vocabulary, and grammar), but also the cultural code. The cultural code involves knowing how to act, what to wear, how close to stand to someone when you are talking to them, what to do with your hands, body language, facial expressions, gestures, turn-taking, and so on. In other words, it involves culturally coherent communication or "speaking, writing, and responding to speech in ways in which natives of the target culture expect people to speak, write, and respond" (Christensen and Warnick 2006, p. 68). Native Chinese people should not have to adapt their behavior (including speech) to accommodate communicating with learners of Chinese.

Bringing Culture into the Classroom

In our foreign language classrooms we impart two kinds of knowledge: declarative (or factual) knowledge and procedural knowledge. O'Malley and Chamot (1990, p. 20–25) refer to this as "language as the object of study" (declarative) and "language as a skill" (procedural). In other words, declarative knowledge involves learning *about* the language, such as grammar, the sounds and tones of the language, the meaning of vocabulary items, cultural knowledge, and so on. Procedural knowledge involves performing *in* the language — that is, practicing using the language through speaking, responding to speech, reading, and writing. Inasmuch as it is easier and faster to learn *about* a language than it is to learn how to *speak and read that language*, it makes sense to spend the bulk of our time in the classroom giving students opportunities to *use* the language in socially and culturally appropriate ways. In other words, we need to provide ample opportunities for our students to perform in the classroom.

Thus, we bring culture into the classroom through performance. In order to instill in students culturally appropriate behavior, teachers must let students practice those behaviors in and out of the classroom. For this learning to be more meaningful it is important for teachers to contextualize the performance. Meaningful practice leads to more permanent learning. Performance is not unlike a task-based approach where opportunities are provided for learners to complete a communicative task, such as asking directions, making an apology, writing a letter, or reading a newspaper article and responding to it.

Bringing behavioral culture into the classroom through performance involves at least two essential steps: providing opportunities for students to perform, and providing a variety of contexts in which to perform.

PROVIDE OPPORTUNITIES FOR STUDENTS TO PERFORM

In providing opportunities for students to perform, teachers must provide an appropriate context. A communicative task or situation can be contextualized through Walker's five elements of a performance (time, place, role, script, audience) mentioned above. The dialogue is an ideal place to start. As students memorize dialogues they "have the opportunity to practice natural intonation patterns, which are determined by the dialogue as whole, not merely individual sentences" (Christensen and Warnick 2006, p. 73). Well-crafted dialogues also provide authentic language in useful contexts that enable learners to develop automaticity with various communicative tasks. Dialogues provide the appropriate social and cultural context needed to understand the function and meaning of the vocabulary and grammar patterns studied. In other words, it provides learners with a reliable foundation of words, phrases, grammatical structures, and cultural behavior from which they can build. Of course we want our students to be able to do more than just perform prescribed dialogues. The dialogue functions as the first step in the process of learning how to behave in the target culture. Since most textbooks do not provide any context for the dialogues that are presented, we can help our students better understand the performance by either discussing or giving to the students in writing the following information: when and where the dialogue takes place, the relationship of the interlocutors, the script, and the audience, if applicable. The teacher can also provide behavioral information, such as information about body language, gestures, and so on, that may be applicable to the situation. I will illustrate how this can be done. In the textbook *Chinese Link* (2006, p. 3), the dialogue on greetings in Lesson 1 begins:

Mary:	你好！
John:	你好！
Mary:	你好！
Mary:	你是学生吗？
John:	我是学生。你呢？
Mary:	我也是学生。

There is no context provided, nor any other information about the language used in the dialogue. With the information provided, learners come away with the impression that 你好 is a simple greeting meaning "hi" or "hello" and can be used just like those greetings are used in American culture. To help learners better understand this dialogue, the following contextual information can be provided to students:

> The greeting 你好！in Chinese is usually used in more formal situations. It is not typically used in informal situations, such as among friends. You would usually use 你好！in the following situations:
>
> - meeting someone for the first time
> - in formal business communication
> - in more formal contexts such as at school between teacher and student
> - someone in an inferior position speaking to one in a superior position

In casual, informal situations, such as among friends and acquaintances, the following greetings are common:

- **Acknowledgment of Action:** this simply means that you state what the person is doing. For example, if you walked into your apartment and saw your roommate reading a book, you might say as a greeting, 看书啊！, meaning 'you're reading.'
- **Vague Question:** typical questions, used for greetings, include, 去哪儿？, meaning 'where are you going.' This question would be used if you bumped into someone out on the street. Another greeting question is, 吃饭了没有？ or 吃了吗？ meaning, 'have you eaten yet?' This greeting is used

around mealtimes. The purpose of these greeting questions is to express interest or concern in the other individual. When asking these questions, a lengthy response is not intended and vague answers are expected.

▪ **No Greeting**: In many communicative contexts, no verbal exchange of greeting or other pleasantries is used. In most of these situations, in an American cultural context a greeting would usually be used and expected. For example, greetings are typically not used with strangers (unless being introduced or meeting for the first time), such as vendors on the street, or asking for directions, etc. With family members or close friends, greetings are often not used.

In the Lesson 1 dialogue, the greeting is between two students who are meeting for the first time. As such they use the more formal 你好. Handshaking is becoming more and more common in Chinese speaking communities, but is not always used as freely as in Western countries. Lesson 1 dialogue can be contextualized as follows:

Performance: Meeting (and Greeting) for the First Time.
Time: During a school day.
Place: A college campus.
Roles: Two students (equals).
Script: Since they are meeting for the first time, they use 你好 and shake hands as they greet. Appropriate body language requires that you keep your hands out of your pockets and that you shake with one hand, while nodding the head slightly.
Audience: Perhaps other students walking around on campus.

With this information learners understand that 你好 is a rather formal greeting used when meeting someone for the first time. They also understand that there are other greetings that are used in different greeting contexts.

It is imperative that learners understand the nature of performing in the language. A dialogue performance is not simply a recitation of memorized strings of language. A performance involves actually pretending that one is participating in the communicative situation. This involves not just what comes out of your mouth but also your behavior (i.e., how you act, gestures, body language, and so on).

The beginning of the instructional cycle thus begins with highly controlled, highly structured performances, like a memorized dialogue. This is followed with activities that are semi-controlled and semi-structured, such as role plays or other similar activities. With the dialogue as the foundation, learners are exposed to variations of that dialogue and are allowed to perform in different, though related, scenarios. The behavior is partly predictive because the contexts and roles are provided by the instructor. But learners also have some freedom to express their own intentions, within the context and parameters provided by the communicative situation. Toward the end of the instructional cycle learners perform in open-ended, loosely controlled activities. This is where learners fully personalize the material. They are free to respond according to their own ideas and intentions, within the general framework of the content of the lesson (i.e., vocabulary, grammar, and communicative tasks) and within culturally appropriate parameters. Below, I illustrate how this progression, from memorized dialogue to open-ended, creative expression can be done. In the example below, excerpted from *Integrated Chinese, 2nd edition* (2005, p. 79–80), a simple dialogue dealing with scheduling time between two friends is portrayed.

小白：王朋，你明天忙不忙？

王朋：我今天很忙，可是明天不忙。有事吗？

小高：*明天我请你吃晚饭，怎么样？*

王朋：为什么请我吃晚饭？

小高：因为明天是小高的生日。

王朋：是吗？好。还有谁？

小白：还有我的同学小李。

王朋：那太好了，我也认识小李。几点钟？

小白：明天晚上七点半。

王朋：好，明天七点半见。

After the dialogue has been performed verbatim at the beginning of the instructional cycle, provide a similar situation, but change the context. For example, you might say that two students want to arrange a time to meet to study. Give the students two schedules with the instruction that they need to find a compatible time to get together in the time frame you provide. Have the students then perform the role play. This level of performance can be done with multiple variations, such as scheduling a time to go out to eat, arranging a time to meet with a teacher, and so on. At first you can tightly control the exercise by outlining specifically what you want the learners to do. For example, you might direct your students to schedule an evening out together next Saturday evening. They then will only have to negotiate the time. Then you may instruct them to arrange a time to go out to eat sometime next week. In this way learners are given increasing amounts of freedom to use the language creatively, but still within a specified controlled context.

The next level of performance would be more open-ended, and less structured. You might create a situation like the following:

You need to arrange to meet with a classmate to work on your Chinese homework. You hope your classmate can help you with your character writing in particular. Arrange a time and place to meet that is compatible with both of your real life schedules.

Or:

> You need to set up an appointment to meet with your teacher. You need help with pronunciation, particularly tones. Arrange a time to meet that is compatible with your schedules. As a student speaking with a teacher, you will be more deferential with your time.

Students would then perform according to the instructions. This kind of activity allows students freedom to speak according to their individual circumstances and preferences. An even more open-ended activity might be something like:

> Arrange with a classmate to go out this weekend. Since you are both living and studying in Beijing, decide on an activity (or location of a cultural site), day, and time. Prepare to report back to the teacher (class) what you decided.

This kind of activity has the least amount of structure. Students are free to decide and negotiate what they want to do, when, and where. By following this progression, learners are carefully led from predictable, highly structured activities to open-ended, improvisational activities.

PROVIDE A VARIETY OF CULTURAL CONTEXTS

Providing a variety of contexts in the classroom equips learners with the ability to improvise, an important skill. It is impossible to arrange every kind of situation a learner may encounter in the target culture. But we can provide a variety of cultural contexts for them to perform, thus teaching them the ability to adapt to a new situation by relying on related rehearsed performances. By changing the variables of the performance, the performance changes, both linguistically and behaviorally. It is also important for learners to understand that when you change one of the elements of the performance, such as the roles, then the performance changes as well. For example, if the roles were changed in the greeting dialogue cited above, then the language and behavior would also change. Instead of two people meeting for the first time, have students greet each other as if they were close friends. The improvised dialogue then might look something like:

Time: At the end of a school day.
Place: In your apartment.
Roles: Two roommates who are also close friends.
Script: This is a casual environment where the two people are close to each other. As such, the greeting is more of an acknowledgement than a more formal greeting. You come home to find your roommate sitting on the couch watching television.
Audience: None.

A: 看电视啊。
B: 嗯。

Or, if one person is a teacher and the other a student, the greeting would likewise change to the more formal:

A: 老师好。
B: 你好。

Greetings may also change according to time or season, such as around Chinese New Year, or in the morning. The important thing to remember is that we teach our learners how to do something, then we provide variations that simulate situations they will likely encounter in the target culture. Walker and Noda (2000, p. 190–91) refer to this type of rehearsal as "remembering the future." That is, students build memories of how to do things in the classroom through repeated performances, so that in the future, in a Chinese-speaking situation they can rely on these memories to perform appropriately. The answer to the question, *how do the Chinese greet each other*, then depends on the specific situation (who is greeting whom, where you are, when, and so on).

The same principles discussed above also apply to bringing the socio-cultural aspects of the language to reading and writing exercises. The social and cultural aspect of reading a given text in Chinese involves understanding the conventions of that written genre. For example, different genres of written discourse have certain conventions that are followed, such as newspaper writing, correspondence, essays, and so on. Some of these conventions may not differ drastically with English language conventions, such as newspaper writing. However, some genres of written discourse, such as correspondence do have significant differences. In a Chinese letter, for example, a specific format is followed based on the nature of the letter. In a Chinese personal letter between friends it is customary to begin with the person's same, but not the equivalent of "dear" as we do in English. This is followed by a greeting, like 近來好吗? The conclusion of a personal letter usually contains some kind of closing remark expressing good wishes, such as 祝好 or 敬祝安好. The physical layout of the page also follows a specific format in personal and business Chinese correspondence. It is helpful for learners to know what these conventions are, or the appropriate format in which these things are written. It is also important for learners to understand the role that a given text plays in society. So often in our classes, teachers focus exclusively on helping learners understand the content of a text, with little or no discussion of *context*. Christensen and Warnick state,

It is important to keep in mind, however, that understanding the content of the text is not the ultimate goal: The next level is to help learners understand what to do with the text *after* the content is understood (Walker

1984). Texts are produced to fill a particular role in society. To become participating members of the target culture, learners need to understand the social role of the given text. They need to understand why natives of that culture read the text and what they do as a result. Reading activities in the foreign language curriculum therefore, should be sociolinguistically appropriate and should focus on the social nature of the text. (2006, p. 123)

Reading activities can be divided into three phases: the pre-reading phase, the reading phase, and the post-reading phase. Traditionally, teachers tend to spend a great deal of time on the actual reading phase, using much valuable classroom time reading the text aloud and explaining the meaning of vocabulary and grammar patterns. While this is not without merit, the act of reading itself is an activity that learners can do quite effectively on their own, outside class. The pre-reading phase is the time to help learners understand the social and culture context of the text. This may include information not only about the author, but also about when the piece was written and for what purpose. Helping learners understand the format or conventions of the genre of text is also helpful in this phase, as is information about the topic and its importance and/or relevance in the target society. For example, if you were teaching a literature or advanced language course and assigned your students to read the short story 祝福 by Lu Xun, you might do one or more of the following in the pre-reading phase:

- Discuss the traditional Chinese Confucian family structure
- Discuss the role of women within this structure, particularly the role of widows and mother-in-laws.
- After discussing the above, have a discussion about what students may anticipate in the story.
- Have students read an essay or other information about traditional Chinese families
- Compare these traditional Chinese views with traditional American views on the family and role of women.
- Discuss, show a film clip, or have students read about the political climate of the time in China.
- Give a brief biographical sketch (orally or in writing) of the author Lu Xun.
- Show a film version of 祝福 so they understand the story line.
- Preview the vocabulary and grammar patterns that appear in the story.

All this information helps learners not only better undertand the story, but also better understand the role of the story in Chinese society and the author's intentions. By coming to the story better prepared the likelihood that they will understand it and appreciate it as it was intended is much greater.

Perhaps the most important activities occur in the post-reading phase. Once learners understand what they have read, now what? What do you do with the text now? One way is to explore what natives of the target culture do with this kind of text. Each text will play a different role in society, from a Lu Xun short story to a newspaper editorial. Post-reading activities may include discussing student opinions about the text (whether they agree with the author's point of view), oral reports, debates on the topic, or writing a synopsis of the text in a letter to a friend. (For a more detailed discussion of reading strategies and activities, see Christensen and Warnick 2006).

By adopting the strategies above, learners are dealing intimately with the social and cultural implications of Chinese. This is another way to bring culture into the Chinese language classroom.

Social and Cultural Authenticity

We could design the most interesting interactive classroom activities, but if the language is not authentic, then it will not be of much benefit to our students. Authentic language is that kind of language that is spoken by native Chinese in normal circumstances. Using this definition, it is acceptable to use "textbook" language such as dialogues and reading passages as long as the language is authentic.

When we think of authenticity we often refer to the language, but it is equally relevant that we have our students perform authentic tasks in the classroom. We can have 100 percent authentic language, being grammatically correct, with native-like pronunciation, but if learners use that language in ways that native Chinese do not, or would find odd, then it is not a useful task. One kind of situation where this is often apparent is when we allow beginning, or even intermediate learners, too much freedom with the language too early. We may have them create their own skit using the lesson vocabulary and grammar. What often happens is learners come up with a situation that is very funny in an American cultural context; they end up speaking English in Chinese. That is, they use accurate, authentic Chinese, but in ways and in situations where native Chinese would never use it. They may be speaking Chinese but they are behaving and speaking like Americans. For this reason it is important that we have enough structure early on so that our students learn when and how to use Chinese in ways that native Chinese speakers expect people to behave, linguistically, socially, and culturally. Tasks we provide for our students should be socially and culturally authentic *and* useful. Useful tasks are those that learners will likely encounter in Chinese-speaking communities.

Conclusion

We bring culture into the Chinese language classroom by first rethinking our definitions of culture and what kinds of cultural phenomena are relevant to foreign language study. Though other aspects of Chinese culture will undoubtedly benefit our students, behavioral culture is inextricably tied to language performance. As we contextualize student performances in the classroom through authentic language and tasks, learners understand not only what to say, but how to behave in a variety of communicative situations.

Performance is the vehicle we use to bring culture into the classroom; contextualization is the method we use to help students practice using the language in a variety of different situations.

By providing a clear context for each performance, teachers can help learners gain a deeper understanding of why and how the language is used. By providing a variety of related contexts or variations of communicative situations, teachers can equip learners with the ability to improvise and better understand that communication (linguistic and non-linguistic) varies depending on the role you are playing, who you are communicating with, where you are, when the situation occurs, what script is involved, and who else may be passively participating. Ultimately we need to get beyond thinking that culture is a separate and distinct skill that we treat differently from language skills. Speaking, listening, reading, and writing are cultural in their very nature and should be taught within authentic social and cultural contexts.

Discussion Questions

1. How does the teaching of culture in this article differ from the way you learned about culture in the foreign language classes you studied?
2. Do you think performed culture, as described in the article, can be applied to all levels of Chinese language learning? Explain your answer.
3. Do you think performed culture can be applied to the learning of all four skills — speaking, listening, reading, and writing? Explain your answer.
4. Young adults have a hard time learning to behave appropriately in their own culture. Is it possible to train them to behave in a culturally appropriate manner in a foreign language context? How can this be done?
5. What kinds of materials (props) can be used to help contextualize student performances in the classroom?
6. How can multimedia resources be useful to facilitate performance and cultural understanding in Chinese language classes?

References

Agar, Michael. 1994. *Language shock: Understanding the culture of conversation.* New York: William Morrow and Company.

American Council on the Teaching of Foreign Languages. *Standards for foreign language learning: Preparing for the 21st century.* http://www.actfl.org/i4a/pages/index.cfm?pageid=3324.

Brooks, Nelson. 1997. Teaching culture in the foreign language classroom. In *Pathways to culture*, ed. Paula R. Heusinkveld, 13. Yarmouth, ME: Intercultural Press.

Christensen, Matthew B., and R. Paul Warnick. 2006. *Performed culture: An approach to East Asian language pedagogy*. Columbus, OH: National East Asian Languages Resource Center, The Ohio State University.

Hammerly, Hector. 1985. *An integrated theory of language teaching and its practical consequences*. Blaine, WA: Second Language Publications.

Jorden, Eleanor, and A. Ronald Walton. 1987. Truly foreign languages: Instructional challenges. *Annals of the American Academy of Political and Social Science* 496: 110–124.

Morain, Genelle. 1986. Kinesics and cross-cultural understanding (pp. 64–76). In *Culture bound: Bridging the cultural gap in language teaching*, ed. Joyce Merrill Valdes, 64–76. Cambridge: Cambridge University Press.

Omaggio Hadley, Alice. 2001. *Teaching language in context*. 3rd ed. Boston: Heinle and Heinle.

O'Malley, J. Michael, and Anna Uhl Chamot. 1990. *Learning strategies in second language acquisition*. Cambridge: Cambridge University Press.

Schank, Roger C. 1990. *Tell me a story: A new look at real and artificial memory*. New York: Scribner.

Schumann, John H. 1976. Social distance as a factor in second language acquisition. *Language Learning* 26 (1): 135–143.

Walker, Galal. 1984. Literacy and reading in a Chinese language program. *Journal of the Chinese Language Teachers Association* 19 (1): 67–84.

Walker, Galal. 2000. Performed Culture: Learning to Participate in Another Culture (221–236). In Richard D. Lambert and Elana Shohamy (eds.), *Language Policy and Pedagogy: Essays in Honor of A. Ronald Walton*. Amsterdam: John Benjamins.

Walker, Galal and Mari Noda. 2000. Remembering the future: Compiling knowledge of another culture. In *Reflecting on the Past to Shape the Future*, ed. Diane W. Birckbichler, 187–212. Lincolnwood, IL: National Textbook Company.

Wu, Sue-mei, et. al. 2006. *Chinese Link*. Upper Saddle River, NJ: Pearson Education, Inc.

Yao, Tao-chung, et. al. 2005. *Integrated Chinese: Level 1, Part 1*. 2nd edition. Boston: Cheng & Tsui Company.

Chapter 3

Focusing on the Learner in the Chinese Language Classroom

Moving from "Talking the Talk" to "Walking the Walk"

Cynthia Ning

University of Hawaii at Manoa

The driving principle behind standards-based approaches to language teaching is the focus on the learner. This simple, straightforward statement of purpose — to focus on the learner[1] — implies a requisite sea-change in teacher behavior.

There is general agreement among educators that a good curriculum is best determined by the real-life needs of the student, and tempered by the ability of the student. Furthermore, the effectiveness of the curriculum is monitored by checking student performance of the real-life tasks laid out in the curriculum (see the *ACTFL Performance Guidelines for K–12 Learners*, at http://www.actfl.org). And there is widespread discussion of various principles guiding how instruction might proceed, if a curriculum and classroom are to be truly learner-centered[2]. Transferring cognitive "knowledge about" principles into behavioral "how to" practices that become second nature even in the most difficult classroom continues to be a primary challenge to the field of Chinese language education. Though growing numbers of teachers are beginning to "talk the talk" by becoming increasingly

---

[1]My sincere thanks to the anonymous reviewers of this chapter for these and many other thoughtful comments that have led to several revisions of my original draft.

[2]For a useful overview, see Nunan (1999).

familiar with and accepting of research-driven theories, finding educators who actually demonstrate learner-centered teaching in the classroom is still disappointingly rare. This essay focuses on the implementation of effective standards-based, learner-centered approaches in the Chinese language classroom — "walking the walk," in other words.

Defining Goals

The overall goal of instruction is not to "cover" a textbook, or to survive a school day without incident while maintaining the type of classroom we remember from our own student days. Our goal is not to drive students to achieve at a hoped-for level on a classroom-based or standardized test. Given the acceptance of standards for instruction in world languages, our goal is to produce students who can function at the target proficiency level of any given course — say, "Intermediate Low" for a beginning/intermediate class — who demonstrate appropriate levels of both linguistic and cultural competency while interacting effectively in a real-life, Chinese context.

The performance standards (see Everson, The Importance of Standards, this volume) widely adopted by U.S. schools articulate this overall goal in terms applicable to the classroom, in gradations that facilitate assessment. The Minnesota Department of Education, for example, lists the following guidelines for Grade 9–Level One for a Mandarin Chinese curriculum (2007):

STANDARD 1.1 INTERPERSONAL

- Greet and respond to simple greetings and farewells with appropriate level of politeness for different age groups, social positions, relationships.
- Exchange simple biographical information: Name, age, address, phone number, etc.
- Exchange information about your family: how many people are in your immediate family; family members.
- Give simple description of yourself, your friends, and your family members: name, age, appearance, personality.
- State what you, your friends, your family like to do, don't like to do.
- Make arrangements to meet with someone for an appointment, meeting, or activity.
- Express feelings: Happy, sad, ill, etc.

Guidelines such as these focus on what it is the *student* will be able to do as a result of instruction. Then, following the suggestions given in *Backwards Design*[3],

---

[3]Minnesota Department of Education (2007).

the teacher can construct her assessments, syllabus and lesson plan, keeping a vision of the target *student (learner) performance* in mind as a constant.

A First Step: Recognizing the "Look" of Learner-Centered Instruction

Many of us have spent most of our lives learning in teacher-centered classrooms, with the teacher at the front of the classroom and the students sitting together facing the teacher. Since these teacher-centered approaches have been drilled into us for hours and months and years, it is challenging for us to "un-learn" these approaches and move towards learner-centeredness. As the anonymous reviewer of this chapter wrote:

In my class observations, I often find teachers unknowingly copy what their own teachers did. To succeed, our teachers need to first unlearn their old approach and then learn the new one. This is not easy. The learner-centered approach includes, besides attention to students, learner-directed materials/activities, multiple directions of communications (teacher to students, students to students, etc.) Also, how the teacher posits himself in the classroom affects the learning tremendously. A teacher-centered teacher would view himself as the authority and stand "on the other side" of the class. On the other hand, a learner-centered teacher would view himself as "part of the class," and hence build up a rapport with the students and make the students feel they are liked and cared about.

The question, then, is how do we recognize learner-centeredness? Suppose we were to make a film featuring learner-centered approaches to teaching Chinese. We might begin by obtaining footage of effective, learner-centered instruction in practice, with the goal of interspersing such footage with descriptions of the principles of standards-based, learner-centered language instruction, to illustrate the implementation of these principles in teaching.

As with any screen test, we would set up one or more cameras to film *only the students in a class*. If we are looking for learner-centered classes, it would be reasonable to feature learners, not teachers, on screen. There would be no camera or microphone recording what the teacher says or does; since we are focusing on the learner, the equipment would be arranged only to record what the students say and do.

If, at the end of a class period, the captured footage reveals only students sitting, listening to the teacher, taking notes, and responding only when called upon by the teacher, we would suspect that the point of interest — the focus of attention — in this classroom lies not with the students, but with the teacher. This is a teacher-centered class. The highest level of energy, the peak of the "action" in this class, emanates from the teacher, not from the student. Attention in this class is therefore centered on what the teacher says and does, not the students. Therefore, with cameras trained on the students only, the peak of interest in the class would not be recorded and revealed onscreen. We would not "cast" this class, because it is not a learner-centered class.

If, on the other hand, cameras focused only on the students obtained significant footage of dynamic energy emanating from the students — if the highest level of interest emanates from students actively engaged in creative processes of learning, deciding what to say and when to say it, deciding what to write and when to write it, initiating an interaction or a transaction and deciding when the task is done, standing up, milling around, focused on interlocutors and actively engaged most of the time in the class, asking and answering questions, laughing in pleasure at small successes and pressing for clarification from classmates or teacher when confused — then it is apparent that students are the major point of interest in this class. If a visitor were to enter the classroom and scan the scene, his or her eyes would lock on the students, because they are visually the most interesting feature. The teacher is present, but not dominant. The teacher is not the "sage on the stage" and the focus of all attention, but the "guide on the side," actively engaged in a support position vis-à-vis the students, who are the stars.

If, in the course of a class, we can obtain such "student-centered" footage lasting for at least **half** of the duration of the class, we have likely found a learner-centered class.

Teachers in the learner-centered classroom "place students at the center of education and limit their own role to arranging the best conditions for learning, to guiding and assessing students' performance, and to providing them with helpful feedback. The students themselves help to determine the content, activities, and assessments and carry out the tasks within thematic units, researching information for themselves as they need it" (College Board 2007, p. 7). Whereas it may on the surface appear that this move from "sage on the stage" to "guide on the side" is downplaying the role of the teacher, reducing her impact on the student's development to something secondary and reactive, the reality is the polar opposite: the role of an effective "guide on the side" is an enormously challenging one, that entails a confident, pro-active and purposeful intervention in the student's academic life. An effective "guide on the side" requires the student to take responsibility for his own learning, and enables and empowers him to do so[4].

Moving Onwards: Attaining the Reality of a Learner-Centered Classroom

All classroom activities can be classified as constituting one of two types: "skills-getting" and "skills-using."

In skills-getting, students learn new vocabulary, sentence patterns, and culturally appropriate interactional techniques. Language classes have always included skills-getting work.

---

[4]See Wiggins and McTighe (2004).

Skills-using presents the greater challenge: it is getting the student to recognize contextual cues, to decide for themselves what language and other communicative strategies to use when — how to initiate or respond to an interaction, how to continue communication or conversation, how and when to take a turn, when to press ahead and to back off, how to recognize when the objective of the interaction has been met, how to conclude the interaction or transaction with grace.

SKILLS-GETTING IN THE LEARNER-CENTERED CLASSROOM

This begins not with what teachers want to teach (based on a pre-set curriculum or on what is available in a given textbook), but, not surprisingly, on what the learner needs and wishes to learn.

A survey of learner needs is a good place to begin. Its results might lead to a reassessment of the curriculum, perhaps to bring it into closer alignment with learner needs.

The next step might be to consider Stephen Krashen's notion of $i + 1$, where "i" represents the student's current level of competency, and "+1" indicates input just beyond the current level of competency[5].

DETERMINING THE "I" OF "I + 1"

A primary challenge in the classroom is to stay constantly apprised of students' changing "i" levels, which can be determined *only by autonomous student performance*. In the learner-centered classroom, "i" can ONLY be assessed by student performance, independently motivated, and never by teacher behavior. If a teacher has "covered" certain points multiple times, generally by telling the class repeatedly about them, but student reaction does not demonstrate that they have taken in the information and modified their behavior, then the "i" has still not shifted. Often, simply telling the students about something does not work; students need to work things out for themselves, arrive at the appropriate conclusions, then demonstrate time and again that they can incorporate the new knowledge into their behavior, in order for the "i" level to shift.

Conversely, if the teacher had intended to tell (or re-tell) the class certain points, but student behavior indicates that these points have already been absorbed, then the "i" level has already shifted; discussing the points under these circumstances would constitute "i − 1," which is a waste of time and effort at best, and at worst irritating to the students[6].

---

[5]College Board (2007), p. 7.

[6]Some may conclude that the role of this "guide on the side" is a peripheral one. On the contrary, teaching effectively in a learner-centered classroom requires an enormous amount of preparation, energy, and effort on the part of the teacher—first outside of the classroom to find and plan activities that will be productive for students, and second in the classroom to achieve the right balance between giving students enough structured guidance to learn from their mistakes, while encouraging them to

For example: many Chinese language teachers point to the bǎ-construction as a relatively difficult form for beginning language students. Many teachers begin their instruction by TELLING students about the bǎ-construction: describing the pattern, analyzing it, and giving several examples of sentences using the pattern[7]. This typical activity of the teacher-centered classroom is often followed by the teacher calling on several or all the students in turn, to repeat a bǎ- sentence or create one of their own, following cues given by the teacher. (Teacher: "打開門 Open the door." Student: "把門打開 Open the door.")[8] This type of student work is not autonomous — the STUDENT did not decide what to say when, but is simply responding to teacher management of his or her behavior. There is no autonomous student performance on display here, so we cannot say there has been a shift in the "i" level. The class cannot move on to "+ 1" yet.

So how WOULD students demonstrate autonomous performance of the bǎ- construction? Let us consider how bǎ- would be used most extensively in real life. An easy situation for the beginning learner to grapple with involves the physical manipulation of objects, say furniture. In real life, we might hear native speakers saying sentences such as the following:

"把椅子搬進來   *Move the chair inside.*
"把棹子搬出去   *Move the table outside.*
"把燈放在棹子上   *Put the lamp on the table.*

---

take risks with the language. While it is beyond the capacity of this essay to explain the ABCs (甲乙丙s) of how to truly implement a learner-centered curriculum, ACTFL, the College Board, STARTALK summer institutes (see www.nflc.org/projects/current_projects/STARTALK), and a plethora of other public and private institutions offer short- and long-term in-service training opportunities for teachers to learn about, experience, and implement such instructional approaches incrementally. In addition, working long-term with and observing colleagues, perhaps in a different language (including ESL), can be extremely useful for teachers who seek more detailed guidance on how to implement a learner-centered curriculum.

[7]Krashen (1982). There have been objections among theorists that Krashen's "i" is not quantifiable through research, and can therefore be utilized by classroom teachers only in a very general way. Here, we *are* using the term in a very general way, to indicate current competency roughly defined. Although the "i" is undeniably a moving target, it is nonetheless still a target. Consider also Vygotsky's work on the "zone of proximal development (ZPD)," (see Lantolf and Thorne 2006). The ZPD has been applied to language learning as well, to indicate that zone between the level at which a student can perform independently and the level at which she can comfortably perform only with assistance from a more competent learner (or a teacher); the suggestion is that it is in this area that the learner learns best.

[8]Following Krashen, grammar explanations and decontextualized drilling of the sort discussed here constitute incomprehensible input, which, Krashen asserted, does not lead to acquisition. Here, I am not commenting on the veracity of this widely contested claim. Krashen's term "i", however, is commonly used to indicate the level at which the student is currently performing, and this is how I use it. It is true that when I follow up by using "i – 1" in the discussion, I am straying from Krashen's stated intentions, since he was writing of comprehensible target language input. I beg the reader's indulgence for "bending" the meaning of the original term in this fashion.

If moving furniture is difficult to simulate in the classroom, props such as small colored blocks can take the place of furniture. Students could be directed to form pairs, sitting together back-to-back. One member of the pair creates a design of her choosing using her blocks, and then gives oral directions to the partner, to recreate her design using his blocks. For example:

"把紅的放在中間，把黃的放在左邊，把黑的放在紅的右邊，把白的放在紅的上面 *Put the red one in the middle, put the yellow one on the left, put the black one to the right of the red one, put the white one on top of the red one.*"

If the design the partner creates matches that of the student giving directions, her oral performance is satisfactory.

In this situation, the learner has more autonomy in determining what to say, and deciding when she has said enough. This is a first example of a student demonstrating she has gained some familiarity with the *bâ*-construction. To follow up with another consolidating activity, the teacher might suggest that students play "obey me" with a list of familiar nouns they brainstorm, based on objects on hand and the useful utterances " 遞給 X *Hand it to X*" and "交給 X *Turn it over to X.*"

Say the students have access to the following objects, and therefore brainstorm the nouns "筆 *pen,*" "書 *book,*" "紙 *paper,*" "書包 *book bag,*" etc. They could place these objects in a pile on the floor in the center of the room (or on the teacher's desk), and take turns instructing their classmates:

"把書遞給我　　　　*Hand me the book.*"
"把紅筆傳給林大明　*Pass the red pen to Lin Daming.*"
"把錢包交給老師　　*Turn in the wallet to the teacher.*"

Again, here the students have a greater degree of autonomy than in the first (teacher-centered) example, and their performance in this activity gives some insight into their "i" level — we could probably say that at this stage the students are demonstrating partial control of the bâ-structure[9].

---

[9]Many believe it is necessary for the instructor to explain/analyze the pattern and make sure students understand it before engaging them in practice, otherwise students would produce unacceptable patterns such as *我把作業寫。*他把我打。*我把他喜歡。 The point is, though, in a standards-based curriculum, the teacher would never set the students loose to make such uninformed, ungrammatical sentences. In a *grammar*-based curriculum it might be important to explain the grammar first, and then have the students try to produce grammatical sentences to demonstrate that they "understood" or "mastered" the grammar. In a *task*-based approach, however, the point of departure is a task: for example, "Put these three blocks in order, as instructed." If the teacher demonstrates "把紅的放中間，把白的放左邊，把黃的放右邊 *Put the red one in the middle, put the white one on the left, and put the yellow one on the right,*" the students hear the structure and are limited to a small vocabulary set; therefore, it is highly unlikely that they would go astray. Prior to performing this task, it is *not* necessary that the teacher explain the grammar—they would be obfuscating the task at hand. Perhaps *after* performing a series of tasks involving the *bâ*-construction in various contexts, the students might begin to wonder, what is the *bâ*-construction anyway? This would be a very good

Of course, to determine their REAL "i" level, we'd have to follow them into a Chinese speaking community and record them speaking Chinese entirely independently, unprompted by the teacher. Though it is possible to conduct research in this manner, this is not a realistic pedagogic recommendation for the teacher! We might keep in mind, though, that our ultimate goal is precisely independent student performance. If our students can demonstrate using the *bâ*-construction truly autonomously and appropriately in real life, in nearly *every* situation that requires it, then we could say their "i" includes full control of *bâ*.

OFFERING NEW MATERIAL AT THE " + 1" LEVEL

Once you are comfortable that you know, approximately, what the "i" student performance level is, you can determine the " + 1" content amount by watching your students' response patterns. How much new information can they absorb into their behavioral output without their eyes glazing over?

Let's consider an example from what is likely an earlier piece of the curriculum than the bâ- structure used earlier. Say your "i" student performance level in self-introductions includes the ability to describe members of the immediate family, including name, age, and family relationship. You might decide that the "+ 1" instructional content (input) could include information about what members of the family do, professionally. You might pick a handful of nouns identifying professions for the students to learn. Such core terminology might include the following:

student, teacher, nurse, doctor, lawyer, accountant, business person.

How would you best support your students' learning of these terms[10]? The LAST thing you want to do is give them a vocabulary list with English, *pinyin*, and characters, and read over the list with them. How is the student to actively engage with such a list? If a camera were trained on your students, what live energy would it record, in focusing on their reading a list? You might want to give them such a list (better: have them work with you to DEVELOP such a list) AFTER they've been actively involved in taking in these terms.

How could you set up a learning experience focusing on the students speaking, questioning and performing that would allow you to step to one side, so that a

---

time to have a grammar lesson, beginning with an explanation and followed with grammar drills. In my experience, a grammar lesson at this point is like dropping a seed on ground that has been thoroughly tilled and prepared. The germs of information quickly take hold. Conversely, grammar explanations that precede task-based manipulation of the relevant structures by the students is like casting seeds on hard, unworked soil: too many of them simply go to waste.

[10]Swain (1985) argues that it is important for students to have opportunities to produce and modify comprehensible output, since this process leads to acquisition.

videographer in your room would naturally be drawn to your students, rather than to you? You might play a pantomiming game with your students. Call a volunteer to the front of the room, show her a card with the term "accountant" written on it in English, and have her pantomime "accountant" (as if the class were playing charades) while you repeat "會計; 會計; 會計; 會計; 會計; 會計...." until the class correctly guesses "accountant." Once it does, you can ask, "Accountant 中文 怎麼說?" and likely several of the students will correctly say "kuàiji," since they will have heard you say the term upwards of 20 times. Repeat with the remaining vocabulary.

It might take you perhaps 30 minutes of class time to go through the terms on your list, but during the activity, the students will have been fully absorbed and using auditory, visual, kinesthetic and cognitive faculties to process incoming information. If you were then to follow up by doing a dictation, during which the students write out the terms in *pinyin* as you or a student volunteer recites them (if students recite the terms, you can correct as necessary); and then an exercise in which the students write the English next to each of their *pinyin* terms; and THEN an exercise in which the students match Chinese characters which you write on the board or post in character flashcards for each of the terms, with the *pinyin* and English that they have written — then you and your students would have developed a vocabulary list together. Chances are, your students will already be very familiar with the contents of this list, and will be much closer to being able to USE the terms on the list, than if you had simply handed them a prepared list to begin with.

Following such an activity, you might wish to give the students an opportunity to truly develop their own list, including terms in which they are genuinely interested. If you were to give the students a blank index card each, and have them write on it the English term for their dream career, chances are you would be returned vocabulary items not on your original list. You might get back terms such as "sports agent," and "rock star," and "software designer." In your unit on careers, you should arguably save half of your class's energy to focus on terms of their own selection, regardless of what is provided in the textbook you are using. (You'll likely need some help coming up with the Chinese equivalents of some of the terms your students will select, but such assistance is widely available, face-to-face in your community or via web-based resources.) Then you can "process" these terms the same way you did the original list, and eventually test them the way you do the rest. If you end up with too long a list, you could tell the students they need only to develop full control of all or some of the original core vocabulary, plus the term they contributed themselves, plus maybe 3–5 terms they select from the list their classmates developed. Such full (or active) control might mean they should be able to understand as well as PRODUCE these terms as needed. For the remaining terms, tell them that partial (or passive) control suffices — if someone else uses the term, they should understand it, but they themselves may not be able to produce the term.

MOVING TO SKILLS-USING: FACILITATING MEANINGFUL INTERACTION

Skills-getting is something that language classrooms everywhere offer. What is too often missing is the critical next step: classroom training that supports the students USING the skills they have learned in simulated real-life situations, so that they make the transition from classroom to life with greater ease. Skills-getting focuses on the language tools themselves: words and grammar and syntax. Skills-using trains the students to recognize when to use which tools, and how to use these tools in culturally appropriate ways.

For example, when do native-speakers tend to use bâ-sentences in real life (rather than non-bâ sentences)? Contexts that beginning Chinese learners are likely to encounter involve performing actions on specific objects. These include the following:

- setting the table according to specifications;
- moving furniture around, following directions;
- putting clothing away in a specified fashion;
- putting food away following specifications, etc.

Skills-using exercises for the classroom might involve these contexts, then.

What do we consider when designing skills-using exercises? The following list is a start:

Language Objective

This is foremost. Without a language objective, there is really no reason to do any activity in a language-training classroom. The language objective can be formulated using function ("giving directions") as a point of departure, or using a specific form-based element (practicing a particular grammatical point, such as the bâ-structure). Ultimately, we generally end up combining function with form, whether we began with a focus on the function or on the form. In real life, form follows function, and functions cannot be completed without form. An effective classroom should follow suit. In our example, an appropriate language objective might be: "Practice giving and following instructions."

Contextualization

If the classroom simulates life, then we need to take context into consideration, always. Every interaction in real life takes place within a context, a setting. So for our exercise(s), we should determine and specify the context in which we might situate it. Specifying simulated contexts also helps the student recognize when he should reach for the specific linguistic tool which we are manipulating in the exercise.

In our example, viable contexts given our deliberations to date might include the following.

- For "setting the table in a specified fashion," the context might be: "You have invited Chinese friends over for dinner. You are just finishing up preparing the food, and have already brought out the eating utensils you will need. Your friend offers to set the table. You accept his offer. Give him specific instructions on how to place the dinner (large) plate, salad (small) plate, dinner (long) fork, salad (short) fork, knife, spoon, glass, and napkin at each place setting."

- For "moving furniture around," we might consider the following. "You are moving into a room. You have several items of furniture piled up near the door, but as you begin to move them, you twist your ankle slightly. Your friends happen to walk in, tell you to sit down on the floor, and offer to put away your furniture for you. Give them specific instructions on where to put the sofa, desk, chair, bed, big lamp, small lamp, bookcase, rug, and wastebasket."

- "Putting food away in a specified fashion" might be called for given the following context: "You have accompanied your Chinese friend grocery shopping, and you return to your apartment completely exhausted. You collapse on the couch. Your friend suggests the groceries should be put away immediately, but you can't get up. Give directions on where (where in the refrigerator? Which shelf in which cupboard?) to put the milk, eggs, apples, bananas, bread, fish, vegetables, and cookies."

To implement task-based activities using these contexts, we might use pictures, individualized sets of cartoon objects, or computer-based picture and image presentations.

Focus on Task

In real life, people generally do not talk simply to demonstrate that they know how to talk; we talk to accomplish an end, a task. This task might be instrumental (we need to get an object purchased or moved, or a form filled) or social (we would like to establish or maintain a connection with someone). For our skills-using activities in the classroom, it would be beneficial to our students to practice accomplishing such real-life tasks, using the language they have learned.

Example social tasks might include:

- "Turn to your partner. Chat for a few minutes, and find out five things about his/her background, including birthplace and what languages were spoken at home. Respond to his/her questions about your background." This activity might be followed up by reporting back to the class (the teacher might make a list of where everyone was born, for example), or telling another student in the class what was learned during the course of the conversation.

- "Tell your partner five details about what you did this past weekend, and find out the same about her/him."
- "Find out from your partner five details about her/his taste in clothes. Tell the same about yourself."

Transactional tasks simulate accomplishing real-life chores in the classroom. Role-plays are a common way to structure these. For example:

- Partner A will play a hair stylist; partner B is the customer. B tells A exactly how he wants his hair cut, colored, highlighted, etc; A renders a drawing of her understanding of how B's hair will look at the completion of the treatment.
- Every student in the class receives three blank index cards. On these, they draw three items of their choice, and write a price (say, under $20) for each. (For example, a student might draw an mp3 player at $18.75; a lollipop at $.50; and a teddy-bear for $15.) Next, every student receives an index card with "$25" written on it. This is a debit card. The students circulate around the classroom, shopping (and bargaining) for their classmates' items, and selling their own. After a set period of time, everyone sits down again. Students share information about their purchases with others in the class. "Winners" can be those who sold all three items.
- The activity for Unit 5d on pp. 111–12 in the Teacher's Activity Book for *Communicating in Chinese* (available for free download from http://www.yalebooks.com/cic) is an example of a transactional task. There are many more examples of transactional tasks in this volume[11].

Focus on Form[12]

A standards- or performance-based curriculum is extremely concerned with the issue of accuracy in student use of the target language; the belief is, though, that accuracy in language use is best attained through learner-centered skills-getting and skills-using activities such as the ones described above, followed <u>afterwards</u> by a discussion (likely in the native language) of issues of form — pronunciation,

---

[11]It has been suggested that vocabulary such as "accountant" and "sports agent" or "rock star" (as appear later in this chapter) do not belong in an elementary curriculum. I disagree. In a *teacher*-centered approach, the teacher (and textbook authors) decide what the student should learn, and these people might decide that students should learn "common" terms such as "teacher," "doctor," "nurse." In a more *learner*-centered approach, however, the learner has an opportunity to decide for herself what to work on. Learning to answer the question "What do you do?" or "What profession are you interested in?" is a Novice-Intermediate Low sort of task, on par with "Where are you from?" and therefore belongs in an elementary curriculum. The answer should be based on what the student actually wants to say. Therefore, terms such as "accountant" and "rock star," which have not traditionally been part of the curriculum in Chinese, deserve a place there. For a suggestion on how to incorporate student-generated vocabulary, see the next paragraph.

[12]See Ning (1993).

grammar, syntax, pragmatics — and form-based exercises as necessary. A focus on form is often most effectively implemented when the *student* initiates the discussion, to confirm a hypothesis she has been developing about a grammar point, or to clarify a certain usage that has been confusing her. Alternatively, when the teacher notices an emerging pattern of incorrect usage or performance, she might resort to a mini "grammar clinic," to point out specific issues. Teacher-initiated "focus on form clinics" ideally will not interfere with communication-based activities, though. Beginning learners can be expected to make many errors in communication; excessive attention to error-correction can inhibit student willingness to take risks, and risk-taking is necessary for the student to build confidence in his own ability to communicate[13]. Teachers are likely well-advised to take their cues from the students on issues of form — when they indicate a curiosity about grammar, the focus in the classroom should turn to grammar; when their curiosity seems to be sated, the focus on grammar might be dropped.

Spiraling to Reading and Writing

With the exception of heritage learners who already know how to speak but need to learn how to read, beginning learners generally need to gain some listening and speaking competence in the target language before they can begin to tackle reading (see Wen, this volume).

Continuing the focus on the learner in moving to a new skill, we might begin by a survey of *what* students will be faced with reading in life, when teachers and parents and administrators are not around to influence the environment. What authentic Chinese language items will cross the learner's field of vision, that he might wish or need to read? The list might include the following:

> Road signs, maps, written announcements, personal notes, letters, e-mail messages, forms, cartoons, subtitles on movies, newspaper articles, weather reports, novels, product labels, instructions, essays, journal entries, etc.

These items might appear in printed or hand-written formats, *in simplified or full-form (traditional) characters.* Regardless of what the teacher believes regarding the ideal instructional sequence or approach to gaining a working knowledge of Chinese characters — (teach traditional only to privilege Taiwan and traditional China, teach simplified only because of the PRC's increasing geopolitical power, teach simplified first and then switch to traditional because simplified might be easier to learn since simplified characters involve fewer strokes, teach traditional first and then switch to simplified so that students can see the basic structures of characters when they first learn them) — the fact is that the world the students face beyond the classroom includes BOTH traditional and simplified characters, and

---

[13]For an overview of the role of calling students' attention to language form, see Schmidt (1995).

Chinese texts come in both forms. A can of food produced in Taiwan has a label in traditional characters. An advertisement from a Beijing travel agency will be printed in simplified characters. A karaoke program of Hong Kong pop songs presents lyrics in traditional characters. A children's storybook featuring a tale told in Chinese from Singapore is likely in simplified characters. Street signs and store fronts in most Chinatowns in the United States feature traditional characters. Native speakers can extract the information they need from both forms, and write either one form or the other. Regardless of the teacher's personal conviction, the reality is that sooner or later, students need to deal with both forms. Students who learn Chinese by studying abroad in Taipei will at first be surrounded by traditional characters, but chances are, they will be faced with texts in simplified characters as well. Conversely, students trained in Shanghai will at first be immersed only in simplified characters, but later may be faced with a letter or email message from Taiwan or Hong Kong in traditional characters[14].

If the students are exposed to and trained in both forms concurrently, they can accept the reality that both forms exist in the Chinese world, and, regardless of their teachers' or parents' biases, THEY can learn to navigate in both traditional and simplified universes. This is a very emotional issue for Chinese language teachers, but from the student's point of view, it need not be difficult to recognize that 謝 — 谢 are different forms of the same character, as are 這 — 这 and 們 — 们. Furthermore, keep in mind that at least half to two-thirds of the characters that students are likely to encounter in any given text will be the same in both forms.

For example, in the following exercise in which students match all three columns, matching A and B is likely going to be the easiest and therefore most motivating part of the exercise, and doing the matching gives students that much more exposure to Chinese characters.

A	B	C
紅	白	green
藍	黑	blue
黃	红	white
白	绿	black
黑	黄	red
綠	蓝	yellow

For another example, once the student has learned the meaning of sign A below from a Taipei street corner, if you show her the sign B below from a Beijing street

---

[14]For a discussion of the role of "re-casting" in response to student errors, see "Recasts in SLA: The Story So Far" (Chapter 4; p. 75–118) in Long (2007).

corner, chances are she'll be able to tell you what it says ("do not enter, please go to the right"), and think herself rather smart for having done so! And in showing your students BOTH signs (in such a fashion as to maximize their chances of success in decoding them), you will have helped introduce them to a world of diversity.

A. 禁止進入 ／ 請走右側
B. 禁止进入 ／ 请走右侧

Writing is a different issue. Remember: native speakers tend to write either one form or the other, not both. It therefore suffices that students, too, write only one form or the other, as long as they try not to mix them up (remember, though, that native writers from Taiwan will simplify characters as well — most people write 台灣, not 臺灣, so if a student who writes traditional characters occasionally simplifies one or two, he can sometimes be justified in doing so). When I give my students the choice to write one form or the other, I find that about half pick traditional (because a parent or grandparent writes traditional characters, or because they simply find traditional characters more aesthetically pleasing, or because they enjoy a challenge!) and the other half pick simplified (because they want to go study in Beijing, or do business with China, or prefer fewer strokes).

Going back to the issue of reading, *what* might students practice reading? Following a standards-based approach, they should practice reading in the classroom what they will likely have to read in real life. If they are children, they might practice reading children's songs and games and stories (or pieces of these). If they are teenagers, they might practice reading e-mail love notes from other teenagers! (And street signs and menus and sports reports and movie ads, etc.) Adults might practice reading forms and instructions and newspaper articles, etc.

The only time adult native speakers read written versions of speech is when reading play scripts, movie subtitles, or closed captioning. That is only *part* (perhaps a rather small part) of the reading universe. Therefore, we should not spend *all* our time in class reading character versions of everything we practice *saying*. Reading textbook dialogues has always struck me as a bad idea: Textbook authors limit what they will put in these dialogues because they don't want to burden the students with useful spoken expressions that are not high priority for reading. Content such as the following do not often appear in beginning level Chinese textbooks:

今天得加一件襯衫，天氣涼了。也不好穿涼鞋了，得把襪子穿上！
Put on an extra shirt today, the weather's cool. And don't wear sandals, you should put on socks!

The point is that while terms such as 襯衫 "shirt" and 襪子 "socks" are basic vocabulary words that belong in a beginning curriculum for a student to *say* and *understand,* they are often withheld because the *characters* have many strokes and are low frequency in written texts, so textbook authors don't want to burden students with having to read them. So the spoken curriculum is deprived because of considerations for the reading curriculum[15].

Conversely, signs such as the following definitely belong in the beginning reading curriculum for teenagers and adults, because they are important in the real universe of written texts:

此路不通   *no thoroughfare*
售票處   *ticket office*

But is it important for beginning students to practice *saying* these expressions? You might agree that it is NOT important for a student to be able to say all content they know how to read.

As for writing, proceeding from a focus on the learner — what is important for a learner to know how to *write,* in calibration with his stage of learning? Surely a beginning learner need not know how to write 售票處, even if it's useful for him to know what it means. And since we proceed from passive (listening, reading) to active (speaking, writing) skills, it is easy to determine that the writing curriculum should be a subset of the reading — there is no reason to make the students write everything they can read. Conversely, we might say that we do not need to with-hold reading texts from students, waiting for their writing capacity to catch up. In other words, it makes no sense to restrict the students' reading diet to, say, 150 characters per semester, simply because you don't want to make them WRITE any more than 150. Their reading vocabulary might easily expand to 300 characters or more (although character counts vis-à-vis reading skills are problematic in their own right; the standards-based curriculum focuses on text-types and tasks, not character counts). Following is an illustration of the writing curriculum vis-à-vis reading and listening/speaking: the listening-speaking curriculum should perhaps be the most extensive; the reading curriculum overlaps largely but not entirely with listening-speaking; and the writing curriculum is a much more limited subset of both the listening-speaking and reading curricula.

---

[15]I realize that this is a very controversial issue with most Chinese language teachers, for reasons that have very little to do with the language forms themselves. It has been suggested that, sooner or later, one or the other of the two forms will simply "go away" or be absorbed by the other. Arguments promote both scenarios: people say, "Look at what's happening with the U.N.; their documents will only be retained in simplified Chinese. The traditional form will eventually disappear." Or they say, "Look at what's happening in China; more and more signs and other materials are being published in traditional characters. Eventually the simplified forms will be discarded." Based on current reality, though, and the increasing emphasis on diversity in the United States, I hold that teaching both forms concurrently obviates the tension for our students, and in the long run serves their best interests. I sincerely doubt that teaching both forms "doubles the cognitive load," as has also been claimed. See the following paragraphs.

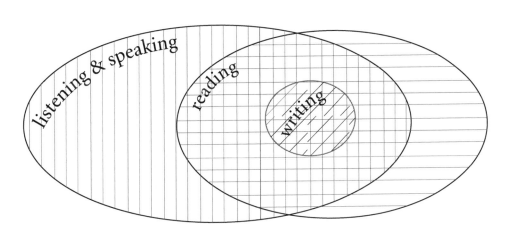

As for the implementation of the reading and writing curricula — not surprisingly the same principles that hold for listening-speaking apply here as well. Learning proceeds most effectively at the level just beyond the student's current level of competency; reading and writing texts and tasks should be contextualized; skills-getting (learning individual characters) should be balanced with skills-using (extracting as much information as possible from a real-life text); and the focus on real-world tasks should be followed by a focus on form (discussion of the linguistic forms of the language) when necessary.

Interactions with Authentic Texts

Giving students classroom training in extracting information from authentic texts is an important thing for teachers to do, because, as the national standards indicate, our goal is to produce target language users who can operate independently in the target culture.

Generally, students benefit by beginning with *pre-reading* exercises when they tackle an authentic text, in order to "activate schema" (elicit information drawn from background knowledge they already possess, on the topic of the reading) and to prepare to interact with the text — to maximize their chances of success in interpreting authentic texts <u>without</u> a prepared glossary in hand. For example, if the students are going to tackle a McDonald's Restaurant menu in Chinese, it would help to elicit from them such details as the following, based on their previous contact with McDonald's menus[16]:

---

[16]One might raise the point that most Chinese language classes would not consider working with a McDonald's menu because the characters/vocabulary used in such menus are less/least frequently used ones. The problem with "less frequently used characters" only arises if the expectation is that *all* characters in any given text must be studied. The problem fades if it is understood that meaning can be derived from infrequently encountered characters simply from the placement and format of these characters in the text and from the students' background knowledge: "麥當勞", for example. In the

What are some items McDonald's sells? List these.
What are the approximate prices of each of these items?
Do you know any of the Chinese terms for any of the items on this list?
For example: hamburger, French fries, cola? Large, medium, small? Brainstorm to see if you already know any of these words.

This activity is a good example of a learner-centered exercise: the teacher cannot tell the student anything, because the object is to find out what the *student* knows. The teacher *facilitates* the gathering of information, perhaps by taking notes (as a secretary would) on what the students say on the blackboard or on an overhead projector transparency. The advantage of doing it on the transparency is that you can photocopy it for passing out to the students later, if you choose to do so.

The second step in interacting with the text might be what is often called a *global reading exercise*: or *skimming* the text to block out the major divisions, and to extract main ideas. This is reminiscent of what a native reader does when she picks up a newspaper or magazine: she skims to obtain an idea of what the key content is. With the McDonald's menu, for example, students might use their knowledge of key menu items, range of prices, and previously encountered Chinese terminology to figure out the following:

Where are the key sections of the menus? Where are the burgers?
How many kinds are there?
Where are the accompanying items such as French fries? Dessert items? Drinks?

Remember, it is not necessary to read *every last character* on the menu. The point of the exercise is for the student to be able to extract information that would be useful to him from target language texts. In fact, the student should be encouraged to *tolerate ambiguity,* to be satisfied to confirm what he *does* know, and discard what he does not, as long as he can ascertain that what he does not know does not invalidate what he does.

The next step after reading for main ideas is to *scan for supporting details* or *specific information,* much like native readers do with a newspaper. Once they have determined the main topic of an article (perhaps by skimming the headline, and looking at any accompanying photos, captions, or highlighted sentences), they often scan through the article, looking for information that interests them. Readers

---

words of a reviewer, "麥當勞 is a three-character visual unit, highly constrained by context, so the frequency of these particular characters is regulated more by how often (students) see the word 麥當勞 than by the frequency of the individual characters themselves." Beyond recognizing the Chinese characters for "McDonald's," however, it wouldn't make sense to require the students to do too much with individual characters in the term; you would never ask them to use 麥 or 當 or 勞 in sentences, for example. Conversely, there are many characters on such menus that are *very* frequently used, and would be useful to see in context: 大, 中, 小, and 元, for example. Besides, looking at familiar and real life texts can be more *motivating* than teacher-concocted texts.

seldom read every last word of any given article, and they certainly hardly ever read every last word of the entire paper. Similarly, our students can begin to scan for specific information on the McDonald's menu. For example:

Is there a Big Mac? How much does it cost?
How much is a cheeseburger?
Is there a chef's salad? How much is it?
Is there milk? How much is it?

The task for the students might be: Find out how much it would cost to order your favorite McDonald's meal in Chinese.

Again, the point here is for the *students* to tell the teacher what they can extract from the text. In a performance-based curriculum, the learners must be constantly performing. It would entirely defeat the purpose of the exercise for the teacher to *tell* the students what they *should* be able to read — that would be teacher (not learner) centered. The teacher is useful only in as far as she can incite and support the *student's* performance; from the point of view of student learning, we are entirely uninterested in having the teacher demonstrate how well she can read the text!

After all the necessary information has been extracted from the text, the students might begin focusing on form: galvanizing their linguistic gains. What new vocabulary items have they learned? Are there unfamiliar sentence or phrase structures on the menu? This is the point at which it would be most useful for the students to *develop* a vocabulary list, complete with characters (in simplified and traditional formats, if possible), romanization, and English.

Thereafter the class might spin off into a different modality, after this reading sequence has been completed. The students might *discuss* the menu, or their individual reactions to fast food (oral/aural exercises); or they might *write* a note to a friend, requesting that he purchase certain items from a McDonald's on their behalf (writing exercises).

The Role of Literacy Training Texts and Graded Readers

Reading in Chinese is a particularly challenging adventure for the English-speaking learner (see Everson, Literacy Development in Chinese as a Foreign Language, this volume). In addition to attending to extensive reading in authentic texts, students would also be well-served by working through graded readers, a growing number of which are available (*The Lady in the Painting* (2007) being an example of a widely used one calibrated to the second level)[17]. Pairing authentic texts with readers for

---

[17] Also consider the graded readers recently published by Cheng & Tsui Company, including *Tales & Traditions: Readings in Chinese Literature Series*, edited by Xiao, et. al. (2007, 2008); as well as *How Far Away Is the Sun? and Other Essays* and *The Moon Is Always Beautiful and Other Essays*, both part of the *Readings in Chinese Culture Series* by Huang and Ao (2007, 2008). See www.cheng-tsui.com.

"literacy training" (in which students work on recognizing characters, and "becoming aware of the basic units of spoken language, the basic units of the writing system, and the mapping between the two" is the pedagogic version of China's "兩條腿走路 (walking on two legs)". This wise adage describes a process that helps propel the learner towards the goal of independent reading fluency!

Writing in Chinese involves learning the mechanics of producing the characters by hand — stroke for stroke, word-processing Chinese on a computer or digital device using software, and composing cogent Chinese for real communicative purposes. Since native speakers can read (or at least puzzle out) both forms of Chinese characters (traditional and simplified), and our non-native and heritage learners have varying reasons why they wish to become competent in Chinese, it would make the most sense to allow *them* to choose which form of Chinese they would prefer to write — simplified or full — as long as they adhere to that form conscientiously. With writing, as with speaking, after determining what our particular learners' communicative needs are, we can tailor our curriculum and classroom activities to respond to those needs. For example, students may list writing objectives such as the following:

- Text-messaging Chinese friend
- Writing a letter to a grandmother in Taiwan (or Shanghai)
- Prepare for business communication in a future career

By teaching writing as a *process* (students develop an outline of what they intend to write, list and confer with others about key vocabulary they might use, write a draft, have the draft checked by a classmate or the teacher, produce a corrected proof, submit that proof to the teacher and their classmates for feedback, respond to feedback as appropriate and produce a final draft), students can carry over skills they are working on in their native language classrooms into their foreign language classrooms as well. Also, keep in mind that corrected texts written by students themselves make excellent reading material for the class as a whole, since these texts are likely

√ at the *i + 1* level, since they are by authors who are themselves learners;
√ meaningful, since they reflect circumstances and a context familiar to the students;
√ empowering, since for the authors of the pieces being read, having the class become responsible for reading and discussing their work is a form of publication; and
√ motivating to students as authors, since they understand who their audience is to be.

Testing Language Competence

The guiding principle in a standards-based, learner-centered classroom is simply that "we test what we teach." Since we are teaching students to carry out language functions, to accomplish tasks, we might continue to do exactly the same thing for a test, except now we are grading the student's performance, based on a rubric we might develop in consultation with the students.

At the end of a semester, for example, the teacher might ask the class to brainstorm "20 topics" they are prepared to speak on for a minute, impromptu, in the target language. A beginning language class might come up with topics such as the following:

√ a self-introduction, including name, age, level in school, information about family, etc.
√ my favorite foods
√ my favorite weekend activities

An intermediate student might list topics such as the following:

√ what I like about my best friend
√ directions to get from the classroom to my home
√ how to make my favorite dish

An advanced student might choose to talk about the following:

√ the plot of my favorite book or movie
√ a funny incident that happened to me last year
√ how my family celebrates Thanksgiving

The point of the brainstorming session is to come up with a communally determined list of what has been "covered" in the course of the past semester — what content with which the students are supposedly reasonably comfortable. Each student is technically able to speak on (or, if you are brainstorming topics for a writing task, write X number of sentences about) EACH of the topics on the list. Therefore, on the day of the test, the teacher could write the topics on index cards and have the student draw (as in drawing a lot) one to perform. She is not going to know ahead of time which one she will draw, and should be ready for ALL the topics. Assessment of her work on the topic selected might be based on the following rubric, for a speech sample:

- Content: speech provides
  - a substantial amount of information relevant to the topic (4 points)
  - a reasonable amount of information relevant to the topic (3 points)
  - barely enough information relevant to the topic (2 points)
  - some but not enough information relevant to the topic (1 point)

- Accuracy: speech
  - is essentially error-free, and easy to understand (4 points)
  - has a few errors which do not interfere with comprehension (3 points)
  - has errors which make understanding more difficult (2 points)
  - leaves the interlocutor guessing at meaning (1 point)
- Fluency: speech
  - proceeds at a natural or normal rate of speed (2 points)
  - is halting (1 point)

If there is time, students might practice rating each other using the rubric, so they are quite clear on what the *performance* standards are, for the class. Rating each other is also an empowering activity, and helps build confidence.

For a writing sample, the assessment rubric used might be the same, except that in place of *fluency* the teacher might substitute something like

- Richness of expression: writing sample uses
  - a variety of apt and vivid terms and vocabulary (2 points)
  - limited vocabulary and more repetition (1 point)

Testing the receptive skills can be done in the native language, if feasible. Taking notes in the native language on the basis of a target language text is a very natural real life behavior. For example, if the student is skimming and scanning through a newspaper article about tourist sites in Xishuangbanna, assuming he has never seen an article about this particular city before, he might be required to produce a 3-day itinerary in English of what he might visit in Xishuangbanna. Or, if she has studied many menus in class, she might be tested on a menu she has never seen before, and asked to recommend (writing in English) 3 dishes for her vegetarian friend (or a friend who adores seafood).

The Role of Culture

Following is a citation from the College Board's *World Language's Framework*:

> Cultural perspectives underlie the ways in which people use languages for communication, and the patterns of behavior and products of a society; therefore, the Culture standards demonstrate the interaction of perspectives, practices, and products. A language curriculum oriented to the standards integrates these aspects of culture throughout, as they are pertinent to communicating effectively within the culture and understanding cultural phenomena "from the inside."[18]

---

[18]College Board, *World Languages Framework*, pp. 11–12.

Although what language teachers commonly teach as "culture" — big "C" culture such as historical facts and philosophic concepts, as well as small "C" culture including making ethnic foods such as jiaozi and celebrating Chinese New Year — is undeniably a part of the culture curriculum, it is necessarily only perhaps of lesser importance in that curriculum. More urgent are the subtler and more pervasive *attitudes* and *perspectives* that underlie a culture, that determine what, when, and how one says what one does, how one holds oneself, what one does when and to whom, what one wears, how one lives, what decisions one makes for one's life course, etc. (See Christensen, this volume).

Following are "cultural objectives" for units in the integrated, media-based language curriculum yet to be named, currently under development by Yale University Press (of which I am a lead author):

- Display appropriate body language (eye contact, tilt of head, amount of interpersonal space, hand movements) in polite interactions. Demonstrate tolerance for same-sex physical contact, and circumspection in opposite sex interactions.
- After viewing of video introductions to public transportation in a variety of Chinese communities, demonstrate tolerance for and familiarity with varying degrees of passenger density in various public modes of transport.
- Demonstrate familiarity with the etiquette of a Chinese restaurant meal, in which one person orders for all, or everyone participates in ordering for all, and the sharing of food as each dish arrives. Demonstrate ability to use chopsticks. Demonstrate ability to be politely tolerant of each dish, and not express either strong like or strong dislike of any. Demonstrate familiarity with and tolerance of "communal" values in eating together (communal vs. private space, for example).
- Demonstrate tolerance for clothing patterns that allow you to harmonize rather than "stick out" in Chinese communities. Demonstrate ability to interact in a friendly and accepting fashion with persons whose tastes and customs in clothing do not match your own.
- Demonstrate tolerance for notions of repressing personal desires and wants in favor of communal needs. Demonstrate ability to consider group needs in assessing personal preferences and action.

Demonstration of cultural understanding can be accomplished by real behavior (how one conducts oneself vis-à-vis the other, for example), expression in the target language (how to thank or apologize with the *right* degree of effusiveness or abjection, for example), or discussion in the native language. ("How do you feel when you are standing in a packed elevator, and people are jammed up to you?") Of course, thoroughgoing cultural understanding takes a lifetime to develop, and remains a long-term goal for everyone involved in intercultural exchange.

Conclusion

Here's a basic issue: China and Chinese are monumentally high-achieving, and absolutely deserving of nothing but the deepest admiration and respect, and ultimately will elicit respect and admiration from all. We need to *believe* this statement implicitly in order to "walk the walk" of effective standards-based instruction. We don't have to try to force our students to respect the culture that we are trying to introduce to them by being stern in the classroom, or by making our textbooks look intimidating, or by giving scholarly monologues on language structure or syntax or high C culture. It's okay to have textbooks that *look* easy, and present students classroom activities that are fun and doable (EVERY thing we do in the classroom needs to be calibrated to be achievable by all the students — so that they walk away with a sense of accomplishment and triumph). If *they* can't do it, *I* haven't presented it right, and will need to retreat to the drawing board to recalibrate. It's not about my impressing them in the classroom with my knowledge and control, it's about their impressing me with what they have learned and can do.

Except for giving directions and responding to student questions, I as the teacher only say what I hope the students will be able to say themselves, either at the present time or in the near future. Anything else I say in the classroom is "wasted speech." What percentage of time do I spend on wasted speech in every class period? I must try to get that percentage down, as much as possible.

In the final analysis, and in reiteration, it doesn't so much matter what I as the teacher say or do; it's what I can get my STUDENTS to say and do that counts. If I can get my students to talk communicatively for a minute each in the target language without doing anything at all, then congratulations to me — I'm going to keep doing what I am doing (and not doing). If on the other hand I talk rapid fire for much of my class period and I still can't get my students to say much that is meaningful, then I'll consider shutting up, and trying something other than talking at them. This essay has focused on providing some ideas on how to get students to perform. Teacher improvement, however, is a lifelong endeavor. In the words of "the great sage" (Confucius):

三人行，必有我師焉，擇其善者而從之，其不善者而改之.
In strolling in the company of just two other persons, I am bound to find a teacher. Identifying their strengths, I follow them, and identifying their weaknesses, I reform myself accordingly[19].

I look forward to continuing to stroll and learn from teachers and students alike.

---

[19] *The Analects of Confucius*, translated by Roger T. Ames and Henry Rosemont, Jr. Book 7, Number 22, p. 115–16.

Discussion Questions

1. What were some of the ideas presented in this article that you most strongly disagree with, or find most different from the way you yourself were taught in school?

2. What were some of the ideas presented that you most strongly agree with, that you will try to implement in your own teaching?

3. What were some issues you will try to explore in greater depth, through action research, observation of other people teaching, observation and feedback of your own teaching by video-recording, discussion with colleagues, reading on the topic, attending seminars and workshops, or by other means?

References

American Council on the Teaching of Foreign Languages. (n.d.). *ACTFL performance guidelines for K–12 learners.* http://www.actfl.org. (Summary only; full guidelines may be purchased from this site.)

———. *ACTFL Proficiency Guidelines — Speaking.* Revised 1999. http://www.actfl.org/i4a/pages/index.cfm?pageid=3325.

———. *ACTFL Proficiency Guidelines — Writing.* Revised 2001. http://www.actfl.org/i4a/pages/index.cfm?pageid=3326.

Analects of Confucius: A philosophical translation (1998). Trans. Roger T. Ames and Henry Rosemont Jr. New York: Ballantine Books.

Annenberg/CPB, WGBH Boston, and ACTFL. 2003. *Teaching World Languages K–12: A Library of Classroom Practices.* http://www.learner.org.

——— 2004. *Teaching Foreign Languages K–12 Workshop.* http://www.learner.org/resources/series201.html.

College Board. *World Languages Framework* (2007). http://www.collegeboard.com.

Cook, V. 2001. *Second language learning and language teaching.* London: Hodder Arnold.

Huang, Weijia and Ao Qun. 2007, 2008. *How far away is the sun?* (Volume 2) and *The moon is always beautiful* (Volume 3). Readings in Chinese Culture Series. Boston, MA: Cheng & Tsui Company.

Krashen, Stephen D. 1982. *Principles and practices in second language acquisition.* Oxford: Pergamon Press.

Lantolf, James, and Steven Thorne. 2006. *Sociocultural theory and the genesis of second language development.* Oxford: Oxford University Press.

Long, Michael. 2007. *Problems in SLA.* Mahwah, NJ: Lawrence Erlbaum Associates.

Minnesota Department of Education. *Chinese Language Programs Curriculum Development Project: FY 2007 Report to the Legislature.* Retrieved July 1, 2007 from http://education.state.mn.us.

National Standards in Foreign Language Education Project. 2006. *Standards for foreign language learning in the 21st century.* 3rd edition. Laurence, KS: Allen Press.

Ning, Cynthia. 1993. *Communicating in Chinese* (series). New Haven: Yale University Press.

———. 2007. *Exploring in Chinese* (series). New Haven: Yale University Press.

Ning, Cynthia, and John Montanaro. Forthcoming. *Mandarin Chinese: Scope and sequence for instruction in the first year.* New Haven, CT: Yale University Press.

Norris, J. M., and L. Ortega, eds. 2006. *Synthesizing research on language learning and teaching.* John Benjamins: Amsterdam/Philadelphia.

Nunan, David. 1999. *Second language teaching and learning.* Boston: Heinle & Heinle.

Ross, Claudia, Jocelyn Ross, and Fang-yu Wang. 2007. *The lady in the painting: A basic Chinese reader.* New Haven, CT: Yale University Press.

Schmidt, Richard, ed. 1995. *Attention and awareness in foreign language learning (Technical Report No. 9).* Honolulu: Second Language Teaching and Curriculum Center.

Swain, M. 1985. "Communicative competence: Some roles of comprehensible input and comprehensible output in its development." In *Input in second language acquisition.* Eds. S. Gass and C. Madden. Rowley, MA: Newbury House.

Wiggins, Grant and Jay McTighe. 2004. *Understanding by design. 2nd ed.* Alexandria, VA: Association for Supervision and Curriculum Development.

Xiao, Yun, et al. 2007, 2008. *Tales and traditions: Readings in Chinese literature series. Volumes 1 & 2.* Boston: Cheng & Tsui Company.

Chapter 4

AP® Chinese Language and Culture

Pedagogical Implications and Applications

T. Richard Chi

The University of Utah

With the launching of the first Advanced Placement® Chinese course in Fall 2006 and the first AP® Chinese exam in May 2007 by the College Board, teaching of Chinese as a foreign language has reached a new milestone. As one of the first new language offerings in the College Board's AP Programs portfolio since 1955,[1] the AP Chinese Language and Culture course and exam have effected, in very tangible ways, a timely response to the needs of teachers and students at the K–12 level, a real effort for curriculum articulation between colleges and secondary schools, and a heretofore unseen high level of enthusiasm among teachers of Chinese to discuss and seek new cutting-edge strategies to take their profession to a higher level of expectations and possibilities.

This article will exam the philosophy of the College Board's AP programs, the pedagogical principles of — and their curricular applications for — AP Chinese, and the likely impact of AP Chinese on the Chinese teaching profession now and in the future.

---

[1]The other new language offerings are Italian, Japanese, and Russian. See the *AP Chinese Language and Culture Course Description*, May 2007, May 2008, p.3, http://apcentral.collegeboard.com/apc/public/repository/ap07_chinese_coursedesc.pdf.

Why AP?

The mission of the College Board, as stated at the beginning of *AP Chinese Language and Culture Course Description* (College Board 2007, 2008) and the Board's many other publications, is "to connect students to college success and opportunity" through some of its best known programs such as the SAT®, the PSAT/NMSOT®, and the Advanced Placement Program® (AP®). The AP Program currently offers 37 courses with corresponding exams in 22 subject areas.

Based on various research findings and reports from college administrators and students, the College Board believes that the AP Program gives students a head start on college by allowing them a better chance at college admission, college credit and placement into advanced courses. The College Board reports that students who take AP courses and exams are much more likely than their peers to complete a bachelor's degree in four years or less.[2] While 61 percent of the students who had taken two or more AP classes completed a bachelor's degree in four years or less, the graduation rate stood at 45 percent for those who had taken one AP course and only 29 percent for those who had not taken any AP classes.[3]

Another crucial component of the College Board AP Program is equity, namely, equal access to the AP courses regardless of the student's socioeconomic background. The College Board states in its Equity Statement that "[the College Board] is committed to the principle that all students deserve an opportunity to participate in rigorous and academically challenging courses and programs," and that the College Board advocates "the elimination of barriers that restrict access to AP courses for students from ethnic, racial, and socioeconomic groups that have been traditionally underrepresented in the AP® Program" (The College Board 2004).

Why AP Chinese?

As China's fast growing economy and geopolitical influence continue to expand around the globe, so has interest in studying Chinese. Various surveys and estimates have put the number of secondary school students taking Chinese at 20,000 to 24,000. According to an American Council on the Teaching of Foreign Languages (ACTFL) estimate, the number of K–12 students taking Chinese today is much higher — at 30,000 to 50,000.[4] As for heritage students, surveys have put the number of students studying Chinese in Chinese heritage schools and other private schools across the United States at about 150,000. A 2002 Modern Language Association survey of foreign language enrollments in institutions of

---

[2]This information is based on a study conducted by Camara (2003), connecting the AP Program to college graduation rates.

[3]This information is provided in *AP and Higher Education*, a report published by College Board (2004).

[4]This information is provided in an article entitled "More U.S. schools pin fortune on Chinese" written by Pauline Vu of Stateline.org on March 16, 2007.

higher education in the United States indicates a 20 percent enrollment growth, from 28,456 in 1998 to 34153 in 2002, and a 51 percent increase in 2006 (over 2002) (MLA 2007). Although these numbers are very small compared to the four to five million American students taking Spanish in over 90 percent of secondary schools offering foreign language classes, the country is seeing an unprecedented growth of enrollments in Chinese classes in various institutions across all levels.

In 2003, the College Board conducted a survey among U.S. high schools to determine the extent of their interest in offering an AP Chinese course and exam; 2,400 schools expressed such an interest.[5] Following the survey, "[in] June 2003, the Trustees of the College Board approved a plan for four new AP courses and exams in world languages: Chinese, Italian, Japanese and Russian — the first new language offerings to be added to the AP Program's portfolio since its inception in 1955. The introduction of the AP Chinese Language and Culture course and exam is an important step in a commitment by the College Board to further multiculturalism and multilingualism in secondary school education." (The College Board 2007, 2008). An AP Chinese task force was assembled in August 2004 to establish the guidelines and develop the framework for the AP Chinese Language and Culture course and exam. These guidelines include the following curricular and pedagogical decisions:

- The AP Chinese Language and Culture Course is equivalent to a regular fourth-semester college level course. There are intensive language courses (6 credits per semester) parallel to non-intensive courses (3 credits).
- The AP Chinese exam is designed for students whose experience in learning Chinese language and culture comes from taking Chinese courses in secondary schools — i.e., these students are non-heritage learners. However, due to its commitment to providing access to the AP Exams to home-schooled students and students whose schools do not offer AP, the College Board does not require students to take an AP course prior to taking an AP exam. This means that all students of Chinese, including the heritage learners, can take the AP Chinese exam.
- The AP Chinese course and exam are designed to teach and assess students' culture and language proficiencies (listening, speaking, reading, writing) in three modes of communication (interpersonal, interpretive, presentational) across the five content goal areas of the National Standards (Communication, Culture, Connections, Comparisons and Communities), as outlined in the *Standards for Foreign Language Education: Preparing for the 21st Century* (ACTFL 1999).

---

[5]This information is provided in a College Board press release entitled "China National Office for Teaching Chinese as a Second Language and the College Board Announce New Chinese Language and Culture Initiative: New Agreement will Build Chinese Language Programs in U.S. Schools" on April 19, 2006.

- The course is taught predominantly in the target language.
- Both traditional and simplified forms of Chinese characters are taught and used in the course and the exam respectively.

The first AP Chinese Development Committee was assembled in the Fall of 2005 to start designing test items for the exam. A total of 3,261 students took the first AP Chinese exam in May 2007.

The AP Chinese Exam: Format and Specifications

The AP Chinese Exam has two sections. Section I, which tests students' listening and reading skills, consists of 70 multiple choice questions that take one hour and twenty minutes to complete. In the Listening section, students listen to and answer questions on various types of verbal stimuli — 10 minutes on 10–15 rejoinders in conversations and another 10 minutes on announcements, conversations, instructions, messages, and reports. In the reading section, students spend 60 minutes to read and answer questions on advertisements, articles, emails, letters, notes, posters, signs and stories.

Section II, which tests students' writing and speaking skills, consists of 12 free response questions that take one hour and twenty minutes to complete. In the writing section, students read and answer questions on a number of written texts — 15 minutes to write a story narration based on a set of four pictures, 30 minutes to write a personal letter, 15 minutes to write an email response, and six minutes to write a note relaying a telephone message. In the speaking section, students spend five minutes to answer six questions in a conversation, seven minutes to make a presentation on a Chinese cultural practice or product, and seven minutes to present a plan for an event.

Sample questions from the exam can be found in the *AP Chinese Language and Culture Course Description* (College Board 2007, 2008), and the 2007 exam questions and sample students' responses are available online at http://apcentral. collegeboard.com/apc/Pageflows/usermanagement/login/fromEPL.do after registering on AP Central.

What is AP Chinese? Pedagogical Principles and Applications

As can be gleaned from the *Course Description*, the AP Chinese Language and Culture Course has the following pedagogical requirements:

1. Design and teach a standards-based curriculum. The course is designed to teach what all students should know and be able to do, as defined by the content standards outlined in the American Council on the Teaching of Foreign

Language's *Standards for Foreign Language Learning in the 21st Century* (ACTFL 1999) (see Everson, "The Importance of Standards," this volume).

2. Provide students with a learning experience that immerses them in the Chinese language and culture. The course focuses on practicing the three modes of communication, introduces students to appropriate traditional and contemporary cultural topics, and maximizes students' exposure to authentic language and culture.

3. Engage students in doing meaningful learning activities to enhance their learning strategies and problem-solving skills.

4. Provide frequent and varied formative and end-of-unit summative assessment and use rubrics to assess students' performance.

5. Use effective teaching strategies to provide students from all backgrounds, including both heritage and non-heritage students, with a positive learning experience. Consider the multiple intelligences of the students and learn to teach classes with students that have multi-level skills.

Design and Teach a Standards-Based Curriculum

The National Standards for Foreign Language Education project was launched in 1993. In 1996, ACTFL introduced the general National Standards in *Standards for Foreign Language Education: Preparing for the 21st Century*. In 1999, an expanded version of the 1996 document was published that contained K–12 and K–16 language-specific standards for seven languages, including the Chinese K–12 standards.

The *"Communication"* standards focus on interpersonal, interpretive and presentational communication. The main goal of communication is to learn to communicate in languages other than English. The *"Cultures"* standards emphasize the ability to demonstrate knowledge and understanding of the products, practices and perspectives of other cultures. The *"Connections"* standards refer to the ability to connect to other disciplines and gain knowledge through the foreign language, including those distinct viewpoints and perspectives accessible only through the foreign language and culture. The *"Comparisons"* standards describe students' ability to develop and demonstrate insight into the nature of language and culture by comparing the target language and culture with the learner's own language and culture, respectively. Finally, *"Communities"* aims for students to use the foreign language in the classroom and in other settings for practical and other personal enrichment purposes.

The *Course Description* stipulates that the AP Chinese course must incorporate the five content standards into its curriculum. Therefore, the five standards have essentially become one of the most crucial organizing principles for curriculum, course materials and assessment design. In addition, they can be used as guidelines for teachers to select and adapt their instructional resources to the learning goals specified in the standards.

Focus on Practicing the Three Modes of Communication

Traditionally, course designs center around the acquisition and assessment of the four skills — listening, reading, speaking and writing. However, the national standards advocate teaching and practicing communication in the three modes of interpersonal, interpretive and presentational communication. This shift in no way diminishes the importance of the four skills when learning a foreign language. On the contrary, the national standards embrace the four skills in a way that more accurately describes the way the four skills are used in communication.

As specified in the *Course Description*, interpretive communication involves the interpretation of a broad range of oral and written messages. In AP Chinese, students use listening and reading skills to identify and summarize main points and supporting details. They learn how to use listening and reading skills, cultural knowledge, personal experience and contextual clues to guess and make inferences to interpret spoken and written messages.

Interpersonal communication involves all four language skills since a speaker/writer's ability to interact with an interlocutor depends on the speaker/writer's ability to understand the interlocutor's spoken or written message. Interpersonal communication takes place when people are having a conversation or writing emails to each other.

The presentational mode of communication involves using speaking and writing skills to present either spoken or written messages in a variety of forms and settings. Presentations can take the forms of giving a speech or report, narrating or describing an event, or producing a newscast or video. Students can make coherent and cohesive presentations on topics they have researched. While continuing to practice their handwriting skills in composing their written work, students are also given intensive training on computer keyboarding to meet the needs of modern day technology as well as to prepare them for the an internet-based AP Chinese exam.

Introduce Students to Appropriate Traditional and Contemporary Cultural Topics

The AP Chinese Language and Culture Course aims to provide the students with a learning experience that immerses them in the Chinese language and culture. To that end, students must be introduced to both traditional and contemporary topics. Selecting and addressing appropriate cultural topics serves a number of crucial purposes for the AP Chinese course. First, it allows students to learn about various aspects of contemporary Chinese society and culture in various regions in and outside China. Second, it introduces students to significant persons, events, products and perspectives in Chinese history. Third, selecting themes related to contemporary and traditional Chinese culture naturally includes vocabulary items that need to be covered in the AP Chinese course. Fourth, it provides students with the opportunity to work with all five standards. For example, students make comparisons and contrasts between target cultural products, practices and perspectives with those of their own, leading to a deeper understanding and appreciation of both cultures (Cultures and Comparisons). Studying appropriate topics also enables them to acquire knowledge in other areas of subject matters (Connections). Finally, they become resourceful, independent language users in communities that extend beyond their Chinese language classrooms (Communication and Communities).

The AP Chinese *Course Description* provides a list of general cultural topics to guide teachers in selecting specific topics for exploration in the course. In an effort to identify appropriate contemporary and traditional cultural topics for the AP Chinese course, the author of this article surveyed the participants of AP Chinese summer institutes he conducted in 2006 and 2007. Specifically, the participants were asked to identify topics perceived to be interesting to and appropriate for the middle and high school students. The topics proposed by the participants can be placed into ten thematic categories. While some of the themes and topics may seem familiar at first glance to teachers who may have taught them in classes, others are actually not usually covered in Chinese classes. The chart below is a summary of the proposed topics.

Main Themes	Topics
1. Everyday Life	• Food: favorite foods, cooking, recipes, eating out • Clothing: what's hot and what's not, weather and climate • Living quarters: floor plans, arranging furniture, cleaning house • Transportation: transportation vehicles, routes and maps • Shopping: purchase for personal needs at various venues • Banking: currencies and exchange rates, online banking • Emailing and chatting with friends • Health and medicine: illnesses, going to the doctor's and hospitals, taking medicines, reading instructions, Chinese herbal medicine and acupuncture
2. School Activities	• Selecting classes and making schedules; favorite classes • Talking to counselors and teachers • Signing up for clubs and extra-curricular activities • Participating in school events: fashion shows, stage presentations of Chinese stories, field trips • Discussing topics of interest: drugs and smoking prevention, sex education, sexual preferences, dating, divorce and impact on children, summer Olympics in China, global warming and environmental issues, current events

Main Themes	Topics
3. Interpersonal Relations	• Family and societal relationships • Making friends • Interacting with a friend's elders • Attending social events: birthdays, dinners, potlucks • Social customs: giving and receiving gifts, invitations; meeting someone for the first time; being a guest at a friend's home; offering congratulations and condolences • Applying for a job
4. Spare Time and Recreation Activities	• Hanging out with friends at the mall, sports events, night market, karaoke, movies, and watching television • Inviting friends to go to concerts and art exhibits • Reading books (literature, genre novels), magazines, comics and cartoons on various topics • Participating in community activities, public debates and performances • Playing online games; YouTube and podcasts • Emailing and chatting with friends • Traveling: checking out famous tourist sites, making an itinerary and ordering tickets
5. Pop Culture	• Popular online games • 新潮手機 (i-Phone, m-phone) • Hot movies and music groups • Popular TV shows • Celebrities such as 姚明，周杰倫，郎朗
6. Holidays and Festivals	• Important holidays in the target and students' own cultures • Important cultural practices: legends and historical figures, ceremonies and celebrations (foods, music, dances and community activities) • Important cultural perspectives: significance of family and societal relations, philosophies and value systems underlying the activities
7. Traditional Thought and Culture	• Family relationship and obligations: 家庭倫理，孝順 • Teacher-student relationships: 尊師重道 • Societal relationships: 小我 vs. 大我 • Famous philosophers and their thoughts: 孔子，老子 • Chinese maxims and idioms: 吃得苦中苦 方爲人上人
8. Literature, Arts and Performing Arts	• Popular poetry and novels • Calligraphy and painting • Famous writers and artists • Chinese opera, costumes

Main Themes	Topics
9. Interactions between China and Other Cultures	• Individualism vs. benevolence (個人利益超越對他人謙讓) • Capitalism vs. traditional ethics (資本主義超越傳統倫理道德) • Globalization vs. isolationism (全球化取代閉關自守)
10. Language for Emergency Situations	• Medical emergencies • Automobile accidents • Earthquakes and typhoons • Getting lost • Losing valuables

Maximize Students' Exposure to Authentic Language and Culture

In order to help students develop an understanding and appreciation of Chinese culture by directing them to explore contemporary and historical Chinese culture, teachers must introduce students to a wide range of authentic materials in AP Chinese. The use of authentic materials, such as travel brochures, train and plane schedules, menus, registration forms, signs, labels, newspaper editorials, magazine articles, conversations between native speakers, radio or TV broadcasts and commercials, announcements, etc., as teaching aids has long been advocated by language instructors. This is because authentic materials directly acquaint learners with elements of the language and culture they are studying (Hadley 1993).

The AP Chinese exam assesses students' ability to interpret and interact with culturally authentic language in both multiple-choice and free-response questions. The stimuli of the test items for the interpretive, interpersonal and presentational tasks are culturally and linguistically authentic. Test takers listen to conversations, messages and narratives. They read notes, letters, emails, and realia of various kinds such as ads, songs, posters, stories, and newspaper articles. They are required to perform verbal exchange tasks such as job interviews, describe an event plan, and give a presentation on a chosen cultural topic. They respond in writing to a written message (a note, letter, or email) or to an aural message (a phone message).

Engage Students in Meaningful Activities That Enhance Problem-Solving Skills

Savignon (1983) characterizes communicative competence as "a dynamic rather than a static concept that depends on the ***negotiation of meaning*** between two or more persons who share some knowledge of the language . . . [and that] it applies to both written and spoken language." AP Chinese advocates engaging students "in constant and *meaningful* language use" and that "teachers make use of varied performance-based activities . . . [to] ensure that all students are fully engaged in the *meaning-making* process of language acquisition. . . ." *Negotiation of meaning* as a means to achieve the end of communication is a central pedagogical strategy in AP Chinese. As outlined in the *Course Description*, meaning-making activities designed for AP Chinese include, but are not limited to, "conversations based on daily life activities, role-plays, debates, oral reports, storytelling, and discussion of Chinese films. Written tasks include writing letters or emails in Chinese to Chinese pen pals, writing papers on aspects of traditional Chinese culture, using calligraphy to copy couplets in preparation for a Spring Festival celebration, making and writing New Years' greeting cards that include Chinese proverbs, and reading and reciting classical Chinese poetry. Authoring and editing a class newspaper, with reviews of contemporary Chinese films, painting, and song lyrics, can also engage students actively in their learning." Engaging students in doing meaningful tasks prepares them to handle the challenges of the real world. Students learn the Chinese language and culture by practicing meaningful language in appropriate contexts in which they get ample experience to learn how to communicate interpersonally, interpretively and presentationally.

Central to these instructional strategies and activities is engaging students to perform, to enhance their learning strategies, and to develop strong problem-solving skills on their own. Teachers must design learning activities that challenge the students to use their linguistic, cultural and world knowledge and their cognitive skills to complete the tasks successfully — which they are likely to perform in the real world — on their own. They will be challenged to interpret what they hear and read, determine how they should respond in speech or in writing, and demonstrate how they should behave in culturally and socially appropriate ways. Teachers must allow their students to take risks in solving their own problems, even if they make mistakes. All language users make mistakes while learning the language in and outside the classroom. During this process of trial and error, they mispronounce words, construct incorrect sentences, misinterpret the main themes and supporting details of written and spoken messages, write incorrect characters, or misuse discourse styles in speech and writing, or use registers inappropriate to the situation. Their mistakes often cause them to be misunderstood or to not being understood at all. But they do learn to guess, hypothesize, make inference, generalize, and draw conclusions. They learn on their own.

While it is every teacher's dream and hope that their students will learn to interpret and produce correctly the language they are learning, teachers must also remember that, despite all the correct information they give to their students, the students must be given the opportunity to internalize and use the information to solve real problems on their own. It is essentially the students who must do the learning, while the teachers do their coaching on the sideline, because the ultimate goal is to train our students to become independent, resourceful, and life-long language learners.

Traditionally, teachers have placed a disproportionate emphasis on having students memorize information — Chinese characters, vocabulary, idioms, sentence patterns, and piecemeal or disjointed cultural information. However, to help students sharpen their skills to search for answers on their own, students must learn to use other cognitive skills as well, as listed below.

- 假設　　　hypothesizing
- 推理　　　making inference
- 分析　　　analyzing
- 綜合　　　synthesizing
- 歸納　　　generalizing
- 結論　　　concluding
- 預測　　　predicting
- 猜測　　　guessing
- 比較　　　comparing
- 對比　　　contrasting
- 自我檢查　self-monitoring
- 自我改錯　self-correcting
- 自我評估　self-assessing
- 自我學習　self-learning

Below are two sample activities illustrating how students can be guided to complete a grammar task and a reading task. The key strategies used in these activities are asking leading questions, requiring the students to think on their feet and weigh different options, and ultimately guiding them to find the answers on their own.

Sample Activity 1: When do Chinese speakers use the question particles 嗎 ma, 吧 ba and 呢 ne when asking questions?

Communicative Functions: making inquiries; confirming information

Context: daily routines

I. INITIAL PRESENTATION

Present some initial information about the question particles such as 吗，吧，呢, etc., illustrate the use of the three particles, and guide the students to analyze, hypothesize and generalize to figure out the grammatical rules on their own.

Question particles: Unlike English, the structure of a Chinese question sentence is not different from that of a non-question sentence. The question sentence uses a "question particle" at its end.

Examine the following three dialogues and determine what message each question particle is used to convey. A and B stand for Speaker A and Speaker B respectively. Q stands for "question particle." Question particles occurring for the first time are underlined with the corresponding literal English translations also underlined. Each Chinese sentence is written in pinyin, with a word-for-word translation and a colloquial translation in English.

Dialogue 1

A: 你好吗?
   (you good q)
   How are you?
B: 我很好, 谢谢.
   (I very good thanks)
   I'm fine. Thanks.

Dialogue 2

A: 你好吗?
   (you good q)
   How are you?
B: 我很好, 你呢?
   (I very good you ne)
   I'm fine, and you?
A: 很好. 忙吗?
   (very good. busy q)
   Fine. You busy?
B: 很忙. 你呢?
   (very busy. you ne)
   Quite busy, and you?

Dialogue 3

A: 你是李先生吗?
   (you are Li Mr. q)
   Are you Mr. Li?
B: 是. 你是百先生吧?
   (am. you are Bai Mr. ba)
   Yes. You are Mr. Bai, right?

II. DRILLS AND ACTIVITIES

1. Work with your study partner to draw a line to connect each of the question particles on the left with its communicative function listed on the right. Be ready to present this information to the class.

   嗎 **ma** The speaker already has an answer and is merely seeking an affirmation from the hearer.

   呢 **ne** The speaker is asking the same question already asked of him/her by the hearer without repeating it.

   吧 **ba** The speaker is simply raising a yes/no question and does not know if the answer is going to be "yes" or "no."

2. Using the question particles, you and your partner ask each other a few questions to find out who you are, how you are, what you are, where you are from, etc.

3. Imagine you have to communicate in writing with your partner who has lost his/her voice because of a severe cold. Do the same activity in #2 above by writing down and exchanging with each other your questions and answers on a piece of paper.

III. ASSESSMENT TASK

The teacher can have the students complete the task below to assess if the students have truly conceptualized the usage of the question particles — and their ability to read in the Chinese characters already taught in the unit.

   Fill in the blanks in the dialogue below with the choices given. A choice may be used more than once.

   Choices: 嗎，吧，呢

   A: 最近忙 1 ？
   B: 不忙，你 2 ？你的工作怎麼樣？
   A: 還好。你的工作 3 ？還好 4 ？
   B: 忙是不忙，就是沒有意思。
   A: 忙總比不忙好。要是沒有工作，就更沒有意思了。是 5 ？

IV. ANALYSIS OF THIS ACTIVITY

1. Students are given the opportunity to analyze language data and figure out the grammatical rules in a meaningful way. As a result, they enhance their cognitive skills and develop learning strategies to solve problems on their

own. They also retain this grammatical information better than if they are simply fed this information by the teachers or the textbook.

2. They get to compare question constructions in Chinese and in English, providing evidence that the Comparisons standard is integrated into their learning.

3. They get to practice interpretive, interpersonal and presentational communication in a meaningful way, demonstrating that the Communication standard is integrated into their learning.

4. The assessment task is contextualized. Students are required to use their cognitive skills to analyze the context to connect what they know about the question particles to how they would use them in the appropriate contexts.

5. The assessment task also measures students' ability to determine if a context can be interpreted in different ways to allow the usage of more than one question particle in the same context (either 嗎 or 吧 can be used in 4 and 5), thus reflecting their understanding of language ambiguity.

Sample Activity 2: Interpreting an authentic reading text.

Authentic language refers to what is said, heard, and seen in Chinese-speaking communities. As mentioned before, using authentic language as instructional material familiarizes students with various aspects of the Chinese culture. In addition, engaging students in working on tasks involving authentic materials also sharpens their ability to use cognitive skills, helps them develop strong language learning strategies, and strengthens their problem-solving skills.

Below is an invitation to an art exhibit. Both the cover of and the content of the invitation are displayed, followed by activities to be performed by the students.

I. PRE-READING 讀前活動

1. Based on your own experience, what information do you expect to hear or see in an invitation?

2. Write down in Chinese (in pinyin or in characters) the vocabulary for the information you expect to hear or see in an invitation.

II. READING 閱讀活動: SKIMMING AND SCANNING (略讀與細讀)

1. Skim the text to find the main categories of information.

2. What does the word 請柬 on the cover of this invitation mean? What words does the character 請 remind you of (for example, words whose meanings might be connected to 請柬)?

3. How long will the exhibit last? What do the words 起 and 止 mean in the context of dates?

謹 訂 於 2月 21日 起 至 3月 4日 止 假 本 畫 廊 舉 辦
"無 名 氏 書 法 展" 敬 請 光 臨 、 觀 賞 、 指 教 。
酒 會 : 2月 21日 （ 星 期 六 ） 下 午 3 時 ～ 5 時

龍 門 畫 廊 敬 邀
（ 上 午 10： 30至 下 午 6： 30星 期 一 休 假 ）

4. What does the character 至 mean? It is between two dates. It is also similar to the character 到. Use this information to guess the meaning of 至.

5. What kind of exhibit is this? Does the word 畫 help?

6. Two sets of hours can be found in this text. What are the hours of the exhibit? What is the other set of hours for? Is the exhibit open seven days a week? How do you know? Notice one set of hours is connected to 酒會, and the other to 休假.

7. Who is the host of this exhibit? Examine the words to the left of the character 邀.

III. POST-READING 讀後活動

1. Call a friend to inform her or him about this invitation. Give your friend the information in this invitation. Invite your friend to go with you. Make an arrangement with your friend to meet.

2. Write an email to your friend about this invitation. Give your friend the information in this invitation. Invite your friend to go with you. Make an arrangement with your friend to meet. Ask your friend to write you back.

3. How would an invitation of this kind look in your own culture, in terms of the kinds of information included in it and how it is organized and presented in the invitation?

IV. ANALYSIS OF THIS ACTIVITY

1. The pre-reading tasks activate the learners' background knowledge of the language and culture and help the learners understand the perimeters of the reading task at hand.
2. The skimming and scanning tasks require the learners to use their cognitive skills to hypothesize, analyze, guess, make inference, and draw conclusions about the meaning of messages presented in the text. Learners are guided to identify the main categories of information, find supporting details, and guess the meaning of unfamiliar words and phrases.
3. The post-reading tasks connect what they learn from the reading text with their personal experience (Communities).
4. By doing such a meaningful learning activity, students get to analyze authentic materials, practice their problem-solving skills, and use what they learn to complete tasks emulating real life situations. They get to practice the three modes of Communication (interpersonal, interpretive, presentational), compare the cultural products from Chinese and their native cultures (Comparisons), and do research on related topics to connect to other subject areas, such as cultural studies (Connections).

Assess with Rubrics to Measure Students' Progress.

According to the *Course Description*, "the AP Chinese course reflects the proficiencies exhibited throughout the Intermediate range as described in the American Council on the Teaching of Foreign Languages (ACTFL) *Proficiency Guidelines*." The ACTFL *Proficiency Guidelines*, first published in 1986,[6] provide global definitions of listening, speaking, reading and writing proficiencies for integrated performance at the Novice, Intermediate, Advanced and Superior levels (see ACTFL 1999 and ACTFL 2001). The assessment criteria for each of the four skills define proficiencies in four areas:

1. Functions: global linguistic functions such as asking and answering questions, narrating, and describing.
2. Content and context: topics in various thematic contexts about which the functions are performed.

---

[6]The Speaking and Writing Proficiency Guidelines were revised in 1999 and 2001, respectively.

3. Text type: Information can be presented in memorized words and phrases, sentences, paragraphs, or connected discourse.
4. Accuracy: The level of precision with which communication is performed.

In 1998, ACTFL introduced the *ACTFL Performance Guidelines for K–12 Learners* (see ACTFL 1998). The performance guidelines, which draw from both the *Proficiency Guidelines* and the National Standards, describe the language skills and cultural knowledge of K–12 learners in a standards-based curriculum up to the Pre-Advanced (Intermediate High) level. While the National Standards define "what all students should know and be able to do," thus providing information on "what" should be taught in the K–12 foreign language classrooms, the *Performance Guidelines for K–12 Learners* describe "how well" students can be expected to do the "what" within the school setting.

These performance guidelines are organized according to the three modes of communication in terms of: **Comprehensibility** (How well is the student understood?), **Comprehension** (How well does the student understand?), **Language Control** (How accurate is the student's language?), **Vocabulary Usage** (How extensive and applicable is the student's language?), **Communication Strategies** (How do the students maintain communication?), and **Cultural Awareness** (How is their cultural understanding reflected in their communication?). The *Performance Guidelines* contain rubrics that describe characteristics of performance for each of the three modes of communication at the three proficiency levels (Novice, Intermediate and Pre-Advanced) in terms of each of the five assessment areas listed above. The AP Chinese course prepares students to demonstrate their proficiencies through the Intermediate level as articulated in the *Performance Guidelines*.

To assess students' language and cultural proficiency, the AP Chinese course stipulates that both formative and summative assessments should be conducted to evaluate students' ability to perform in the three modes of communication. The result of formative assessment, given typically within each unit of study, informs the teacher and the students of the students' progress, which can also in turn help the teacher make necessary instructional adjustments. Summative assessments, often timed and typical of the AP Chinese exam, can be given within a unit of study or after completing several instructional units.

Informed and inspired by the *ACTFL Proficiency Guidelines, the ACTFL Performance Guidelines for K–12 Learners*, and the National Standards, the AP Chinese course requires teachers to set learning goals and design assessment procedures and criteria to identify evidence of learning. The AP Chinese course also advocates that the assessment criteria should take the form of rubrics against which students' work will be evaluated. Also, these rubrics should be given to and reviewed with the students before the assessment takes place. An example of such assessment criteria can be found in the rubrics-based scoring guidelines used to assess students' performance in the free-response questions of the 2007 AP Chinese Exam, as shown in the following tables (see The College Board 2007).

TABLE 1.   Free-Response Questions

Communication Mode	Language Skill	Tasks
1. Presentational	Writing	Story Narration
2. Presentational	Writing	Personal Letter
3. Interpersonal	Writing	Email Response
4. Interpersonal	Writing	Relay Personal Message
5. Interpersonal	Speaking	Conversation
6. Presentational	Speaking	Cultural Presentation
7. Presentational	Speaking	Event Plan

TABLE 2.   Assessment Areas

Task Completion	Delivery	Language Use
• Response to prompt	• Pace	• Vocabulary
• Text type	• Pronunciation	• Grammatical constructions
• Organization of information	• Register	

TABLE 3.   Rating Scale

Score[7]	Definition
6	Excellent: demonstrates excellence
5	Very Good: suggests excellence
4	Good: demonstrates competence
3	Adequate: suggests competence
2	Weak: suggests lack of competence
1	Very weak: demonstrates lack of competence
0	Unacceptable: contains nothing that earns credit

Table 4 below contains the complete scoring guidelines for the free-response questions for Conversation. There are six congruent questions in each conversation. The response to each question is scored separately and holistically based on the scoring guidelines. To become further familiarized with how students' responses are scored, please do the activity below.

Using the Conversation scoring guidelines below, the readers gave the score of "6: Excellent" to Student A and "3: Adequate" to Student B. The question and the responses from Student A and Student B are given below, along with comments from the readers.

---

[7]These are scores assigned to each student response. They ARE NOT the final AP Grades, which are 5: Extremely well qualified; 4: Well qualified; 3: Qualified; 2: Possibly qualified; 1: No recommendation.

TABLE 4.   2007 Scoring Guidelines for Conversation

Interpersonal Speaking: Conversation

		TASK COMPLETION	DELIVERY	LANGUAGE USE
6.	**EXCELLENT** Demonstrates excellence in interpersonal speaking	• Directly addresses prompt and provides a very thorough and appropriate response; includes elaboration and detail • Smoothly connected sentences	• Natural pace and intonation, with minimal hesitation or repetition • Accurate pronunciation (including tones), with minimal errors • Consistent use of register appropriate to situation	• Rich and appropriate vocabulary and idioms, with marginal errors • Wide range of grammatical structures; with minimal errors
5.	**VERY GOOD** Suggests Excellence in interpersonal speaking	• Directly addresses prompt and provides a thorough and appropriate response; may include elaboration and detail • Connected sentences	• Smooth pace and intonation, with occasional hesitation and repetition • Occasional errors in pronunciation (including tones) • Consistent use of register appropriate to situation except for occasional lapses	• Variety of grammatical structures; with minimal errors
4.	**GOOD** Demonstrates competence in interpersonal speaking	• Directly addresses prompt and provides an appropriate response • Sentences may be loosely connected	• Generally consistent pace and intonation, with intermittent hesitation and repetition • May have several errors in pronunciation (including tones) which do not necessitate special listener effort • May include several lapses in otherwise consistent use of register appropriate to situation	• Mostly appropriate vocabulary and idioms, with errors that do not generally obscure meaning • Mostly appropriate grammatical structures, with errors that do not generally obscure meaning

TABLE 4.   Continued

		TASK COMPLETION	DELIVERY	LANGUAGE USE
3.	**ADEQUATE** Suggests competence in interpersonal speaking	• Directly addresses prompt and provides a basic but appropriate answer • Disconnected connected	• Inconsistent pace and intonation, with hesitation and repetition that interfere with comprehension • Errors in pronunciation (including tones) sometime necessitate special listener effort • Use of register appropriate to situation inconsistent or includes many errors	• Limited appropriate vocabulary and idioms, with frequent errors that sometimes obscure meaning; intermittent interference from another language • Mostly simple grammatical structures, with frequent errors that sometimes obscure meaning
2.	**WEAK** Suggests lack of competence in interpersonal speaking	• Directly addresses prompt and provides an appropriate but incomplete answer • Fragmented connected	• Labored pace and intonation, with frequent hesitation and repetition • Frequent errors in pronunciation (including tones) necessitate constant listener effort • Frequent use of register appropriate to situation	• Minimal appropriate vocabulary; with frequent errors that obscure meaning; repeated interference from another language • Limited grammatical structures, with frequent errors that obscure meaning
1.	**VERY WEAK** Demonstrates lack of competence in interpersonal speaking	• Addresses prompt minimally or marginally • Very disjointed sentences or isolated words	• Very labored pace and intonation, with constant hesitation and repetition • Frequent errors in pronunciation (including tones) necessitate constant listener effort • Constant use of register appropriate to situation	• Insufficient, inappropriate vocabulary; with frequent errors that significantly obscure meaning; constant interference from another language • Little or no control of grammatical structures, with frequent errors that significantly obscure meaning

TABLE 4. Continued

		TASK COMPLETION	DELIVERY	LANGUAGE USE
0.	**UNACCEPTABLE** Demonstrates lack of competence in interpersonal speaking	• Mere restatement of the prompt • Clearly does not respond to the prompt • "I don't know," "I don't understand," "Please repeat," or equivalent in Chinese • Not in Chinese • Blank (although recording equipment is functioning or mere sighs		

Examine the two students' responses and the scoring guidelines in Table 4 to determine if you agree with the readers' ratings. Remember, your ratings must be based solely on the students' responses and the scoring guidelines. What you do not hear in the responses and what you do not see in the guidelines cannot enter into your considerations.

Instructions for the student followed by Conversation Question 1:

• You will have a conversation with Li Ming, your host parent greeting you at the airport about your arrival for a stay as an exchange student in Beijing. "你好，我是李明。欢迎你来北京。坐了这么长时间的飞机，累坏了吧？"

Below is Student A's response to the question above, followed by the evaluator's comments.

• "Uh … 其实还好。我很高兴有这个机会能够来到这边当交换学生。我希望在这边的经验 uh 能够很丰富，而且我可以学到很多不同的.. 知识。希望这 次来这趟旅行是很快乐而且我可以玩得非常开心。"
Sample: A
Score: 6

The student directly addresses the prompt and provides a very thorough response that includes an elaboration on the reasons for being excited to visit Beijing. Sentences are smoothly connected and delivered at a natural pace without hesitation or repetition. Pronunciation is accurate, vocabulary is rich and suitable, and grammatical structures are varied and appropriate.

Below is Student B's response to the same question, followed by the evaluator's comments.

> ▪ "还好，是不是..时特别累。因为..?? 是因为有一个是比较很..是好的睡眠，在.. 在飞机上。 那 uh 是?? 是我想了解一下 是北京的一些情况。那是因为这是我第一次到达北京。"
> Student: B
> Score: 4

The student directly addresses the prompt and provides an appropriate answer in loosely connected sentences. However, the answer does not contain any elaboration. The pace of delivery is generally consistent. Vocabulary is mostly appropriate, but there are some grammatical errors, such as 是不是时特别累；有一个比较..好的睡眠在飞机上；但是因为这是我第一次到达北京。

Develop Instructional Strategies That Address Learner Variability

In order to achieve effective teaching and learning, language teachers must also consider individual learner differences such as age, motivation, family language background, language learning aptitude, personality, cognitive styles, affective states, beliefs about language learning, learning strategies, proficiency in the native language, etc. (Altman 1991; Skehan 1989; Larsen-Freeman and Long 1991; Ellis 1994). To make the AP Chinese course accessible for every student, AP Chinese teachers also need to become aware of individual learners' differences. As shown in the studies cited above on individual learner differences, these variables interrelate and interact in complex ways. However, by always being aware of the individual differences of the students and incorporating learning activities addressing differences such as individual students' learning styles, a teacher can lead more students to success.[8]

While a verbal/linguistic learner enjoys speaking and writing and learning about language, a visual/spatial learner learns more effectively with illustrations and visual designs and patterns. While an interpersonal learner enjoys doing work in groups, an intrapersonal learner prefers to work alone and introspectively. To ensure effective learning, teachers will need to use different instructional strategies to meet the needs of these different learning styles. The verbal/linguistic learner will most likely learn well by doing role plays, reading stories, writing letters and analyzing grammatical structures. The visual/spatial learner would enjoy doing communicative tasks such as drawing maps and making illustrations. The

---

[8]Adapted from Diehl and Helbing's *Pre-AP: Strategies in World Languages and Cultures—Building Proficiency, Leader's Notes.*

interpersonal learner learns most effectively by doing group projects, and the intrapersonal learner may enjoy making cross-linguistic and cross-cultural comparisons and contrasts.[9]

While some factors for individual learner differences are stable and are likely to be influenced by the environment (Carroll 1981), such as language learning aptitude and age; other factors, such as motivation, could change due to learning experiences (Crookes and Schmidt 1989). Classroom observations have also shown that factors for individual differences such as beliefs about language learning, learning strategies, and even affective states could change as a result of teacher sensitivity to individual differences, use of varied and effective instructional strategies, and cultivation of a more congenial and cooperative classroom atmosphere. To learn more about the application of the multiple intelligences theory (Gardner 1993) in the classroom, see Christison and Kennedy (1998).

Today, a common problem facing many Chinese language teachers and programs is teaching a multiple-skills and multi-level class in which they find true beginner learners as well as heritage learners of various backgrounds. Such a class requires differentiated teaching. Wu (2007) in her study entitled "Robust Learning for Chinese Heritage Learners: Motivation, Linguistics and Technology," goes into detail explaining the differences between the Chinese Heritage Learners (CHL) and the Chinese True Beginners (CTB). Based on data collected from classroom observations, Wu discovered CHL and CTB can be distinguished in terms of their motivations and goals for learning Chinese, their perspectives toward the learning of the culture, and their various approaches toward learning the linguistic aspects of the Chinese language. Wu's theoretical framework for developing robust learning opportunities for the two groups of learners argues that the notion of learner-centeredness and the pedagogical implications of the National Standards must be adopted as the central organizing principles for the curriculum of such a course. She provides detailed sample learning activities and online exercises as well as illustrations for both instructional and assessment procedures. This study addresses all relevant aspects of the issue of teaching CHLs with well argued and very credible recommendations.

AP Chinese Course Audit Curricular and Resource Requirements

To request authorization to label a course "AP," teachers must complete and submit an AP Course Audit form, on which the teacher and principal attest that their course includes or exceeds the curricular requirements listed below. The AP Chinese teachers must also submit an electronic copy of the course syllabus that demonstrates inclusion or improvement on the curricular requirements. Although

---

[9]Adapted from *The Massachusetts world languages curriculum framework: Making connections through world languages.* 1995. Malden, MA: Massachusetts Department of Education.

the College Board supports the principle that each school develop its own AP curriculum, the audit procedure provides AP teachers with a set of expectations to ensure that the approved AP course meets the expectations of a college-level course established by college and secondary school faculty nationwide. The audit procedure also provides guidelines that ensure that the each curriculum submitted for auditing follows the guidelines specified in the *AP Chinese Course Description*, and that the school provides the resources necessary for the students and the course.

The curricular requirements for the AP Chinese course audit mirror the pedagogical principles articulated in the *AP Chinese Course Description*. These curricular requirements, listed below, constitute the indispensable components of the AP Chinese course.

1. The teacher has read the most recent *AP Chinese Language and Culture Course Description*.
2. The course prepares students to demonstrate their level of Chinese proficiency across the three **communicative** modes, as articulated in *Standards for Foreign Language Learning in the 21st Century* (Standards); and at the Intermediate level, as articulated in the *ACTFL Performance Guidelines for K–12 Learners*.
3. The course also addresses the Standards' other four goals: **cultural** competence, **connections** to other school disciplines, **comparisons** between Chinese language and culture and those of the learners, and the use of the language within the broader **communities** beyond the traditional school environment.
4. The teacher uses Chinese almost exclusively in class and encourages students to do likewise.
5. Language instruction frequently integrates a range of Chinese cultural content that exposes students to perspectives broader than their immediate environment, such as the fundamental aspects of daily life in China, Chinese family and societal structures, and national and international issues.
6. Assessments are frequent, varied, and explicitly linked to the standards' goal areas. Prior to assigning an assessment task, teachers share with their students the criteria against which their performances will be evaluated.
7. The teacher chooses from among both conventional print and aural materials such as textbooks, audiovisual materials, and web-based content designed for language learning. They also make use of materials generally used by native Chinese speakers, such as print and web-based texts; animated computer programs; and video-, CD-, and DVD-based products. Teachers scaffold students' experiences with these texts, particularly those that would normally be considered beyond the grasp of high school students.
8. The course teaches students to develop both communication and language learning strategies, such as inferring meaning either through socio-cultural context or linguistic features.

9. The teacher plans and implements structured cooperative learning activities to support ongoing and frequent interpersonal interaction, and employs a range of instructional strategies to meet the diverse needs of his or her learners.
10. The course provides students with opportunities to develop both Chinese handwriting skills and word processing skills in *Hanyu Pinyin* or *Bopomofo*.

Aside from the above curricular requirements, there are two additional resource requirements.

1. The school ensures that each student has a copy of the texts utilized in the course for use inside and outside of the classroom, and has access to an in-school computer capable of inputting and displaying Chinese characters.
2. The school facilitates student use, outside of instructional time, of in-school or public library computers capable of inputting and displaying Chinese characters.

Additional course audit information on audit timeline, review process, syllabus self-evaluation checklist, and course authorizations can be accessed on AP Central (http://apcentral.collegeboard.com/apc/public/courses/teachers_corner/46361.html).

AP Chinese and its Possible Impact on the Chinese Teaching Profession

The rapid growth of Chinese programs in U.S. secondary schools and colleges since the early 1990s has brought new challenges as well as new opportunities to the Chinese teaching profession. Increasing numbers of students and programs also increase the need for more professionally trained teachers. Both pre-service and in-service professional developments are needed for new and experienced teachers, including guest teachers from China under the auspices of the College Board Guest Teacher Program[10]. The need for instructional materials and pedagogy designed specifically for K–12 is also a critical issue that must be addressed without further delay. And, the newly launched AP Chinese course and exam are already making their impact on the profession.

First, to familiarize high school teachers with the content and pedagogy of the AP Chinese course and the format and specifications of the AP Chinese exam, the College Board launched its first AP Chinese workshops and summer institutes in

---

[10]A College Board press release dated Aug 13, 2007 reports that a second group of 64 guest teachers from China arrived in the United States in early August, increasing the number of teachers in the program by a nearly 200 percent and making it the largest guest teacher program in the United States.

2006. A large number of teachers from secondary and community language schools have participated in AP Chinese workshops and summer institutes[11] in 2006 and 2007. In addition, Chinese Language Teachers Association (CLTA) and Chinese Language Association of Secondary-Elementary Schools (CLASS) sponsored two articulation forums in 2006 and 2007 which drew gatherings of K–12 and college teachers in unprecedented numbers. And the topic of AP Chinese dominated the discussions.

Second, the AP Chinese course audit procedure[12] and the AP Chinese Exam will lend impetus to secondary Chinese programs streamlining their AP Chinese curriculum and, quite possibly the courses leading up to AP Chinese. Vertical articulation at the K–12 level in programs that offer multi-level courses can be expected to happen over time. College programs anticipating increasing enrollment of high school students who have taken the AP Chinese exam will likely begin to feel the pressure to make a concerted effort, sooner than later, to articulate with the secondary school curriculum. Making this effort at the college level is essential to ensure continuity and constancy in these students' Chinese learning experience in college.

Third, the AP Chinese course and exam could potentially make a big impact on the teaching of second and third year Chinese in college. As indicated in the *Course Description*, the AP Chinese course is designed to provide students with a learning experience equivalent to a fourth semester college course that develops students' proficiencies throughout the Intermediate range and deepens students' immersion into the language and culture of the Chinese speaking world. Students who took the AP Chinese course and exam, received AP scores of 3 and above, and wished to continue studying Chinese after entering college will likely enroll in intermediate and advanced level classes. Gone are the days and practice in some colleges where entering freshman students who had taken Chinese classes in high schools were placed in beginning level or less challenging courses.

These students are likely to pose some new challenges to program directors and teachers who may find it necessary to adjust the content and pedagogy of second and third year courses to accommodate heterogeneous groups of students due to age differences, possible disparities of language proficiencies, and adoption of topics and instructional approaches appropriate for the diversified groups.

Anticipating college-entering freshmen who did well in the AP Chinese exam to seek granting of college credits and enrollment beyond the second year is not

---

[11]In 2007, 99 teachers of Chinese received scholarships to attend AP and Pre-AP Chinese summer institutes on four Chinese university campuses in Beijing, Shanghai and Nanjing. There were additional AP and Pre-AP Chinese summer institutes held in the United States.

[12]Based on AP Chinese course audit information made available to the AP Chinese Development Committee in its February meeting by Keith Cothrun, Associate Director, College Board World Languages and Cultures Advanced Placement Programs, there were 185 AP Chinese curriculum submissions for course audit for 2008–2009. As of January 29, 2008, 144 had been fully authorized.

unreasonable. Granting credits and allowing placement into courses beyond the beginning level have been a long standing practice among many colleges and universities in the U.S. The College Board is quoted as saying in its *Bulletin for AP Students and Parents, 2007–2008*[13]:

> With qualifying AP Exam grades, you can qualify to earn credits, placement, or both at more than 90 percent of four-year colleges and universities in the United States, as well as at colleges and universities in 40 other countries. At many of these institutions, you can earn up to a full year of college credit (sophomore standing) once you've attained a sufficient number of AP Exam grades. (p. 5)

In a recent College Board study conducted by the Crux Research, Inc. in 2007, college language department chairs were contacted to find out about their institutions' credit granting and placement policies for students with qualifying AP Exam grades. In total, 100 language chairs were interviewed — 3 for AP Chinese, 39 for AP French, 15 for AP German, 6 for AP Italian, 7 for AP Japanese, and 63 for AP Spanish.[14] These interviews generated a number of interesting findings relevant to our discussion:

- Two-thirds of colleges interviewed give students credit if they score a 3 on the AP Exam; this jumps to 90 percent for scores of 4 or 5.
- Three-quarters of College Faculty report that students who score a 5 or higher on the AP language exam will be <u>placed</u> in a third semester or higher course.
- Eighteen percent of respondents would place a student scoring a 4 on the AP Exam into the fifth semester of language study or higher.
- Thirty-six percent of respondents would place a student scoring a 5 on the AP Exam into the fifth semester of language study or higher.
- Colleges appear to be more generous with placement policies than with credit policies for scores of 4 or 5.
- Most faculty (74 percent) feel that AP's Language curriculum is a good fit with their curriculum.
- Most college respondents agree (85 percent) that AP Language experience in high school helps students be successful in their college language courses.

---

[13]This document can be accessed on AP Central http://www.collegeboard.com/student/testing/ap/about.html.

[14]This information was relayed to the AP Chinese Development Committee at its winter meeting on February 28, 2007 in a Power Point presentation entitled "AP World Languages Summary of Findings: AP Teachers/College Faculty Research" by Keith Cothrun, Associate Director, World Languages and Cultures Advanced Placement Programs, the College Board.

Although the three Chinese language chairs represented only a small three percent of the study group, as expected since the AP Chinese exam was administered for first time in 2007, one would hope that the institutions with existing credit granting and enrollment policies for French, German and Spanish would consider implementing similar policies for Chinese based on equity.

When discussing the issues of credit granting and placement, we must take a close look at the 2007 AP exam data. As shown below, two sets of performance data were presented — one for the Total Group of 3,261 students that took the first Internet-based AP Chinese exam, and the other for the Standard Group[15] that the exam targeted.

As shown in the Total Group chart below, the majority of the students did quite well on the exam: 81 percent (2,643) of these test takers received the score of 5 (Extremely Well Qualified), 11.8 percent (386) received 4 (Well Qualified), and 4.5 percent (146) received 3 (Qualified). Of particular interest is the fact that, as shown in the Standard Group Chart, nearly 85 percent the Standard Group of test takers, who were non-heritage learners and who made up a little over 11 percent of the total number of test takers, received a score of 3 or above. Among them, 48.8 percent (177 students) received a score of 5; 19.6 percent (71 students) received a score of 4; and 16.5 percent (60 students) received a score of 3. In other words, the majority of the students in the Standard Group did extremely well in the 2007 exam.

These statistics pertaining to the performance of the non-heritage learners clearly show that a higher percentage of these true beginners were in fact quite competitive in handling the challenge of the AP Chinese exam. These initial test data further suggest, quite strongly, that true beginners can indeed succeed in attaining very respectable amounts of language and literacy acquisition during their high school years.

One might suspect that the success of nearly 10 percent of the total number of test takers who were true beginners could be attributed to the possibility that the test was too easy or that the readers were too lenient since none of the students could have finished the AP curriculum, which was launched in Fall 2006, before the exam was administered in May 2007. Such a possibility could not have existed due to two facts. The first fact is that validity of the AP Chinese exam was established

---

[15]Standard Group refers to students who generally receive most of their foreign language training in U.S. schools. They did not indicate on their answer sheet that they regularly speak or hear the foreign language of the examination, or that they have lived for one month or more in a country where the language is spoken. Based on this definition and for practical reasons, it is this author's opinion that the Standard Group test takers should be characterized as non-heritage learners, who can be loosely referred to as the true beginners. And the other test takers fell into the category of heritage learners. Pronunciation, grammar and the ability to complete tasks as demonstrated by student responses to the interpersonal (Conversation) and presentational (Cultural Presentation and Event Plan) speaking tasks also left the impression that the great majority of the test takers were heritage students.

using college professors' grading in a college comparability study conducted in 2007. During this college comparability study, a portion of the exam was administered to college students enrolled in the fourth semester courses — the level at which the AP Chinese course and exam were pitched. The college students' responses to the Free Response questions were scored in AP Reading, along with the responses of the AP Chinese test takers. The results of this college comparability study were considered when setting AP grades to ensure that the AP grading standards were comparable to or higher than the grading standards used by the college professors when they evaluated their own students in the corresponding college fourth semester courses. The resulting AP Chinese exam grading standards were applied to evaluate the performances of all AP Chinese test takers. The second fact is when evaluating the performances of the test takers, the AP Chinese readers were not given — nor did they have access to — any background information about the test takers. The readers applied the same scoring guidelines in their evaluations of the test takers' responses.

Given these facts and the test result data, one can logically conclude that the successful performances of these true beginners in the AP Chinese exam spoke voluminously to the high quality of their high school Chinese programs and the skills of their teachers, despite the suspicion and criticisms sometimes directed at the level of rigor and depth of high school Chinese programs.

Again, one might surmise, quietly reasonably, that it is likely that many of the 92 percent of the students who took the 2007 AP Chinese Exam and received a score of 4 and 5 may pursue college credit and/or placement beyond the second year course. Language departments offering Chinese language courses will likely address this matter in the very near future by reviewing existing policies for other languages and making new policies to accommodate these students of Chinese. If a majority of the students who performed well in the AP Chinese exam indeed enter

Total Group

Examination Grade	Chinese Language and Culture	
	Number of Students	**Percentage**
5	2,643	81.0
4	386	11.8
3	146	4.5
2	36	1.1
1	50	1.5
Total	3,261	
3 or Higher / %	3,175	97.4
Mean Grade	4.7	
Standard Deviation	0.74	

Standard Group

Examination Grade	Chinese Language and Culture	
	Number of Students	**Percentage**
5	177	48.8
4	71	19.6
3	60	16.5
2	24	6.6
1	31	8.5
Total	363	
3 or Higher / %	308	84.8
Mean Grade3.93		
Standard Deviation	1.30	

Chinese classes in college, Chinese programs may anticipate an immediate impact on their advanced level courses in the coming academic years as a result of increasing enrollment and the pressure to find additional resources to accommodate these students.

Third, with the AP Chinese exam data, college teachers will not only know the students' AP scores and have some general understanding of their proficiencies, but will also be able to access more specific information about the weaknesses and strengths of the students' performance in the AP Chinese exam. Teachers can find information on the exam questions, scoring of the exam, samples of and commentaries on students' response, and AP grade distribution. All of this specific and detailed information will assist college teachers in placing these students in the proper courses and in creating strategies to teach these students who had studied Chinese in secondary schools. For instance, the free-response questions scoring statistics below provide information about the weakness and strength of student performance, as shown in the charts below.

Teachers can also find specific information on, and recommendations for, improving student performance. For example, regarding student performance in the 2007 exam on the task of Story Narration, which required the students to narrate a story based on a series of four pictures, the Chief Reader noted in his report a common failure by students when organizing and writing their paragraphs. The Chief Reader also made the recommendation: "Students need to practice writing in paragraphs, not just in isolated sentences. Teachers should have students write in paragraphs with appropriate connectors."

Also, the overall picture of student performance, as shown by the statistics, suggests that the topic Relay Telephone Message would have been the most difficult task in the exam. However, as observed by the Chief Reader, this could be due to the fact that "some students did not understand the nature of the task.

Free-Response Questions Scoring Statistics
All Students

Question	Mean	Standard Deviation	Number of Points Possible
Writing			
Story Narration	4.41	1.27	6
Personal Letter	4.62	1.16	6
Email Response	4.81	1.38	6
Telephone Message	3.42	1.6	6
Speaking			
Conversation	27.51	5.53	36
Cultural Presentation	4.23	1.43	6
Event Plan	3.98	1.38	6

Standard Group

Question	Mean	Standard Deviation	Number of Points Possible
Writing			
Story Narration	3.62	1.14	6
Personal Letter	4.12	1.07	6
Email Response	4.86	1.62	6
Telephone Message	2.91	1.45	6
Speaking			
Conversation	21.39	7.53	36
Cultural Presentation	3.34	1.41	6
Event Plan	3.15	1.35	6

They thought that the phone message was directed to them, so they answered the message instead of relaying it." Such information can be very useful to college instructors in their effort to develop new and varied strategies to meet the needs of these students coming into their advanced level classes.

Finally, AP Chinese can potentially have a further impact on the pedagogy of Chinese courses at all levels. A close examination of the pedagogical principles of the AP Chinese will lead to two important observations. First, the course encompasses some very crucial pedagogical philosophies and applications that came out of the Proficiency and Standards movements in the 1980s and 1990s. Second, the pedagogical principles of the AP Chinese course and exam can be — and perhaps should be — applied to Chinese courses at ALL levels, from kindergarten through college.

At the AP Chinese workshops and summer institutes in 2006, a great majority of the participants who planned to launch AP Chinese in the fall thought the course and the exam would be too difficult for their students who had studied Chinese for two to three, or even four, years. The biggest reason for their concern, as explained by these teachers, was their students lacked the background and training in their pre-AP experience necessary for them to succeed in AP Chinese. To properly prepare students for the challenging AP Chinese curriculum, Chinese programs and teachers in secondary schools who plan to offer AP Chinese either now or in the future will have no choice but to educate themselves about the philosophy behind the course and start implementing its applications in courses prior to AP Chinese. And to that end, AP Chinese can conceivably become a great motivating and rallying force to bring secondary school teachers together in an effort to update and upgrade their teaching in classes at all levels.

It is unclear if AP Chinese can potentially impact college Chinese programs in a similar way. The AP Chinese course was conceived as being an equivalent to a fourth semester college course. However, it is equally unclear that the fourth-semester courses in colleges across the United States can be typified as sharing and practicing all or some of the pedagogical notions and approaches as articulated in the *AP Chinese Course Description*. There is no horizontal articulation either — or, at least no systematic articulation — between courses purported to be at the same levels among college Chinese programs. Even though many of the AP Chinese students would end up in the advanced classes in college — and some adjustments will need to be made to accommodate these students, as argued above, it is hard to say if college programs will be so inspired by AP Chinese that they will voluntarily implement vertical articulation throughout their offerings — or, if they will, to what degree.

Nevertheless, AP Chinese, as a resource for curriculum design, holds great potential for all Chinese programs and teachers. And, among a great number of Chinese teachers, hopes are high that all the exciting and enthusiastic discussions and activities generated by AP Chinese will continue as a sustained effort to inspire and inform all of us to become ever better course designers and classroom teachers.

References

American Council on the Teaching of Foreign Languages. 1998. *ACTFL performance guidelines.* Available for purchase online at http://www.actfl.org/i4a/pages/index.cfm?pageid=3327.

———. 1999. *ACTFL proficiency guidelines: Speaking.* http://www.actfl.org/i4a/pages/index.cfm?pageid=4236.

———. 2001. *ACTFL proficiency guidelines: Writing.* http://www.actfl.org/i4a/pages/index.cfm?pageid=4236.

———. 1999. *Standards for foreign language education: Preparing for the 21st century.* http://www.actfl.org/files/public/StandardsforFLLexecsumm_rev.pdf.

Altman, H. 1991. Foreign language teaching: Focus on the learner. In *An introduction to second language acquisition research*, ed. Larsen-Freeman, D. and M. Long. London: Longman.

Camara, W. 2003. College persistence, graduation, and remediation. *College Board Research Notes (RN-19).* New York, NY.

Carroll, J. 1981. Twenty-five years of research on foreign language aptitude. In *Individual differences and universals in language learning aptitude,* ed. K. C. Diller. Rowley, MA: Newbury House.

Christison, M., and D. Kennedy. 1998. Applying multiple intelligences theory. *English Teaching Forum* 36 (2):11–13, accessed at http://www.ericdigests.org/2001-1/multiple. html.

The College Board. 2004. *AP® and higher education.* http://www.collegeboard.com/prod_downloads/ipeAPC/04884aphigheredbro_36745.pdf.

———. 2007. *AP® Chinese language and culture 2007 scoring guidelines,* http://apcentral. collegeboard.com/apc/public/repository/ ap07_chinese_sgs_final.pdf.

———. 2007–2008. *Bulletin for AP® students and parents.* http://www.collegeboard.com/ student/testing/ap/about.html.

———. 2007, 2008. *AP® Chinese language and culture course description.* http://apcentral. collegeboard.com/apc/public/repository/ap07_chinese_coursedesc.pdf.

Crookes, G. and R. Schmidt. 1989. Motivation: Reopening the research agenda. *University of Hawaii Working Papers in ESL* 8: 217–56.

Ellis, R. 1994. *The study of second language acquisition.* Oxford University Press.

Gardner, H. 1993. *Frames of mind: The theory of multiple intelligences.* New York: Basic Books.

Hadley, Alice Omaggio. 1993. *Teaching language in context.* Boston: Heinle & Heinle.

Larsen-Freeman, D., and M. Long, eds. 1991. *An introduction to second language acquisition research.* London: Longman.

Massachusetts Department of Education. 1995. *The Massachusetts world languages curriculum framework: Making connections through world languages.* Malden, MA: Massachusetts Department of Education.

Modern Language Association. 2007. "New MLA survey shows significant increases in foreign language study at U.S. colleges and universities." Press release, November 13, 2007, http://www.mla.org/pdf/release11207_ma_feb_update.pdf.

Savignon, Sandra J. 1983. *Communicative competence: Theory and practice.* Reading, MA: Addison-Wesley Publishing Company.

Skehan, P. 1991. Individual differences in second language learning. *Studies in Second Language Acquisition* 13: 275–98.

Wu, Sue-Mei. 2007. Robust Language Learning for Chinese Heritage Learners: Technology, Motivation and Linguistics. In *Teaching Chinese, Japanese and Korean heritage students: Curriculum, needs, materials, and assessment,* ed. by Kimi Kondo-Brown and James Dean Brown. Lawrence Erlbaum Associates, Inc.

Section 2

Teacher Knowledge and Pedagogical Decisions

Chapter 5

Literacy Development in Chinese as a Foreign Language

Michael E. Everson
The University of Iowa

If you ask a student who is currently enrolled in a Chinese language class why she decided to study Chinese, the chances are good she will say that she wanted to learn something different, or that she was fascinated by Chinese characters. Indeed, the elegant and aesthetic design of the characters have for centuries served as not simply a writing system but also an art form that has captured the imagination of those who experience it. Students quickly discover, however, that learning to read and write in Chinese is a labor-intensive endeavor, one that requires significant reserves of time, patience, discipline, and perseverance. As their teacher, you will want to understand the theory and practice behind reading and writing in Chinese so as to help your students find their way as they embark upon this challenging journey.

This chapter is designed to help you take your first steps by learning what it is we think we know about reading and writing in Chinese as a foreign language, as well as understanding some pedagogical principles that will help your students progress. Towards this end, this chapter takes a "Big Issues" approach as its organizing principle and presents these issues in a way that blends theory, research, and practice. That is, you will be introduced to aspects of the reading process that are foundational for you to consider as you seek to build a supportive environment for your students to develop strong literacy skills in Chinese, as well as understand some of the pitfalls and challenges they will experience along the way. These "big issues" are not the only issues related to reading and writing in Chinese, but they encompass the most important theoretical and practical questions that you'll encounter on a daily basis with your students.

Reading

The act of reading is a highly complex process, and one that has always fascinated psychologists and educators. Unlike speech, which a child can acquire through normal interaction with others, reading is a skill that must be learned through instruction. I am reminded of the bumper sticker that I often see on cars that pass me on the highway: "If you can read this, thank a teacher." Yet, reading in their first language (L1) is not a skill that is learned equally well by all children, leading psychologists to be interested in all the factors responsible for variability in children's reading performance. Consequently, how well children are, or are not, learning to read is a major indicator of how well our educational system is faring, for reading is a critical skill to develop if one is to function meaningfully in a modern society.

Reading in a second language (L2) has also received a great deal of interest from researchers in the past few decades (see Swaffar, Arens, and Byrnes 1991; Day and Bamford 1998; Kern 2000; Bernhardt 1991, 2000; Koda 2005; and Birch 2007, among others). This should not be surprising given the number of immigrants who routinely take up residence in the United States, or the fact that citizens who grow up speaking languages other than English in their homes (typically referred to in our profession as "heritage language learners") are often interested in preserving their native language in both oral and written forms. These needs are aligned with those of policymakers who believe that heritage language speakers should maintain their language as part of the overall language capacity of our nation (Brecht and Walton 1993). In addition to research endeavors into L2 reading, both public and private entities are seeking to initiate longer sequences of foreign language instruction in American mainstream education. While the greatest portion of formal foreign language learning in America has traditionally taken place in our high schools, the ambition of producing K–12 and even K–16 foreign language sequences has received a great deal of attention of late by foreign language educators and government funding agencies. Notable are initiatives such as the National Security Education Program's (NSEP) Flagship programs, designed to take language learners to superior levels of language proficiency in Chinese and other less commonly taught languages, levels virtually unreachable in traditional university language programs. It should be noted that The NSEP Flagship programs are also of interest to reading specialists because the majority of the languages that are taught in this program do not employ the Roman alphabet. For example, the Oregon Flagship program in Chinese is implementing a K–16 language learning model (Falsgraf and Spring 2007; Spring, this volume) that provides a coherent and logical sequence between grades to insure continuity in the development of language proficiency. With programs like this in place, we will not only be able to understand the reading process as it develops in students along different points of the K–16 trajectory, but also have the additional benefit of seeing bilingual reading development in students who are studying, from a young age, languages employing writing systems that are distinctly different from the Roman alphabet used in English.

Charting the Way

To help us understand the L2 reading process, Bernhardt (1991) has put forth a model derived from research data based on the experiences of intermediate-level college learners of French, German, and Spanish. The model highlights the following important components that will give you a more comprehensive understanding of the elements in play as your students learn to read in Chinese. The components of the Bernhardt model are both text-based and extratext based, developed from data derived from research studies (for an updated summary of studies, see Bernhardt 2000). The primary data source has been error types that readers made in their recall protocols, comprehension measures completed by research subjects in their native language describing all they can remember about an L2 text they have just read. The text-based components of Bernhardt's model are: 1) word recognition, or how a learner misinterprets the semantic meaning of a word; 2) phonemic/graphemic decoding, or how a learner misinterprets a word that sounds or is visually similar to another word; and 3) syntactic feature recognition, whereby a learner fails to recognize the proper syntactic connection between words, even though the learner has correctly identified the meaning of words individually. The extratext based, or conceptually based, factors include: 1) intratextual perception, which includes how readers reconcile the different portions of the text, therefore providing insight into how readers organize discourse; 2) metacognition, which deals with the extent to which readers reflect on what they are reading, and gives insight into whether they are monitoring their comprehension as to what the text is really about; and 3) prior knowledge, which refers to readers' world, cultural, and domain/topical knowledge or personal experiences that help or hinder their ability to interpret the text. In addition to these factors, Bernhardt added the reader's first-language reading ability as a significant contributor to L2 reading comprehension. This model has been very helpful in elucidating important reading processes, but has been based on data taken from French, German, and Spanish, a shortcoming that Bernhardt recognizes because languages employing non-alphabetic scripts have not been represented. Yet, this model, along with the theory derived from L1 reading, can give us insights into the CFL developmental reading experience and help guide us in developing CFL reading pedagogy. Let us, then, use the components of the Bernhardt model as a guide or a type of map to navigate the makeup of the Chinese classroom to better understand not only what some of our learners' problems will be, but why these problems are happening. To do this, we'll formulate a series of "issues" that this model predicts will occur, and give guidance to you as a teacher about some of the steps that are available to you to deal with these issues.

Jssue #1: Students Coming from an Alphabetic Reading Background

If your students grew up speaking (and reading) English as their native language, their initial literacy development involved learning to read in an alphabetic system. This developmental process is highly complex, and many theorists believe that the process actually starts before a child's introduction to the printed word, that is, when he or she acquires language and determines at some level that words and syllables are composed of even smaller units of sound, or phonemes. Studies have, in fact, found a relationship between a child's awareness of sounds and his or her later reading ability (Goswami and Bryant 1990). Shu and Anderson (1999) have also stated that learning to read involves "becoming aware of the basic units of spoken language, the basic units of the writing system, and the mapping between the two." An advantage of reading in alphabetic systems is that beginning readers can often sound out the pronunciation of unfamiliar words, thereby enabling them to access meaning through the use of so-called grapheme-phoneme conversion rules, or applying sounds to letters and letter clusters to obtain the pronunciation of the word. Chinese characters, however, are not alphabetic, but logographic in nature. That is, they represent words or morphemes, and not phonemes, and only represent the pronunciation of the characters in highly irregular ways, if at all. (For more on this topic, see Yun Xiao's "Teaching Chinese Orthography and Discourse: Knowledge and Pedgagogy," this volume.)

What this means is that native English speakers cannot apply their ability to read in alphabetic systems to their study of Chinese characters in the same way as they would when learning Spanish, French, or German. Because these languages employ alphabetic writing systems, many of the principles students already know for reading alphabets in English can apply in learning to read in these second languages. Students can, for instance, immediately apply approximate pronunciation to new words they encounter in these languages, understand words in these languages that either look or sound the same as their English equivalents (termed "cognates"), and even understand that words in these languages embedded in longer sections of print are demarcated by spaces between them.

Learners of Chinese, however, are hampered on a number of fronts. First, students learn Chinese through the use of romanization, a "helping language" which uses the Roman alphabet to represent Chinese sounds, with diacritical markings used to represent the tones. The primary romanization system used in Chinese as a foreign language classrooms today is *pinyin*, the system used in China to help children initially learn the pronunciation of Chinese characters. Unfortunately, *pinyin* violates many principles of English orthography such as having an initial "q" represent a "ch-" sound yet never being followed by the letter "u" as it must in English, or an initial "c" in *pinyin* representing an aspirated "ts" sound, violations which make it even more difficult for students to correctly master the Chinese sound system (Bassetti 2007). Students learn quickly that this difficulty in discerning the pronunciation of characters makes them difficult to memorize quickly and effortlessly. Researchers also believe that native Chinese readers may have developed processes whereby they process print in a more holistic and visual manner, whereas native English speakers, due to the fact that they have grown up learning to read with an alphabetic system, will be more accustomed to reading in alphabets where individual letters and letter clusters represent the sounds of the spoken language.

WHAT THIS MEANS FOR THE TEACHER

Given this situation, teachers should be patient and realize that learners who come from an alphabetic reading background will not be able to transfer all their alphabetic reading strategies to learning Chinese, especially those involving the complex process of word recognition. That is, because the Chinese writing system is qualitatively different from English, the time it takes your students to gain proficiency in Chinese reading will be longer. Indeed, the federal government has categorized foreign languages according to the time it takes for native English speakers to learn them, with languages such as Chinese, Japanese, Korean, and Arabic being classified as Category IV languages, or those that require learners to spend up to three times more time to reach an equivalent proficiency in languages such as Spanish. As a teacher, then, you must expect your students to learn at a slower rate.

The same will apply to learning to write in Chinese. It is important to remember that native Chinese learners have spent countless hours practicing the writing of Chinese — much more time than learners of Chinese will ever be able to devote in an American classroom setting. Therefore, expecting your students to be able to master Chinese writing quickly, especially writing Chinese characters from memory, will be unrealistic. Since learning to write characters is a long and involved process, it will be important for you to gauge your expectations and the expectations of your curriculum when you begin to demand from your students that a certain amount of Chinese characters be memorized by heart. As you gain experience teaching in your school, you will begin to get a feel for the amount of time your students need to study in order to progress in learning the language according to your expectations. In developing their curricula, Chinese teachers have come to understand that requiring their students to memorize how to write excessive amounts of characters by heart is an unreasonable expectation. Consequently, many teachers choose a strategy whereby certain characters must be written by memory, while others are allowed to be mastered for recognition only. These types of pedagogical trade-offs also enter the picture when the teacher must decide on a strategy for the students to learn both simplified and/or traditional character forms. Students whose parents come from Hong Kong or Taiwan, for example, may wish to learn traditional characters at some point during their study, so the teacher might prepare modules to explain how traditional characters are formed, and what they have in common with their simplified counterparts.

Another important aspect that you will need to become more comfortable with is your students' use of *pinyin*. It's very common for native Chinese teachers to dislike *pinyin*, as they view it as "not being Chinese." Certainly, this is true, but it is important to remember that for a significant amount of time in your students' language learning careers, *pinyin* is their lifeline to spoken vocabulary acquisition and eventual reading development. This again comes from the fact that their native language background is based on an alphabetic system, and until they gain more familiarity with the workings of the Chinese character system, as well as develop a larger inventory of Chinese characters, they will rely on *pinyin* to a significant extent to help them remember and pronounce Chinese characters. Again, it is important to stress that if you wish to develop your students' spoken language proficiency at a rapid rate, you should do this in *pinyin*, as an over reliance on their learning characters when your goal is to improve their spoken language will result in slower development of the spoken language.

Jssue #2: Becoming "Aware" of Chinese Orthography

If students are coming to Chinese from alphabetic backgrounds in their L1 reading experience, what strategies do they perform in learning a script that is not alphabetic in nature? This would come under the component of "metacognition" in the Bernhardt model, the idea that readers make decisions about their own learning and how best to carry out the many processes involved in the act of reading. For example, research indicates that beginning adult learners use a number of strategies to memorize characters, including rote memorization, creating idiosyncratic stories about how characters look or are pronounced, and using the character's semantic and phonetic elements for memorization purposes, though initially it seems that the latter strategy is not beneficial in the long run (McGinnis 1999). Adult learners finishing one year of Chinese also seem to prefer a strategy of learning the meaning and pronunciation of Chinese characters together (Everson 1998), indicating that the retrieval of meaning for these learners is not exclusively a visual process. When tested among beginning learners with more intensive and longer learning experiences, Ke (1998) documented that learners preferred a strategy of writing characters as two-character compounds rather than as single characters. Likewise, he discovered a relationship between learners' valuing and understanding of Chinese character components and their ability to recognize and produce characters. Findings substantiating this relationship were also noted in a study of learners finishing one year of Chinese who were generally able to guess the meaning of unfamiliar characters based on the meaning of the character's semantic radical (Jackson, Everson, and Ke 2003). Highly focused research on radical awareness, defined as an understanding of the role of radicals in forming Chinese characters and the ability to use this knowledge consciously in learning characters, was also found to develop early in the experience of first-year learners, and advance rapidly during the first year of study (Shen and Ke 2007). While continuing to develop, however, this awareness did not increase at such a dramatic rate during the second and third years of study. The authors state that this apparent plateau might be explained by the slow process of restructuring that the students' reading ability might be undergoing as they deal with a new orthography in general, and different types of Chinese characters in particular. It could also reflect the students' attempt at using different types of knowledge sources such as their declarative knowledge of radicals, the procedural knowledge of "how" to use this knowledge, and the strategic knowledge of "when" these knowledge sources can be applied, akin to what Koda (2005) terms "intraword awareness." Shen (2005) also found that students use strategies that pertain primarily to "orthographic knowledge" to learn characters — that is, the strategy of visualizing graphic structures of characters, connecting with previously learned characters, and using semantic and phonetic radicals to learn characters.

WHAT THIS MEANS FOR THE TEACHER

When viewed together, the results of these studies indicate that the understanding and use of the principles that make up the Chinese writing system are not only good for Chinese language students to know as background information, but are also important strategic components for their reading development. There is also evidence that instructors who introduce characters together with purposeful background as to the characters' etymological background, information and analysis of their radicals, and examples of the words as used in different contexts, increase the depth of concept-driven processing for the characters and help students link them more effectively to characters already learned, a strategy that is far more powerful in terms of student retention than is rote memorization (Shen 2004).

Issue #3: Reading is a *Language Activity*

For years the teaching community has been thinking of language instruction in terms of "the four skills"; because of this, there is a tendency to view reading as an isolated skill that is somehow separate from listening, speaking, and writing. In fact, reading is a *language activity* that is heavily dependent upon a learner's experience with the language. Recall again Shu and Anderson's (1999) idea that reading is "becoming aware of the basic units of spoken language, the basic units of the writing system, and the mapping between the two." When young children begin to learn to read, they have already developed a sense of the language that will serve as the foundation for their reading even before their encounter with the printed word. Researchers are adamant that a child's familiarity with how the English language's sound system operates is so important that it can actually predict a child's ability to read later on. In spite of this theoretical and empirical support derived from L1 reading that describes how spoken language development contributes to reading development in a complex process, it is perplexing that we continue to view the confluence of the spoken and written language in CFL as a relatively straight-forward process for our learners, and assume that our Chinese language students should begin to learn to read in Chinese immediately. As stated above, with its poor sound-to-symbol correspondence, Chinese is qualitatively different from the alphabet your students used to learn to read in their first language, and students have virtually no spoken language proficiency in Chinese upon which to build their reading proficiency.

WHAT THIS MEANS FOR THE TEACHER

The ramifications of this fact form one of the most controversial issues in Chinese language pedagogy; namely, when is the best time to introduce characters? This is a highly complex issue, with a host of factors that must be taken into consideration — what are the goals of your program for reading? Does your program stress oral proficiency at the expense of reading proficiency? Do you have heritage learners in the same class with non-heritage learners? Do you have more than one level of Chinese learning in the same classroom at the same time? Despite the many factors complicating this issue, there is enough theoretical and practical justification (see Walker 1984) to support the idea that adult learners may benefit from learning a substantial amount of Chinese via romanization before learning large amounts of characters, and therefore, before authentic reading instruction begins. Let us look at some of the factors that are important to consider.

Because reading is a language activity that depends on other language skills, it is important that Chinese language learners develop listening and speaking skills as quickly as possible. Because the Chinese script has no exact phonetic rendering through which beginning learners can acquire appropriate amounts of vocabulary, unlike their counterparts who are learning Spanish, French, and German, Chinese language students must use a romanization system such as pinyin at the novice level, with reliance on this system tapering off as the students advance in their learning. As was mentioned earlier, it is very clear that the majority of native Chinese teachers do not like pinyin, as it is difficult for them to read and is certainly "not Chinese." Yet, if teachers try to push too many characters on their students too early in the language learning experience, they will simply overload students, causing them to become frustrated, unmotivated, and likely to quit. In the beginning stages of their study, your students are trying to master a number of new things, such as Chinese being a tonal language, a language with a phonetic and morphological system very different from English, and a language that employs a complex written system. Complicating this by throwing in excessive amounts of characters is therefore a recipe for failure. Textbooks, therefore, tend to start students with *pinyin* and an introduction to radicals, then introduce characters together with *pinyin* (see, for example, Yao et. al. 2008). You will learn that one of your most difficult tasks will be balancing your students' progress with the amount of time students can reasonably afford to dedicate to their study. If this balance falls out of alignment to one extreme, students will not be challenged and will not progress; if it falls out of alignment to the other extreme, students will feel overloaded with work and will give up or drop your course, while those remaining in the class may be unmotivated if they perceive the class to be nothing but an endless exercise in learning characters. In addition, one study (Packard 1990) demonstrated that students who delayed learning characters by as little as three weeks after learning Chinese via romanization were better able to discriminate Chinese phonetics and transcribe unfamiliar syllables in Mandarin than were students who began to learn characters from the beginning of the program. This led the researcher to suggest that ". . . the initial focus on non-phonetic character orthography results in a reduced awareness of the sound structure of the language" (p. 174). This study indicates that starting students off with a firm foundation in the Chinese phonetic system as supported by romanization may return long-term dividends for spoken language development.

Jssue #4: The Role of Practice and Experience

The experience your students amass with the Chinese language and the amount of meaningful and effective reading and writing practice your students engage in are crucial to their success in learning the language. In fact, there are a number of reading theories that speak directly to this point. For instance, in their oft-quoted theory of reading, LaBerge and Samuels (1985) state that efficient reading is a matter of "automating" lower-level reading processes such as word recognition, so that attention need no longer be devoted to these processes, and therefore can be devoted to comprehending the message and meaning of the text. To attain automaticity, reading must be practiced. As readers gain more experience reading, it is thought that they actually "restructure" their cognitive processing ability, thus acquiring the ability to read more efficiently.

Yet, until this happens, word recognition and the building of textual understanding is slow. In fact, the research involving L2 language students learning to read in scripts like Chinese and Japanese demonstrates that it is a very laborious process, largely due to the mental effort that students must expend in areas that the native reader takes for granted, areas such as decoding and word recognition (for a summary of the research, see Everson 2002). For native readers of any language, identification of words is rapid and effortless, only taking milliseconds to accomplish. This efficiency in turn enables fluent readers to read at an impressive rate. By contrast, foreign language learners are involved in what we call "cross-orthographic reading," or learning to read in different writing systems, and they spend inordinate amounts of time visually processing the distinctive features of Chinese characters, while also trying to come to terms with how the characters are pronounced. It is not surprising that this lack of fluent reading continues until learners have amassed a respectable amount of characters that they can read quickly and effortlessly, and also gain proficiency with the structure of the language so that they can predict and anticipate structures that are commonly used in Chinese discourse.

WHAT THIS MEANS FOR THE TEACHER

While it would be simple to say that all you need to do is have your students practice reading, the truth is that this is easier said than done. All too often, student reading assignments are translation exercises, or exercises designed more to develop grammatical knowledge than actual reading fluency. What needs to be done is for teachers to develop in their students a desire to read interesting material that is not too far above their level, thus engaging in what is known as "extensive reading" (Day and Bamford 1998). This entails finding the proper materials for your students, a topic that is discussed more below. In addition, class time needs to be set aside for students to be given the opportunity to read silently to themselves with a variety of materials catering to their interests. In this way, students can begin to experience extensive reading without the usual translation assignments that often accompany reading lessons. As will be discussed below, this is also an excellent way to control the recycling of reading vocabulary, thus leading to the all-important automaticity that students will definitely need to develop.

Issue #5: The Role of Background Knowledge

When I began my study of classical Chinese as a third-year Chinese student, I would marvel at how difficult the readings could be. Aside from the enormous amount of new characters we were expected to learn, the grammar was complex and very different from the modern language I was also trying to master. What always amazed me, though, was how I often had translated the text into English, and it *still* didn't make sense to me. What I didn't realize at the time was that I was experiencing a total failure of background knowledge. Omaggio (1993) has stated that in the second language reading process, at least three types of background knowledge are activated: 1) linguistic information, or one's knowledge of the linguistic code; 2) one's knowledge of the world, including what you can expect and predict from personal experience, and topic or domain-specific knowledge, or what helps you quickly and effortlessly read the baseball scores or stock reports while your neighbor cannot; and 3) knowledge of discourse structure, or how texts such as newspaper stories, literary texts, or radio broadcasts are organized. What my classical Chinese course focused on was the linguistic code, so we spent most of the time translating and discussing how the grammar of the language operated. What we spent very little time studying was the world in which classical Chinese operated: the cultural relevance of the text, who among the people in ancient China actually read these texts, and why these issues of history, philosophy, or poetry were important in the Chinese world, and are still revered today among Chinese people.

As it turns out, a great deal of research would be done in both L1 and L2 reading during the 1980s that would be devoted to the investigation of how a reader's background knowledge would influence his or her overall reading comprehension. Theoretically modeled as "schemata," or mental units that contain our background knowledge, schema theory (Anderson & Pearson 1984) was a powerful way of explaining how background knowledge affects reading. Consequently, the importance of background knowledge would become extremely prominent, and would be the driving force behind theories of reading that would be characterized as "top-down," or stressing what is already "inside the heads" of the reader over the importance of the print that is actually on the page.

WHAT THIS MEANS FOR THE TEACHER

When conducting reading lessons, consider your students' backgrounds. This is not always easy, given that students come from different backgrounds and have a variety of personal interests, experiences, and knowledge. Given these factors, one suggestion is that you begin reading any text by initiating a brainstorming session with your students that deals with the general subject of the text, asking them to predict what kinds of information they will likely encounter in the text, and what vocabulary will likely be included. In this way, you will invoke the relevant schema that needs to be in place for students to comprehend the lesson, or more importantly, establish whether the students even have the relevant schemata with which to begin the lesson.

This idea becomes crucial when you begin to teach texts that are more authentic and not designed primarily for pedagogical purposes. Because one's background knowledge is highly influenced by one's culture, it is often difficult to teach the reading of Chinese texts to learners of Chinese who do not possess the cultural understanding to frame the reading in its proper context, an ability that requires not only a great deal of linguistic knowledge, but also cultural and historical knowledge. As previously illustrated through my attempt to read classical Chinese texts written in ancient China, they were opaque and unclear to me because I possessed neither the requisite grounding in language, nor in philosophy, culture, and history. To remedy this problem, your reading classes and reading materials should be accompanied by appropriate cultural and historical context so your students can develop background knowledge against which to understand the text and thus relate it their own knowledge and experience. In this way, students will be able to focus on understanding the content of the lesson as well as its linguistic elements.

Issue #6: The Use of Authentic Materials

There is no question that the ultimate goal of our reading programs should be to lay the groundwork at all levels for our learners to read authentic materials, generally defined as materials that are written by Chinese native speakers for other native speakers. Indeed, if we are to follow the guidance and spirit of the ACTFL National Content Standards, our reading activities will be filled with authentic materials of all types, though we must make sure that these materials are structured in a way that is level-appropriate. Yet, I do want to offer a word of caution here, as it is possible that you will meet teachers and educators who will encourage the *exclusive* use of authentic materials. Let me give you some reasons why this pedagogy is misguided, as well as some things to think about when you decide to use authentic materials (for a review of this debate, see Crossley, et. al. 2007).

First, it is important to realize that we read for different purposes. We sometimes pick up a newspaper and quickly locate the basketball score of our favorite team, a practice known in reading as *scanning.* Or, we might quickly read for basic understanding a story about the United States trade delegation that recently visited China, a practice known in reading as *skimming.* If you think about it, much of our reading of the daily newspaper entails such reading behavior, as we are so familiar with newspaper formatting and newspaper discourse, that we can fly through these texts and acquire the information we seek in almost no time, whereas the L2 reader in this situation is easily overwhelmed by a veritable sea of print. Therefore, they are only taught one way to read — intensively. That is, they are taught to grind through the text for deep meaning, for the purpose of understanding every character of the text, oftentimes being required to show up for class with an almost word-by-word translation. While it is true that we do read intensively in "real life," always requiring this of our students can make them overly reliant on the use of the dictionary. Although new online and computerized dictionaries have made the task of dictionary lookup somewhat easier than the use of paper dictionaries, making the task such that the student is looking up every other word in the dictionary will be a tedious exercise. Therefore, your activities must be developmentally appropriate with your students' reading proficiency. Since it will be impossible for your beginning students to read authentic materials intensively, it is important to follow the mantra that is often used in conjunction with authentic materials — "change the task, not the text." In other words, while you can still use authentic materials, how you use them will be extremely important.

WHAT THIS MEANS FOR THE TEACHER

I mentioned earlier that I disagree with the blanket statement that in Chinese reading instruction, authentic reading texts must be used *exclusively.* I say this because while it is fine to practice intensive reading as a part of the reading curriculum, it is critical that your students begin to practice *extensive* reading in your classrooms, and they simply cannot do this with authentic materials alone. Extensive reading is the reading of larger quantities of materials that are well within the linguistic capabilities of your students. Notice the operative words here are "larger quantities" and "within the linguistic capabilities of your students." All too often, students who are being expected to read extensively with authentic materials are actually engaging in massive decoding exercises enabled by endless dictionary lookup, thus making overall comprehension of the text impossible due to the effort that must be expended in basic word recognition. This problem is compounded when students "chase the curriculum," or find that just as they are beginning to master the characters and structures of the current lesson, they are expected to move on to the next lesson without the mastery that sensible review and re-reading of texts will help facilitate.

To remedy this problem, if your goal is to develop your students' extensive reading ability, it will be important that you give them graded readers that are well within their language competence. "Graded readers" are extended texts, stories, or even books that are specifically designed to be written well within the linguistic proficiency of selected students. Although the notion of graded readers is not particularly fashionable in a discipline that is encouraging authenticity in all we do, graded readers do a number of things. First, since they are written within our learners' linguistic capabilities, students get a sense of "payback," a sense that all the work they have put into their studies has not been for nothing. Indeed, it is very common for a student to finish reading a short book and exclaim to his teacher, "Hey, I just finished my first Chinese book," no mean feat given how much time the student has expended on this text. Secondly, it is important for our students to read extensively to develop their reading stamina. Books that contain vocabulary and structures that are well known to the students solidify what they have already mastered, and give the students a chance to learn some new words while practicing reading words that they already know. All too often, Chinese teachers lose sight of the fact that it is not only important to introduce new vocabulary, but also to review the old: review cannot be overemphasized as the research is very clear that vocabulary words must be encountered frequently in a variety of receptive and productive contexts if it is to be truly learned by the student (Nation 2001). Graded readers that are written with this in mind will be a breath of fresh air for students who view reading as a time consuming and laborious process taken up primarily with dictionary usage and translation.[1]

Conclusion

I hope that this article has given you insights into some of the theoretical and practical issues you will encounter as you teach reading and writing to your CFL learners. Bernhardt's model was used to give you an idea of some of the components that are involved in foreign language reading, components that you will see operating every day in your CFL classrooms. Likewise, this article has attempted

---

[1]Examples of graded readers include *Tales & Traditions, the Cheng & Tsui Readings in Chinese Literature Series* (新编中文课外阅读丛书), Volumes 1–4, by Xiao, et al. Boston: Cheng & Tsui Company; and the *Cheng & Tsui Readings in Chinese Culture Series*, Volumes 1–5, by Weijia Huang and Qun Ao. Boston: Cheng & Tsui Company.

to apply current theory in L1/L2 reading to help you understand not only the processes your students are developing as they read, but also how you can arrange your classroom and curriculum to facilitate this development. It has been said that nothing is more practical than a good theory, so it is my hope that this article has served to demystify reading theory, to allow you to develop reading lessons, materials, and instruction that motivate your students to learn to read in a principled and rewarding manner.

References

Anderson, R. C., and P. D. Pearson. 1984. A schema- theoretic view of basic processes in reading comprehension. In *Handbook of reading research*, ed. P. D. Pearson, 255–291. New York: Longman.

Bassetti, B. 2007. Effects of hanyu pinyin on pronunciation in learners of Chinese as a foreign language. In *The cognition, learning, and teaching of Chinese characters*, ed. A. Guder, X. Jiang, and Y. Wan. Beijing: Beijing Language and Culture University Press.

Bernhardt, E. B. 1991. *Reading development in a second language*. Norwood, NJ: Ablex Publishing Corporation.

Bernhardt, E. B. 2000. Second-language reading as a case study of reading scholarship in the 20th century. In *Handbook of reading research*, Volume III, ed. M. L. Kamil, P. B. Mosenthal, P. D. Pearson, and R. Barr, 791–812. Mahwah, NJ: Lawrence Erlbaum Publishers.

Birch, B. M. 2007. *English L2 reading: Getting to the bottom.* Mahwah, NJ: Lawrence Erlbaum Publishers.

Brecht, R. D., and A. R. Walton. 1993. *National strategic planning in less commonly taught languages.* Washington, D.C.: The National Foreign Language Center.

Crossley, S. A., P. M. McCarthy, M. M. Louwerse, and D. S. McNamara. 2007. A linguistic analysis of simplified and authentic texts. *The Modern Language Journal* 91 (1): 15–30.

Day, R. R., and J. Bamford. 1998. *Extensive reading in the second language classroom.* Cambridge: Cambridge University Press.

Everson, M. E., and C. Ke. 1997. An inquiry into the reading strategies of intermediate and advanced learners of Chinese as a foreign language. *Journal of the Chinese Language Teachers Association* 32 (1): 1–20.

Everson, M. E. 1998. Word recognition among learners of Chinese as a foreign language: Investigating the relationship between naming and knowing. *The Modern Language Journal* 82 (2): 194–204.

Everson, M. E. 2002. Theoretical developments in reading Chinese and Japanese as foreign languages. In *Research in second language learning: Literacy and the second language learner*, ed. Joann Hammadou-Sullivan. Greenwich, CT: Information Age Publishing.

Falsgraf, C., and M. Spring. 2007. Innovations in language learning: The Oregon Chinese flagship model. *Journal of the National Council of Less Commonly Taught Languages* 4: 1–16.

Goswami, U., and P. Bryant. 1990. *Phonological skills and learning to read.* East Sussex: Lawrence Erlbaum Associates, Ltd., Publishers.

Jackson, N. E., M. E. Everson, and C. Ke. 2003. Beginning readers' awareness of the orthographic structure of semantic-phonetic compounds: Lessons from a study of learners of Chinese as a foreign language. In *Reading development in Chinese children*, ed. Catherine McBride-Chang and Hsuan-chih Chen. Westport, CT: Greenwood Press.

Ke, C. 1998. Effects of strategies on the learning of Chinese characters among foreign language students. *Journal of the Chinese Language Teachers Association* 33 (2): 93–112.

Kern, R. G. 2000. *Literacy and language teaching.* Oxford: Oxford University Press.

Koda, K. 2005. *Insights into second language reading.* Cambridge University Press.

LaBerge, D., and S. J. Samuels. 1985. Toward a theory of automatic information processing in reading. In *Theoretical models and the processes of reading*, ed. H. Singer and R. B. Ruddell. Newark, DE: International Reading Association.

McGinnis, S. 1999. Student goals and approaches. In *Mapping the course of the Chinese language field*, ed. M. Chu, 151–188. Kalamazoo, MI: The Chinese Language Teachers Association, Inc.

Nation, I. S. P. 2001. *Learning vocabulary in another language.* Cambridge: Cambridge University Press.

Omaggio, A. C. 1993. *Teaching language in context: Proficiency-oriented instruction.* Boston: Heinle & Heinle.

Shen, H. H. 2004. Level of cognitive processing: Effects on character learning among non-native learners of Chinese as a foreign language. *Language and Education* 18 (2): 167–183.

Shen, H. H. 2005. An investigation of Chinese character learning strategies among non-native speakers of Chinese. *System* 33: 49–68.

Shen, H. H., and C. Ke. 2007. Radical awareness and word acquisition among nonnative learners of Chinese. *The Modern Language Journal* 91 (1): 97–111.

Shu, H., and R. C. Anderson. 1999. Learning to read Chinese: The development of metalinguistic awareness. In *Reading Chinese script: A cognitive analysis*, ed. J. Wang, A. W. Inhoff, and H. C. Chen. Mawah, NJ: Lawrence Erlbaum Associates, Publishers.

Swaffar, J. K., K. M. Arens, and H. Byrnes. 1991. *Reading for meaning: An integrated approach to language learning.* Englewood Cliffs, NJ: Prentice-Hall.

Walker, G. 1984. "Literacy" and "reading" in a Chinese language program. *Journal of the Chinese Language Teachers Association* 19: 67–84.

Yao, T., Y. Liu, L. Ge, Y. Chen, N. Bi, X. Wang, and Y. Shi. 2005. *Integrated Chinese.* 2nd edition. Boston: Cheng & Tsui Company.

Chapter 6

Teaching Chinese Orthography and Discourse

Knowledge and Pedagogy

Yun Xiao

Bryant University

Second language (including foreign language) learning involves acquiring both linguistic and cognitive skills, which include conscious knowledge of the target grammar and second language (L2) strategies such as transfer, simplification, generalization, and restructuring (McLaughlin 1987, p. 133). In this thread, it is essential for L2 teachers to possess the knowledge about the language (KAL) and the pedagogical system for its application. In Chinese as a foreign language (CFL), this concept has been defined as a pedagogical grammar of Chinese, which aims to establish a workable link between linguistic analysis and a pedagogical system (Teng 1997).

In L2 education research, KAL is explicit knowledge about the language systems or rules, which significantly influences teachers' pedagogical systems and practices (Alderson et al. 1997; Andrews, 1997, 1999a, 1999b; Borg 1998, 1999). According to Andrews (1997), KAL is a declarative form of teachers' language awareness, while the application of KAL in teaching is a procedural form of teachers' language awareness. The combination of these two is teachers' metalinguistic awareness. In pedagogical practices, the execution of teachers' metalinguistic awareness includes providing explicit grammar knowledge and corrective feedback (Andrews 1999a, p. 161), in that explicit knowledge and corrective feedback increase the saliency of the target linguistic feature(s) and hence raise learners' attention, consciousness, or awareness of that feature(s). According to information processing theories, learners' attention, consciousness or awareness of target linguistic features is a necessary prerequisite for language processing and permanent acquisition of these feature(s) (Ellis 1990; Schmidt 1990; Fotos 1993). As well, corrective feedback provides an "input enhancing" form of this consciousness raising (Lightbown and Spada 1990; Sharwood Smith 1990).

In the United States, Chinese is taught or learned as a foreign language (i.e., not as the tool of societal communication); thus, it shares many commonalities with other foreign languages. First of all, in a foreign language (FL) context, authentic linguistic input is typically not available, and the classroom is very often the sole context devoted to the learner, where the learner has access to three sources of target language input: (1) teacher, (2) materials, and (3) other learners (Gass and Selinker 2001, p. 311). Since learner input, as shown in FL classroom research, is often limited and full of errors, teachers and materials are often the most reliable resources, of which teachers are paramount because they are the ones who select, create, or decide what materials to teach and what approach to take. Moreover, most of the FL learners in this country come to the Chinese language classroom with an English language background, either with English as L1 (such as the English-speaking American students) or with English as a primary language (such as those heritage language students who have a home language other than English but English becomes their primary or dominant language after they enter the mainstream schools). With the involvement of two languages (i.e., English and a foreign language) in the learner's linguistic repertoire, CFL teachers need to, in addition to developing KAL and pedagogy, be aware of the characteristics of teaching language in a FL context and take into account factors such as cross-linguistic differences and L1 (or primary language) transfer.

CROSS-LINGUISTIC DIFFERENCES

Contrastive rhetoric maintains that language and writing are cultural phenomena. As a direct consequence, each language has rhetorical conventions unique to it (Connor 1996, p. 5), and each language imposes different levels of difficulty to its learners, which means that some languages are harder to learn than others. For instance, Chinese is recognized as one of the most difficult languages by the assessment of the ACTFL (American Council on the Teaching of Foreign Languages) Proficiency Guidelines, in that it takes native English speakers three times the number of instructional hours to reach the same level of proficiency in Chinese as in French or Spanish (Hadley 2001). Recent CFL research studies have provided ample evidence to show that of the many tasks facing CFL learners, character writing is the most difficult (Everson 1998), especially to learners with an alphabetic language background such as English. In their 2000 CLTA (Chinese Language Teachers Association) survey, Ke et al. (2001) report that character learning was identified as the most difficult task by CFL teachers from colleges, pre-college, and heritage Chinese language learners. Moreover, CFL studies investigating Chinese written discourse development also report that Chinese discourse is difficult for learners to comprehend and compose (Cui 2003; Xiao, forthcoming), especially for English-speaking learners whose L1 is strikingly different from Chinese at the discourse level.

L1 TRANSFER

Research in language processing shows that languages differ in their discourse patterns and that L2 learners tend to transfer their L1 discourse processing strategies into L2 (Tao and Healy 1998). Ample evidence has shown that many aspects of learners' L2 usage can be traced back to their L1 (Lado 1957; Kellerman and Sharwood Smith 1986; Odlin 1989). While properties similar in both L1 and L2 tend to transfer, those that are different do not (Kellerman 1983; Ard and Homburg 1992) but tend to result in errors such as avoidance or over-generalization. Such findings are supported by recent CFL research, which have reported that CFL learners with English as L1 are largely influenced by English grammar or avoid using the target features when dealing with Chinese discourse (Jin 1994; Cui 2003; Li 2004a; Xiao, forthcoming).

As discussed thus far, Chinese characters and discourse are both difficult learning tasks for CFL learners. In this chapter, I will focus on these two areas by discussing their major linguistic features and make pedagogical suggestions for each of them. Moreover, as supporting data, I will report the findings of my two recent studies, which examine the linguistic features of Chinese characters and topic chaining. Considering the lack of English equivalents for many of the Chinese orthographic and discourse terms, I will use both English and Chinese for the key concepts, for the ease and efficiency of readership.

Part 1. Teaching Chinese Orthography: Linguistic Features and Pedagogical Suggestions

LINGUISTIC FEATURES OF CHINESE CHARACTERS

Unlike English, which uses an alphabet with a relatively transparent orthography-phonology mapping system, Chinese uses a logographic script with orthography-to-phonology mapping largely unavailable. In Chinese script, strokes are the basic spelling symbol, and characters are the basic analytical unit (Packard 2000). Structurally, strokes form components, and components form characters. Based on their internal complexity, characters are classified as simple characters (about 18 percent of the total number of Chinese characters), which consist of a single un-analyzable component, and compound characters (about 82 percent of the total), which are comprised of two analyzable components with distinct functions: a semantic radical and phonetic element (Shu and Anderson 1999). The traditional Chinese writing system contains 214 radicals and 1,100 phonetics. In principle, the phonetic element conveys the sound of the corresponding character, while the radical contains meaning bearing a semantic relationship with the corresponding character. These recurring components form or assemble the thousands of Chinese characters in multi-dimensional configurations, such as left to right, top to bottom, outside to inside, etc. In such configurations, the radicals and phonetics are in fixed positions. Violation of their positioning causes erroneous variations or non-characters.

To reinforce the orthographic features described above, I will state the key elements, such as the sequence of character formation and various patterns of character configuration, in Chinese terms below.

1. 汉字的生成 (character formation sequence): 笔画 → 部件 → 汉字(张旺熹, 1998)

   如：人 → 大 → 头 → 买 → 卖 → 读

   (1) 笔画
     - 常用笔画有6种：点，横，竖，撇，捺，提。
     - 这些常用笔画共衍生出二十多种笔画，如：横鈎，竖鈎，横折，竖折。
   See http://www.eon.com.hk/estroke for stroke order.
   (2) 部件(components)分成字部件和非成字部件(常用部件有1000个左右)
     - 成字部件，如：口，日，木，女，贝，土，等等。
     - 非成字部件，如：礻，丷，刂，⺮，⻊，等等。
   (3) 完整汉字如
     - 独体字 (常用作合体字的部件)，如：口，日，木，女，贝，土，等等。
     - 合体字(含形/义旁 — radical，和声旁 — phonetic)，如：打，唱，喝，姐，妹，话，花，说，树，桌，椅，等等。

2. 汉字的结构 (patterns of character configurations)大体分四种：
   (1) 独体，如：口，日，木，女，贝，土，等等。
   (2) 包围结构
     - 全围，如：国，园，圆，围，圃，等等。
     - 半围，如：问，周，医，病，句，边，建，用，等等。
   (3) 横向结构
     - 横纵，如：得，慢，摸，别，封，椅，等等。
     - 横围，如：随，腿，氇，褪，等等。
   (4) 纵向结构，如：盘，着，者，参，受，畜，众，药，热，等等。

As shown above, the formation and configuration of Chinese characters are fundamentally different from those of alphabetic languages such as English. With this in mind, when teaching Chinese characters, CFL teachers need to help students develop needed intra-character analytic skills through effective pedagogical practices. In 2005, the writer examined how novice CFL teachers introduced new characters into their classroom teaching and how they formulated preventive and corrective strategies for learners' orthographic errors (Xiao 2005). Participants were six graduate students who took a three-credit CFL pedagogy course taught in the previous semester by the writer. The course focused on linguistic features of Chinese orthography and discourse, and hands-on teaching methods. The participants examined the writing samples collected from 101 CFL learners at low/high beginning and intermediate levels, and analyzed the students' writing samples for phonological, graphemic, and semantic errors. The findings showed that the CFL teacher-trainees were, on average, able to identify over 92 percent of the errors contained in the sample characters, and effectively articulated preventive and corrective strategies. This demonstrated that once teachers were equipped with KAL, they could actively apply it to their pedagogical systems and formulate their working principles accordingly. However, the results of the error identification task also demonstrated that the participants could successfully identify all cases of structural errors in the writing samples, but not all the cases of substitution errors of graphemically similar characters such as 惯 → 慢, 唱 → 喝, 著 → 暑，同学 → 因学，真 → 直，八 → 入；两 → 雨 or semantically similar characters 没有 → 不有，一个朋友 → 一个友朋，明天 → 下天, etc. Since these areas are even challenging to our new CFL teachers, they warrant more attention and consideration in our teaching practice.

Moreover, the correction strategies showed that the participants gave preference to a more "direct error correction" method characterized by "tough" treatments such as directly pointing out the errors, explicitly explaining the errors, and having the students repeatedly write the correct character. Interestingly, these strategies were not promoted in the pedagogy course or current second language teaching approaches; they were instead mere copying of the traditional Chinese teaching methodology experienced in their own prior learning.

PEDAGOGICAL SUGGESTIONS FOR CHARACTER TEACHING

There are many different ways to teach Chinese characters to CFL learners who typically have varied linguistic backgrounds. Below I will make some pedagogical suggestions, which have been field-tested by instructors and teaching assistants in our Chinese program in the past few years. These recommendations consist of (1) a three-step presentation of new characters, (2) methods to prevent orthographic errors, and (3) corrective measures to treat orthographic errors.

1. **Present new characters in a three-step sequence:**
Step 1:
  - Present whole characters with color-coded radicals;
  - Elicit pronunciation and tones from students;

- Model the pronunciation and tones of the target characters;
- Explain the semantic relationship between the radical and the relevant character.

Step 2:

- Present characters a second time with analyzable components further coded with different colors;
- Analyze the configuration and stroke order.

Step 3:

- Group characters with the same radicals together;
- Contextualize the target character in phrases or sentences;
- Have students write the target character and read aloud phrases or sentences containing the target character.

See http://people.umass.edu/Characters/image/index.swf for animated examples of the 100 most frequently used Chinese characters.

2. **Preventive strategies for orthographic errors:**
    - Decompose characters into components;
    - Use explicit orthographic terms in the explanation;
    - Provide new information with visual aids;
    - Reinforce with practice, comparison, and contrast.

3. **Corrective strategies for orthographic errors**:
    - Analyze errors by sound, graph, meaning;
    - Explain the semantic meaning of radicals and their relationship with the relevant characters;
    - Analyze configurations and positioning;
    - Go over the stroke order;
    - Put target characters in context;
    - Repeat writing to reinforce memory.

Part 2. Teaching Chinese Discourse: Linguistic Features and Pedagogical Suggestions

LINGUISTIC FEATURES OF CHINESE DISCOURSE

Typologically, Chinese and English are different from each other in many aspects, such as the role of subject and topic, the use of overt/covert noun phrases (NP) (名/零代词), and various discourse relations. English is a subject-prominent language, in which Subject-Verb-Object word order is predominant, subject plays a prominent role, and NP deletion (i.e., the use of zero pronouns 零代词的使用) in obligatory subject and object positions is not allowed (Li and Thompson 1976).

On the other hand, Chinese is a topic-prominent language, in which the topic rather than the subject plays a prominent role, and coreferrential pronominalized NPs are licensed by the controlling topic to be deleted 同指代词常常省略) (Tsao 1990). At the discourse level, English text connectivity is maintained by various cohesive devices such as reference, substitution, ellipsis, conjunction, and lexical (Halliday and Hasan 1976), whereas Chinese text continuity is largely maintained by topic chains (Chu 1998), as illustrated below.

(1)　(a)　我$_1$愛花，所以Ø$_1$也 愛 養 花。
　　　　　I love flowers so also love grow flowers

　　(b)　可是，我$_1$還 不 是 園藝師。
　　　　　However, I still not am horticulturist

　　　　因爲Ø$_1$ 沒有 時間去 提高 養花 技術。
　　　　　because have no time to improve gardening skills

(《老舍養花》 in Liu, et. al., *New Practical Chinese Reader*, Vol. 3, 2004, p. 49)
*"I like flowers, so Ø also like to grow flowers. However, I am no horticulturist, because Ø do not have time to improve Ø gardening skills."

As shown in Example (1), coreferrential (同指代词) 我 is omitted (省略) in both (a) and (c) to maintain the continuity of the Chinese discourse; such omission is not allowed in English. To make the English discourse acceptable, the omitted "I" must become overt.

TOPIC CHAIN IN CHINESE DISCOURSE

Topic chain (话题链) was introduced into Chinese grammar as the basic unit of communication, which is formed by a sequence of successive topic-comment constructions, controlled by a shared topic (Tsao 1979, 1990). According to Tsao, the controlling topic (控制话题) in the topic chain pronominalizes the subsequent coreferential NPs (使同指名词 代词化) and allows their deletion. The controlling topic and the deleted pronouns (i.e., zero pronouns 零代词) form an antecedent-referent relationship (指代关系), which "chains" the sentence constituents together. Tsao's hypothesis has since been tested and supported by data from both written and oral Chinese discourse studies. Using two modern literature pieces, *Shuǐ-Hǔ Zhuàn* and *Rú-Lín Wài Shǐ*, Li and Thompson (1979) found that topic chains were frequently used in Chinese discourse and that they could extend to over half a dozen clauses. Moreover, the use of zero pronouns is so abundant and so widespread in Chinese discourse that it must be considered a prevailing feature of Chinese grammar. Using data from Chinese native speakers in twelve different speech settings, Tao (1996) also found that the use of zero pronouns was predominant in Chinese oral discourse, with 58 percent of the total in subject positions, and 42 percent in object positions.

STUDIES ON THE EFFECT OF TOPIC CHAIN ON CFL LEARNING

Although an increasing body of research on the structure of the Chinese language has provided strong support for Tsao's theory that Chinese is a discourse-oriented language as evidenced by the predominance of topic chaining, there has not been a consensus in Chinese linguistics as to how to apply this phenomenon to analyze Chinese discourse and to develop a CFL pedagogical system. The writer took a quick survey of the popular CFL textbooks used in this country and found that almost none of them explicitly introduced topic chains or zero pronouns in the grammar notes. Instead, almost all textbooks begin by introducing Chinese grammar as being very similar to English and by emphasizing that Chinese uses a S-V-O structure just like English, which seems counterproductive to reinforcing the discourse-based (as opposed to sentence-based) feature of Chinese grammar. In her many years of Chinese teacher training, the writer noted that many new CFL teachers were never introduced to the concepts of topic chaining or zero pronouns, nor did they pay much attention to these topics in their pedagogical practices. Thus, it is not surprising that recent CFL studies report that students have trouble using these features in discourse comprehension and production.

Using production data, Jin (1994) found that, compared with Chinese native speakers, English-speaking CFL learners tended to overproduce nouns and pronouns and underuse zero pronouns. Cui (2003) reported that CFL learners' errors were often due to the lack of or partial knowledge of Chinese discourse (especially of topic chains), although topic chains frequently occurred in the teaching texts. Li (2004a) found that, although CHL learners were exposed to topic chains early and frequently in the teaching texts, control of the structure was not acquired until later (p. 33). By examining CFL learners' (heritage and non-heritage) diary entries and comparing them with the Chinese native speaker's (NS) re-writes, Xiao (forthcoming) found that both heritage and non-heritage learners did not have much knowledge about topic chains or zero pronouns. Instead, they consistently produced structurally simple and discursively loose SVO structures, with heritage learners not showing any meaningful advantages over their non-heritage counterparts. Below I will give a few samples collected in the study which show the comparison between participants' written production and the native speaker rewrite:

(2)   Amy (non-heritage language learner): 去年我在学校的宿舍住。我不喜欢那里。我觉得房门太小，洗澡间不好。我常常想搬出去。
Native speaker rewrite: 去年我$_1$住在(学校的宿舍)$_2$，可是Ø$_1$不喜欢Ø$_2$，Ø$_1$觉得Ø$_2$房间太小，洗澡间不好，Ø$_1$常常想搬 出去。

(3)   Min (heritage language learner): Michael 的腿很长,所以他很高。他的眼睛得很漂亮。他是美国人。他二十三岁了。我跟他同一个organization/club。

   Native speaker rewrite: (麦克)$_1$的腿很长,所以Ø$_1$很高, Ø$_1$眼睛也很漂亮。他$_1$是美国人，Ø$_1$二十三岁了。我跟他在同一个俱乐部。

As shown in Examples (2) and (3) above, compared with the NS re-writes, the participants, heritage language or non-heritage language alike, tended to use repetitive short and choppy sentences, excessive nouns and pronouns, and insufficient topic chains. Even when they used topic chains, their chains were much shorter and had less complexity than those of the NS. To Chinese native speakers, such discourse is fragmented and causes confusion, because they sound like talking about different people not just one. Moreover, this study found that there was no significant change in the participants' discourse features over the learning of one academic semester, although some level of progress was made by particular individual(s) or with particular feature(s).

As discussed above, discourse learning is, in addition to Chinese characters, another difficult task for CFL learners. To develop learners' Chinese discourse competence in conjunction with grammar competence, it is essential for CFL pedagogy to develop learners' knowledge of Chinese discourse features, especially topic chains. (For suggestions on how to teach and practice the use of topic chains, please see "六. 对外汉语教学的几点建议 (Pedagogical suggestions)" on pages 127–128.)

STRUCTURE OF TOPIC CHAIN AND PEDAGOGICAL SUGGESTIONS

Given its importance and relevance to CFL learning, I will briefly describe below the definition, structure, and linguistic constraints of topic chains, and provide ample examples (see Examples 4–27) *in Chinese* for two reasons: (1) many of the relevant terms do not have agreed-upon English equivalents; and (2) there are as yet no unified linguistic terms to describe these Chinese discourse features, and there are, in many cases, multiple terms for one feature, or multiple features for one term, which has caused difficulty for pedagogical application.

一. 问题的提出 *(Issues of Chinese Discourse in CFL Pedagogy)*

在对外汉语教材中,含话题链的篇章几乎无处不现,而且从初级班开始,学生就要写日记短文,口语讨论交流, 进行口笔语篇章练习,因此这方面的知识对学生来说非常重要。可是据近期调查,国内外对外汉语教材中竟然没有任何一本教课书对汉语篇章现象进行过明确的解释(李文旦,2004a)。本文作者最近翻阅了四本通用的中文实用语法书,也没有发现任何一本对这类现象作过系统的解释。而且语法家们在讨论汉语篇章时使用的术语很多,如: 小句，子句，从句，分句，句段，段句，语段，复句，句群，等等。因为名字太多，概念不一，很难纳入对外汉语教学。笔著以为要想把这种语法现象纳入汉语教学，一定要先定其名，再清楚地回答下列几个问题: 汉语篇章的特点是什么? 是什么样的语法制约把汉语篇章链结在一起的? 汉语教学应该采取什么样的相关措施?

二. "链结" 汉语篇章的话题链 (*The Chaining Effect of Topic Chain on Chinese Discourse*)

曹逢甫先生(1979,1990)对汉语篇章进行了链式分析。他提出汉语篇章中的数个小句，往往受制于一个共同的控制性话题，这个话题使后续同指名词代词化，然后删除成零回指(也叫零代词)，从而将各小句链结在一起，组成话题链，篇章便由此而得以连贯。他发现话题链在汉语实际运用中的出现率是如此之高，以至于汉语应该被称为"篇章语言"。按曹先生的理论，话题链中的话题必须是定指的，毫无例外地位于句首。如，

(4)   (这个人)$_1$ 我$_2$不喜欢Ø$_1$，我妈妈也不喜欢Ø$_1$。(曹逢甫1979, p. 44)

(5)   (这棵树)$_1$ 的(叶子)$_2$又细又长，Ø$_1$ 很难看。(曹逢甫 1979, p. 87)

(6)   他$_1$肚子饿，Ø$_1$ 又找不到东西吃,所以Ø$_1$ 躺在床上。(曹逢甫1990, p. 124)

(7)   他$_1$ 看完了那本书，Ø$_1$ 睡觉了。 (曹逢甫 1990, p. 206)

例(4–7)中各含若干小句，受控于一个话题，将后续同指名词代词化然后承前(anaphoric)省略。这个话题可以是头句谓语的直接宾语 (例4)，头句主语的属词 (例5)，头句的话题 (例6)，也可以是头句的话题兼主语 (例7)。这些句子的句型分别为NP$_1$(话题) NP$_2$ (主语) VP Ø$_1$VP(例4–5)，或 NP$_1$(话题+主语) VP Ø$_1$VP (例6)。也就是说，当句首有两个NP时，第一个为话题 (位于句首的时间,地点等状语不在本文讨论之列)，第二个为主语; 当句首只有一个NP时，话题和主语合二为一。曹先生认为，由于话题和后续小句主语之间存在著一个前词与指词的关系，它们于是形成了一条以话题为核心的的"链"。链中的小句不能独立，之间顺序也不能颠倒。运用话题链这个概念，汉语篇章在一定程度上得到了合理的解释。

在汉语实际运用中，例(4–7)是最常见的话题链,称首连式(曹逢甫1990)。曲承熙先生(1998) 提出，除了首连式话题链(fist-link chain) 以外，还有套管式话题链 (telescopic chain)，如例(8)，

(8)   a.   他手里牵著(一头灰毛驴)$_1$，

      b.   Ø$_1$又瘦叉小，

      c.   Ø$_1$湿淋淋的。(史丁旭，1992:16)

例(8)含三个小句，其控制话题是头句谓语动词的直接宾语"一头灰毛驴"。

从省略与原词的关系来说，例(8)的小句之间只存在一套前词与回指关系(one set of antecedent-referent relationship)，也就是说,这个句子中只存在一个话题链;从话题的位置来说，它属套管式话题链。

三. 话题链中小句主语省略的方向 *(The Direction of Subject NP Deletion in Topic Chain)*

从话题链中小句主语省略的方向来说，前面的例子都属于后续小句承前省略。这种省略往往出现在由联合复句组成的篇章中，即语意上表示事态或行为的继续，语法功能上表示并列，承接，递进，与选择。如，

(9)   a.   (欢迎的群众)$_1$ 一边唱歌，$\emptyset_1$ 一边跳舞。(刘月华等 2001，p. 866)

       b.   *$\emptyset_1$一边唱歌，(欢迎的群众)$_1$ 一边跳舞。

(10)   a.   (王进喜) $_1$听了，$\emptyset_1$二话没说，$\emptyset_1$转身就出了门，$\emptyset_1$一口气走了两个多小时，$\emptyset_1$来到了马家窑。(刘月华等 2001，p. 867)

      b.   *$\emptyset_1$听了，(王进喜) $_1$二话没说，$\emptyset_1$转身就出了门，$\emptyset_1$一口气走了两个多小时，$\emptyset_1$来到了马家窑。

(11)   a.   (困难)$\emptyset_1$不但不会把他们吓倒，$\emptyset_1$反而会把他们锻炼得更坚强。 (刘月华等 2001，p. 869)

      b.   *$\emptyset_1$不但不会把他们吓倒，(困难)$_1$反而会把他们锻炼得更坚强。

(12)   a.   你们)$_1$坐飞机去，$\emptyset_1$还是坐火车去? (刘月华等 2001，p. 869)

      b.   *$\emptyset_1$坐飞机去，(你们)$_1$还是坐火车去?

例(9–12)表明,在表示联合关系的话题链中,主语省略只有一个方向,即只能承前,不能蒙后。如果话题链的方向蒙后省略，就会出现错句，如例(9b-12b)所示。但是当小句之间存在因果,假设,让步,目的,时间先后等偏正关系时，话题链中小句省略则既可承前,也可以蒙后。如，

(13) $\emptyset_1$扎了两针，$\emptyset_1$服了剂药,他$_1$清醒过来，$\emptyset_1$一睁眼$\emptyset_1$便问。(李文旦 2004b，p. 32) 在例(13)中，"他"是第三个小句的主语，也是本句的话题,它通过承前省略控制了后面两个小句"一睁眼,便问"。也通过蒙后省略控制了前面两个小句 "扎了两针，服了剂药"。从语义上来说,前面两个小句表示的是时间背景，后面两个小句表示的是动作的继续。从结构上来说,前面两个小句和 "他"清醒过来有一种时间状语关系,而后面两个小句和他$_1$清醒过来存在一种并列关系。这个句子翻成的英文是：“After he had an injection of camphor and a dose of medicine, he woke up. As soon as he opened his eyes, he asked a question.” 这个句子也可以写成：“他$_1$扎了两针，$\emptyset_1$服了剂药，$\emptyset_1$清醒过来，$\emptyset_1$一睁眼$\emptyset_1$便问”。在汉语实际运用中,这样的句子比比皆是。如，

(14) a. Ø₁想到了这个，Ø₁也马上这么办了,他₁心中痛快了些,好似危险已过,而眼前就是北平了。 (老舍1978, p. 20)

   b. 他₁想到了这个，Ø₁也马上这么办了，Ø₁心中痛快了些,好似危险已过,而眼前就是北平了。

(15) a. Ø₁看电影以前,我₁请你吃饭。 (姚道中等,《中文听说读写》第一册上 1997, p. 97)

   b. 我₁看电影以前，Ø₁请你吃饭。

(16) a. Ø₁看看醉猫似的爸爸，Ø₁看看自己，Ø₁看看两个饿得老鼠似的弟弟，(小福子)₁只剩了哭。 (老舍1978, p. 160)

   b. (小福子)₁看看醉猫似的爸爸，Ø₁看看自己，Ø₁看看两个饿得老鼠似的弟弟，Ø₁只剩了哭。

(17) a. Ø₁为了使教师无后顾之优，(政府)₁不仅给他们提高工资，Ø₁还努力改善他们的居住条件. (刘月华等 2001, p. 869)

   b. (政府)₁为了使教师无后顾之优，Ø₁不仅给他们提高工资，Ø₁还努力改善他们的居住条件。

四．话题链中小句主语承前省略的层次与距离制约 *(The Hierarchy and Distance Constraints of NP Deletion in Topic Chain)*

除了上文谈到的在话题链中主语省略有方向制约外，在承前省略中,还存在层次和距离等制约。按曹逢甫先生的理论，话题链的形成是话题使后续同指名词代词化，然后删除为零回指，从而使各小句"链结"在一起。这个理论预示了在承前省略的话题链中，NP三种形式的出现层次是: 名词(原词) → 代词回指 → 零回指……，或者名词/代词(原词) → 零回指……如，

(18) (祥子)₁真挂了火，他₁不能还说不出心中的话，Ø₁不能再忍。 (老舍1978, p. 146)

(19) 这个(女大学生)₁，由于她₁工作努力，Ø₁知识丰富，Ø₁外语水平高，Ø₁能够直接和外国商人谈判，Ø₁很快地就当上了丝绸部门的副经理。 (Liu and Li 1998, p. 56)

(20) 他₁一点没带感情，Ø₁简单的告诉了虎妞。 (老舍1978, p. 158)

(21) (小福子)₁就是把铺板卖了，Ø₁还上房租，Ø₁只穿着件花洋布大衫，Ø₁戴著一对银耳环,Ø₁回到家中来的。 (老舍1978, p. 158)

例(18)的话题是"祥子"，在后续的两个小句中，"祥子"先被同指代词"他"所代替，然后删除为零回指，即名词(原词) → 代词回指 → 零回指。例(19)也得到了同样的处理。例(20–21)则表明，代词同指和删除可以是同一个步骤，直接用零回指，即名词/代词(原词) → 零回指 → 零回指。除了在特殊语境中，违反这个层次，会造成误解，如下列例子 (22–23)属常见的外国学生病句。

(22) 她觉得孩子更重要，等孩子长大了，小李再自己开个饭店。

(23)　今天早上，他6点钟就起床了。小高一起床，就觉得头有一点儿疼。下午，他头越来越疼，他不能去上课。小高回家了。小高回家以后，他睡了两天，小高头就不疼了。

　　例(22–23)中　尽管每句说的都是同一个人，但由于违反了话题链中主语省略的层次，对说中文的人来说，它们好像在说几个不同的人。

　　至于零回指的使用上限，也就是说零回指可以延伸多远才能回到原词或代词回指，刘月华等先生认为它受制于近距离约束，即离原词(主语或话题)越近，越适合用零回指;稍远的，用代词回指;远到听话人或读者对原型的印象已经模糊时，就重复原词(2001, p. 922)。这在一定程度上预示了话题链在套管式话题链中，零回指离原词或代词的距离很近，因为链中有两个原词交替出现，容易引起混淆，如例(24)。但在首连氏话题链中,如果没有插入语，零回指可以一直延伸，横跨许多小句，如例(25–26); 如果首连氏话题链中有插入语，原词便会立即出现，如 例 (27)。

(24)　(虎妞)$_1$不但不安慰(小福子)$_2$，$\varnothing_1$反倒愿意帮她$_2$的忙: (虎妞)$_1$愿意拿出点资本，$\varnothing_1$教她$_2$打扮整齐，$\varnothing_2$挣来钱再还给她$_1$。(老舍1978, p. 161)

(25)　(穷人的命)$_1$，他似乎看明白了$\varnothing_1$，$\varnothing_1$是枣核儿两头尖:$\varnothing_1$幼小的时候$\varnothing_1$能不饿死，万幸; $\varnothing_1$到了老了$\varnothing_1$能不饿死，很难. 只有中间的一段，$\varnothing_1$年轻力壮，$\varnothing_1$不怕饥饱劳碌，$\varnothing_1$还能像个人儿似的。在这一段里，$\varnothing_1$该快活快活的时候$\varnothing_1$还不敢去干，$\varnothing_1$地道的傻子;　$\varnothing_1$过了这村$\varnothing_1$便没有这店! (老舍1978, p. 93)

(26)　(祥子)$_1$不知道怎么是好了，$\varnothing_1$低著头，$\varnothing_1$拉著车，$\varnothing_1$极慢的往前走，$\varnothing_1$没有主意，$\varnothing_1$没有目的，$\varnothing_1$昏混沉沉的，$\varnothing_1$身上挂著一层粘汗，$\varnothing_1$发著馊臭的味儿。$\varnothing_1$走了会儿，$\varnothing_1$脚心和鞋袜粘在一起，$\varnothing_1$好像踩著块湿泥, $\varnothing_1$非常的难过. $\varnothing_1$本来不想再喝水，$\varnothing_1$可是见了井不由的过去灌了一气，$\varnothing_1$不为解渴，$\varnothing_1$似乎专为享受井水那点凉气，$\varnothing_1$由口腔到胃中，$\varnothing_1$忽然凉了一下，$\varnothing_1$身上的毛孔猛的一收缩，$\varnothing_1$打个冷战，$\varnothing_1$非常舒服。$\varnothing_1$喝完，他$_1$连连的打嗝，水要往上涌! (老舍1978, p. 166)

(27)　我$_1$喜欢喝农民那种带有苦味的茶水，他们的茶桶就放在田埂的树下，我$_1$毫无顾忌地拿起漆满茶垢的茶碗舀水喝，$\varnothing_1$还把自己的水壶灌满，$\varnothing_1$与田里干活的男人说上几句废话，$\varnothing_1$在姑娘因我而起的窃窃私笑里扬长而去。(余华 2003, p. 1)

　　例(24)是套管式话题链，两个话题 — 虎妞 和 小福子 — 交织在一起，互相打断，为了防制混淆，零回指只跨一个小句，便回到原词或代词回指。在例(25)中，话题是 "穷人的命"，紧跟著十四个零回指，没有中断;在例(26)的中，话题是"祥子"，在二十二个零回指之后，才用代词回指"他"。在例(27)中，话题是"我"，由于话题链被插入语"他们的茶桶就放在田埂的树下"打断，在插入语之后，原词"我"立即出现。

上述例子表明，在承前省略的话题链中，NP的三种形式按层次出现，且受制于近距离约束。然而这只是对多元式(即套管式)话题链或有插入语的单元式话题链而言，在首连式单元话题链中，如果没有插入语打断,零回指可以一路通畅，达到二十个以上。

五. 语料调查 *(Discourse Analysis of The Camel Boy)*

为了验正上文所论及的话题链的模式及各种特点，笔著对老舍的《骆驼祥子》中的第十七和第十八章 — 一共二十页 — 进行了语料分析。选择这两章的理由是它们涉及的人物不止一个，有祥子，虎妞，二强子，小福子，二强嫂，等等。不同的人物交织在一起，所用话题链也就多样化，不但有首连式的，也有套管式的。资料分析时，以句号，问号，感叹号为句界，把文章中的句子分成单句和复句，再按主语出现或省略，话题链的种类等等进行分类。分析结果发现这两章著作中，除了引号中的话语以外，共有句子374个，其中单句57个，复句317个。单句中主语出现的有56例，占单句总数的98.25%；单句主语省略的只有一例，占单句总数的 1.75%。复句中小句主语都出现的 (不含话题链)有 22 例，占复句总数的6.94%; 复句中小句主语省略 的(含话题链)有 295 例，占复句总数的93.06%。话题链中首连式有185例，占话题链总数的62.71%；　套管式有110例，占话题链总数的37.29%。在首连式话题链中，跨越句界的有26例，占首连式话题链总数的14.06%; 跨越段界的有7例，占首连式话题链总数的3.78%; 位于句界之内的有152例，占首连式话题链总数的82.16%。(请看下列表格。)

表一：《骆驼祥子》第十七和第十八章中的篇章句子分类

主语出现(不含话题链): 22 例 (22/317, 6.94%)		
主语省略(含话题链): 295 例 (295/317, 93.06%)	首連式: 185 例 (185/295, 62.71%)	
	套管式: 110 例 (110/295, 37.29%)	
	话题链总数: 295 例 (100%)	
复句总数: 317 例 (100%)		

表二：《骆驼祥子》第十七和第十八章中的首连式话题链分类

跨句界	26例 (26/185, 14.06%)
跨段界	7例 (7/185, 3.78%)
句界內	152例 (152/185, 82.16%)
首连式话题链总数: 185 例 (100%)	

上述结果表明，在汉语文学著作的叙述篇章中，绝大多数的句子是复句; 而复句中 绝大多数都含话题链;在话题链中，绝大多数为首连式; 而在首连式话题链中，绝大多数位于句界之内。这表明，在大多数情况下，话题链的链界就是句界，话题链的各种制约也就是句法。需要指出的是以上数

据只基于文学箸作，话题链属中文篇章的主要手法，应用各种语体中，最后结论还有待更广泛深入的调查。

六．对外汉语教学的几点建议 *(Pedagogical Suggestions)*

基于以上几个方面的讨论和本调查的结果,笔著对对外汉语教学提出以下几点建议。

首先，对外汉语教科书和实用语法书要逐步地系统性地介绍汉语篇章特点，将话题链的模式，特点，语法制约，及语言形式标志纳入汉语教学。只有这样，才能帮助学生建立概念。

第二，教学中注意讲解话题链的模式和语法制约。在话题链教学中，重点是首连氏话题链。为帮助理解，可与母语进行比较,如句子结构对比，主语省略对比，名/代/零代词使用对比等等。对于母语为英语的学生，可通过汉英对照，使学生意识到，英语中没有与汉语相对应的主语省略和话题链。英语的句子是通过动词的不同形(时)态和主谓的人性数统一而合成的，篇章连贯则是通过各种指代关联等关系来表达的。 反之，汉语的动词只有一个形态，篇章连贯则主要是通过话题链来控制的。且话题链对内含小句主语省略有方向，层次，和近距离等制约。

第三，要引导学生操作使用。除口语训练外，还要进行语法训练,包括句式变换,句子合并，综合填空等。在分句主语相同的情况下，把后续分句主语代词化，再删除，从而合并成连贯的长句或篇章。如，

I. 句子合并 (Sentence combination)

a. 他吃了饭。他喝了茶。他回家了。→ 他吃了饭，喝了茶，回家了。
b. 第七课的语法很容易，可是第七课的生词太多，第七课的汉字也有一点儿难。

→ 第七课的语法很容易,可是生词太多，汉字也有一点儿难。

II. 选择填空 (Fill in the blanks)

小马很喜欢认识新朋友，所以(小马，他，　Ø)常常住宿舍。这个学期，(小马，他，Ø) 住在学校宿舍，在宿舍(小马，他，Ø) 可以做饭，而且(小马，他，Ø)走路就　可以去学校，所以(小马，他，Ø)觉得很方便。(小马的，他的，Ø)朋友小高不喜欢住宿舍，所以(小高，他，Ø)　租了公寓。公寓比宿舍便宜，但是离学校远，(小高，他，Ø)　　要开车才能去学校。(小马，他，Ø) 没有车，(小马，他，Ø) 觉得买车太贵，所以(小马，他，Ø) 下个学期还住宿舍。

→ 小马很喜欢认识新朋友，所以常常住宿舍。这个学期，他住在学校宿舍，在宿舍他可以做饭，而且走路就可以去学校，所以觉得很方便。小马的朋友小高不喜欢住宿舍，所以租了公寓。公寓比宿舍便宜，但是离学校远，要开车才能去学校。小马没有车，他/Ø 觉得买车太贵，所以下个学期还住宿舍。

最后，作为解读技巧，要指导学生辨认话题，代词回指，零回指，以及回指与原词NP之间的关系。如，

a.   他$_1$吃了饭，$\emptyset_1$喝了茶，$\emptyset_1$回家了。

b.   (第七课)$_1$的语法很容易，可是$\emptyset_1$生词太多，$\emptyset_1$汉字也有一点儿难。

对于母语为英文的外国学生，汉语话题链与他们的母语反差很大。只有不断通过解读，口笔语操作使用，才能逐步地将其内化。

Conclusion

From an L2 education perspective, I discussed the linguistic features of Chinese characters and topic chaining and made relevant pedagogical suggestions in this chapter, with evidence from my recent studies and elsewhere. Linguistically, Chinese is one of the most difficult languages to our learners, especially in character learning and discourse acquisition. Historically, Chinese has been taught in the U.S. for more than a century, but it did not gain national recognition and a momentum for growth until now. The changing world is bringing a great future to our CFL teaching community. This is our time, and the goal is in sight. 任重而道远, together we grasp the opportunity, develop the needed knowledge, and take our first solid step towards our goal.

References

Alderson, J. C., C. Clapham, and D. Steel. 1997. Metalinguistic knowledge, language aptitude and language proficiency. *Language Teaching Research* 1 (2): 93–121.

Andrews, S. 1997. Metalinguistic awareness and teacher explanation. *Language Awareness* 6 (2&3): 147–161.

Andrews, S. 1999a. Why do L2 teachers need to "know about language?" Teachers' metalinguistic awareness and input for learning. *Language and Education* 13 (3): 161–177.

Andrews, S. 1999b. "All these like little name things": A comparative study of language teachers' explicit knowledge of grammar and grammatical terminology. *Language Awareness* 8 (3&4): 143–159.

Ard, Josh and Taco Homburg. 1992. Verification of language transfer. In *Language transfer in language learning*, ed. Susan Gass and Larry Selinker, 47–70. Amsterdam: John Benjamins Publishing Company.

Borg, S. 1998. Teachers' pedagogical systems and grammar teaching: A qualitative study. *TESOL Quarterly.* 32 (1): 9–38.

Borg, S. 1999. The use of grammatical terminology in the second language classroom: A qualitative study of teachers' practices and cognitions. *Applied Linguistics* 20 (1): 95–126.

Conner, Ulla. 1996. *Contrastive rhetoric: Cross-cultural aspects of second-language writing.* Cambridge: University Press.

Chu, Chauncey C. (曲承熙). 1998. *A Discourse grammar of Mandarin Chinese.* New York: Peter Lang Publishing.

Cui, Songren (崔颂人). 2003. 浅谈篇章语法的定义与教学问题. *Journal of the Chinese Language Teachers Association* 38 (1): 1–24.

Ellis, R. 1990. *Instructed second language acquisition: Learning in the classroom.* Oxford: Blackwell.

Everson, M. E. 1998. Word recognition among learners of Chinese as a foreign language: Investigating the relationship between naming and knowing. The *Modern Language Journal* 82: 194–204.

Fotos, S. S. (1993). Consciousness raising and noticing through focus on form: Grammar task performance versus formal instruction. *Applied Linguistics* 14 (4): 185–407.

Gass, Susan M., and Larry Selinker. 2001. *Second language acquisition: An introductory course.* 2nd edition. New Jersey: Lawrence Erlbaum Associates Publishers.

Hadley, Alice Omaggio. 2001. *Teaching language in context.* 3rd edition. Boston: Heinle & Heinle.

Halliday, M. A. K. and Ruqaiya Hasan. 1976. *Cohesion in English.* London and New York: Longman.

Jin, Honggang (靳洪刚). 1994. Topic-prominence and subject-prominence in L2 acquisition: Evidence of English-to-Chinese typological transfer. *Language Learning* 44: 101–121.

Ke, Chuanren (柯传仁), Xiaohong Wen (温晓虹), and C. Kotenbeutel. 2001. Report on the 2000 CLTA articulation project. *Journal of the Chinese Language Teachers Association* 36 (3): 25–60.

Kellerman, Eric. 1983. Now you see it, now you don't. In *Language transfer in language learning*, ed. Susan Gass and Larry Selinker, 112–134. Rowley, MA: Newbury House.

Kellerman, Eric, and Michael Sharwood Smith. 1986. *Crosslinguistic influence in second language acquisition.* New York: Pergamon Press.

Lado, Robert. 1957. *Linguistics across cultures.* Ann Arbor: University of Michigan Press.

Lao She (老舍). 1978. 《骆驼祥子》北京: 人民文学出版社.

Li, Charles N. and Sandra A. Thompson. 1976. Subject and topic: A new typology of language. In *Subject and topic*, ed. Charles N. Li, 457–490. New York: Academic Press, Inc.

———. 1979. Third-person pronouns and zero-anaphora in Chinese discourse. In *Syntax and semantics: Discourse and syntax*, ed. Talmy Givon. New York: Academic Press.

Li, Charles N., and Sandra A. Thompson. 1981. *Mandarin Chinese: A functional reference grammar.* Berkeley: University of California Press.

Li, Wendan (李文旦). 2004a. The discourse perspective in teaching Chinese grammar. *Journal of the Chinese Language Teachers Association* 39 (1): 25–44.

———. (2004b). Topic chains in Chinese discourse. *Discourse Processes* 37 (1): 25–45.

Lightbown, P., and N. Spada. 1990. Focus on form and corrective feedback in communicative language teaching. *Studies in Second Language Acquisition* 12: 429–446.

Liu, Irene and Xiaoqi Li. 1998. *A New Text For A Modern China.* Boston: Cheng & Tsui Company.

刘月华, 潘文娱, 故华. (2001). 《实用现代汉语语法》. 北京: 商务印书馆.

McLaughlin, Barry. 1987. *Theories of second-language learning.* London: Edward Arnold.

Odlin, Terence. 1989. *Language transfer: Cross-linguistic influence in language learning.* New York: Cambridge University Press.

Packard, J. L. 2000. *The morphology of Chinese: A linguistic and cognitive approach.* Cambridge University Press.

Schmidt, R. 1990. The role of consciousness in second language learning. *Applied Linguistics* 11 (2): 129–158.

Sharwood Smith, M. 1990. Consciousness-raising and the second language learner. *Applied Linguistics* 11 (2): 159–168.

Shi, Dingxu (史丁旭). 1992. The nature of topic comment constructions and topic chains. PhD dissertation, University of Southern California.

Shu, Hua (舒华), and Richard C. Anderson. 1999. Learning to read Chinese: The development of metalinguistic awareness. In *Reading Chinese script: A cognitive analysis*, ed. Jian Wang, Albrecht W. Inhoff, and Hsuan-Chih Chen. New Jersey: Lawrence Erlbaum Associate, Publishers.

Tao, Hongyin (陶红印). 1996. *Units in Mandarin conversations: Prosody, discourse, and grammar.* Amsterdam/Philadelphia: John Benjamins.

Tao, Liang (陶亮), and Alice F. Healy. 1998. Anaphora in language processing: Transfer of cognitive strategies by native Chinese, Dutch, English, and Japanese speakers. In *Foreign language learning: Psycholinguistic studies on training and retention*, ed. Alice F. Healy and Lyle E. Bourne, Jr. New Jersey: Lawrence Erlbaum Associates, Publishers.

Teng, Shou-hsin (邓守信). 1997. Towards a pedagogical grammar of Chinese. *Journal of the Chinese Language Teachers Association* 32 (2): 29–39.

Tsao, Fengfu (曹逢甫). 1979. *A functional study of topic in Chinese: The first step towards discourse analysis.* Taipei: Student Book Co., Ltd.

———— (1990). *Sentence and clause structure in Chinese: A functional perspective.* Taipei: Student Book Co., Ltd.

Yao, Tao-chung (姚道中), and Yuehua Liu (刘月华), et al. 1997. *Integrated Chinese.* Boston: Cheng & Tsui Company.

余华. 2003. 《活著》南海出版公司.

Xiao, Yun (萧云). 2005. Raising the orthographic awareness of teachers of Chinese. In *Applied linguistics and language teacher education. Educational Linguistics* Vol. 4, ed. Nat Bartels, 221–234. New York: Springer (former Kluwer Academic Publishers).

————. (forthcoming). Discourse features and development in L2 writing of Chinese. CLTA *(Journal of the Chinese Language Teachers Association)* Monograph #4.

张旺熹. 1998. 从汉字部件到汉字结构. 崔永华主编, 程娟,孟子敏副主编 《词汇文字研究与对外汉语教学》. Beijing: Beijing Languages and Cultures. (北京语言文化出版社).

Chapter 7

Teaching Listening and Speaking

An Interactive Approach

Xiaohong Wen

University of Houston

Listening and speaking are intertwined in the mode of interpersonal communication. The listener and speaker spontaneously convey ideas based on what each hears, request clarifications when there is doubt, and negotiate meanings to reach consensus or to reserve differences. Communication is interactive and bi-directional: When A sends a message, B immediately comprehends it in the context and interprets it according to his/her perspective. The American Council on the Teaching of Foreign Language's National Standards (ACTFL Standards for Foreign Language Learning in the 21st Century, 1999) conceptualize communication into three modes: interpersonal, interpretive and presentational. When learners are engaged in conversation, they are in the interpersonal communicative mode to interpret others' speech and to present their own viewpoints. Under the framework of Communicative Language Teaching, these two skills are practiced in the form of conversation, through interpersonal activities such as dialogues, interviews, discussions, role plays, and debates.

From the perspective of psycholinguistics, listening and speaking are two different processes. Listening is a decoding process that requires comprehension strategies. Speaking is a productive skill that maps concepts and ideas onto correct linguistic forms and appropriate pragmatic functions. Listening is a fundamental source of learning. The development of the listening skill precedes and empowers the speaking skill. Speaking derives from listening, and in turn, enhances the ability of comprehension.

The present article will examine three processing theories: the model of working memory, schema theory, and the input-output model of second language acquisition (SLA) and use. It will discuss the implications of these theories and research findings to the teaching of listening and speaking in the context of Chinese as a foreign language (CFL). It will also present task-based instruction as an effective model that integrates listening and speaking in a highly communicative approach. It will provide pedagogical examples for curriculum design and instructional implementation.

1. The relationship between pronunciation and speech processing: the model of working memory.

The theory of working memory was posited by Baddeley (1986). Working memory is a system that stores information very briefly and allows us to manipulate the information while various mental tasks are performed. We can keep information circulating in working memory by rehearsing it. Baddeley, Gathercole and Papagno (1998) have proposed that phonology and pronunciation are fundamental to the process of listening comprehension. When hearing a phone message such as Sample 1: "大姑于六月9号下午三点乘西北公司179号航班抵虹桥机场，她想知道你能不能去接她", we have to remember the information in the first part of the sentence in order to process the second part. What affects our memory and speed of processing is the phonological store, a mechanism that helps us with working memory (figure 1). The working memory model (Gathercole and Baddeley 1993) states that information we hear in phonological form fades away in seconds. In order to retain the information, one repeats the sound of the word or the phrase silently or aloud, a subvocal rehearsal process (Baddeley 1986). The phonological repetition recycles the sound of words through the articulatory loop back to the phonological store. In other words, the articulatory loop, or phonological loop, is specialized for the retention of verbal information, especially when the words are new and not familiar to us. It mediates and stores unfamiliar sound forms while more permanent memory representations are being constructed.

1.1. IMPLICATIONS OF THE MODEL OF WORKING MEMORY TO CFL LISTENING AND SPEAKING INSTRUCTION.

The model of working memory has two important implications to the teaching of listening and speaking. First, the level of fluency of pronunciation is vital to speech processing and comprehension. Working memory and the listening process are closely interrelated to pronunciation and language use. As Cook (2001) commented, how much one can remember depends on how fast one can repeat, and thus, how fast the information circles round the articulatory loop. Cook posits that "Pronunciation should be taken more seriously, not just for its own sake, but as the

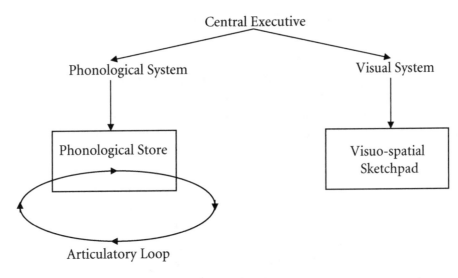

Figure 1. Baddeley's model of working memory (simplified), cited in Cook (2001, p. 84)

basis for speaking and comprehending" (p. 86). Helping learners build a strong foundation in pronunciation at the beginning level fundamentally benefits them in the long run.

Methods to train learners' pronunciation may combine listening and speaking, with listening as the focus (以听带说，听说结合). First comes accuracy in listening, and then correct pronunciation. For example, learners are asked to focus on listening to and practicing the stress and length of the vowel, rhythm, and intonation in varied phonological environments. Instruction can also combine listening and speaking in sentences where grammar plays a role in stress, as proposed by 胡波 (2004). For example, in simple subject-verb sentences, the verb is frequently stressed (as in sentences 1–2 below); when the verb has an object, the object is stressed (sentences 3–4); when a complement is present, the complement is often stressed (sentences 5–6); in questions, interrogative words are often stressed (sentence 7–8).

1. 你说吧！
2. 你喜欢就拿上。
3. 他说出了她的名字。
4. 我不用手机。
5. 张老师解释得很清楚。
6. 他说得有理，做得对。
7. 谁在说话？
8. 你怎么什么都没带来？

The second implication of the model is that teaching should take into consideration memory and processing limitations. Short words and familiar information are easier to process. The sounds of short words are repeated faster, and thus, circulated more quickly and easily back to the phonological store. Familiar information is retrieved directly from memory, saves the capacity of working memory, and consequently speeds up language processing. Different sentence structures require different capacities of memory processing. Passive sentences, for example, take longer to understand than active sentences (Baddeley, 1986). Listening materials should have good control of new words and grammar structures. It is suggested that the material should contain approximately 10% new words and 5% new grammar structures for learners at the elementary and intermediate level. The content of the material should be familiar to learners. Otherwise, a brief introduction is needed before listening. Furthermore, questions in the listening exercise should be immediate and of moderate length. For instance, referring to the information presented in Sample 1, a question such as "大姑几月几号几点乘哪一个航空公司的几号航班抵虹桥机场？" is inappropriate for learners at the elementary level because it is over-loaded with information, and thus requires a large capacity of working memory.

2. The relationship between background knowledge and comprehension: schema theory.

We receive information by listening. The process of listening comprehension, however, is by no means a passive and a receptive skill. Scholars (Clarke and Silberstein 1977, Bransford and Johnson 1982, Carrell 1984) have proposed schema theory, describing comprehension as an interactive process in which listeners actively use both linguistic knowledge and their own knowledge of the world to interact with the content of the input[1], and create new meanings based on their interpretations. What listeners contribute to the process from their memories and experiences is much more than the original input itself, as Clarke and Silberstein (1977) commented:

> Research has shown that reading is only incidentally visual. More information is contributed by the reader than by the print on the page. That is, readers understand what they read because they are able to take the stimulus beyond its graphic representation and assign it membership to an appropriate group of concepts already stored in their memories. (p.136)

Although the topic that Clarke and Silberstein are discussing is reading, schema theory is equally valid and applicable to listening. In the listening process, three steps seem to occur: We first receive the message, then comprehend it in context, and interpret it in each of our own ways. For example, in response to a mother's

---

[1]Input in this article refers to any language to which the learner is exposed.

statement "饭做好了!", everyone in the family might interpret it differently. What the father hears is "Set up the table and get ready to eat!"; the elder brother might think "The food is finally ready; let me go down to the dining room!"; the sister might think "What dishes are they? I hope they are my favorites." The interpretation from the younger brother is different from them all: "There is no chance to go to McDonald's; the food is ready and we are going to eat at home." They all share one thing in common. Everyone actively interacts with the input. They receive the same message but interpret it differently, and create varied meanings based on their concerns and perspectives.

The above example has shown that, as listeners, we selectively associate information in the input to the most relevant knowledge from our memory, compare the input with our existing linguistic and world knowledge, and interpret it based on our own experience. The process is highly interactive and mostly subconscious, and happens in a fraction of a second.

In the process, the listener interacts with the input at different linguistic levels and interprets it based on all possible background knowledge. A listener must understand not only the semantics of a sentence, but also its pragmatic function; not only word meaning, but also the usage in the context. For example, the sentence "有火吗?", although in a question form, is a request. There would be no communication if a person takes the question "有火吗?" as a real "yes" or "no" interrogation. Furthermore, the "light, 火" is definitely referring to a match or cigarette lighter only. In communication, the intent of the speaker is frequently indirect and imbedded. Listeners need to rely on the linguistic and/or non-linguistic context to infer the meaning. For example, when hearing the sentence "麻烦你很不好意思", we do not know if it is an apology, a request for help, or an expression of thankfulness. It is only in the context and based on one's experience that meaning becomes clear.

It is important to note that schemata may be culture specific and vary from one culture to another. For example, when a CFL learner who grows up in the western culture hears the word "婚礼", he / she would activate the schema of "white bridal gowns, fresh white roses, vows, pink flower pedals showering the bride and groom". The learner may become confused and misinterpret the text that describes the wedding with "red bridal dresses, red banners, red signs of double happiness, fireworks, and a big feast with people getting drunk." The misinterpretation is not caused by linguistic elements such as new vocabulary and grammar, but by the lack of target cultural knowledge. Therefore, one of the tasks of second language education is to build up the learner's culturally contextualized schemata. CFL teachers should help learners develop their cultural background knowledge through a variety of activities such as pre-reading, learning vocabularies that convey cultural connotations, making comparisons of cultural practices, and understanding the value behind them. Activities such as visual presentations, flow-charting, or diagramming to develop learners' understanding of the target culture are helpful.

2.1. IMPLICATIONS OF SCHEMA THEORY TO CFL LISTENING AND SPEAKING INSTRUCTION

Schema theory considers listening comprehension not only as a linguistic encoding process but also as a problem-solving process. Listeners use intonation cues, contextual clues, background knowledge, and cognitive skills to associate the input with one's existing experience, activate the relevant content in the mind, and retrieve the pertinent information from memory. When one piece of information is triggered, an associated group of similar categories simultaneously becomes active. Therefore, it is optimal if listeners can make connections between new information and what they already know.

This provides two significant guidelines for classroom instruction. First, teaching must make connections between new learning and what has been already acquired by students. Pre-listening activities serve this purpose. The instructor can initiate activities such as brainstorming to guess the content of the input, having a brief discussion about the title, showing a visual, or telling a brief personal story or an anecdote as a prelude to listening. If there are many new words in the material that are vital to comprehension, a short vocabulary list should be provided. If the material requires cultural understanding that is absent in the learners' repertoire, a brief introduction is in order. Take the previous example "婚礼". Pre-listening activities may include associating color and food with the Chinese wedding; post-listening activities may include a project of examining the meaning and practice of 男婚女嫁 in China. In short, it is essential to help learners acquire the necessary background information applicable to the material, and to create a context that activates learners' existing knowledge.

Post-listening activities also serve the purpose of making connections between learner's existing knowledge and new learning. In post-listening activities, students summarize the learning content and synthesize their understanding. Furthermore, post-listening activities assess the accuracy of comprehension, and combine listening and speaking skills to consolidate learners' comprehension. Post-listening activities should be diverse in form and content depending on the pedagogical purposes and the needs of learners. For example, the first post-listening activity of "你的车找到了" is to answer the listening comprehension questions in the handout. Then learners are asked to exchange their answer sheets with their partners. This gives them opportunities to discuss their uncertainties in listening. As a follow-up, each pair is required to create their own dialogue based on the input of "你的车找到了". The topic may be "你的钱包/手表/车/护照/小弟弟/小妹妹找到了". Since it is a guided composition, learners can produce theirs in a comparatively easy and rapid fashion. (Alternatively, this can be a home assignment so that no classroom time is taken.) Finally, the pair is required to present their new dialogue to the whole class. (If the class has more than 10 students, the instructor can select three pairs. The rest of the students can be selected in future sessions so all students have an opportunity to do a presentation.)

Second, the listening input should be challenging enough so that learners have ample opportunities to employ cognitive skills and learning strategies in the process. While listening, learners not only use bottom-up strategies to understand the meaning of words, but also top-down strategies to grasp the gist of the whole passage, look for internal relationships among the information in the discourse, and infer meaning based on key words. For example, the dialogue in Appendix I (刘珣等 2003) is for learners at the high-elementary level. It has a considerable number of new words. Some (e.g., 丢, 自行车, 派出所, 警察) are essential to comprehension of the whole dialogue; others (e.g., 东升, 城里, 牌子, 永久牌, 取, 拿) are minor and can be easily skipped. It also requires some cultural background, e.g. the local police station in China acts as a "lost and found" for people for such items as bicycles. Before listening, the instructor helps learners focus their attention by asking warm-up questions such as:

1.　如果你的自行车丢了，你会做什么？

Students may give different answers. One might say "告诉 police." The instructor will then write the new word "警察" on the board since it is a key word, and present a visual that shows a Chinese police station with a Chinese police officer and a bike.

2.　谁可能把你的车找到？
3.　警察会问什么问题呢？

(Please see the dialogue in Appendix I.)

During listening, learners are encouraged to first focus on main ideas. If the material is lengthy and presents a certain level of difficulty, listening can be repeated. The first pass may focus on obtaining the major information. The second pass can be more targeted to specific information and details. For example, the instructor may ask learners to "jot down all the numbers," or "jot down the time sequence and names." In the example "你的车找到了", the instructor may ask learners to "jot down the 是……的 sentences" if the purpose of the activity is to practice the "是……的" pattern. Learners are guided toward piecing information together in order to derive complete ideas, and to infer meanings in context. The task of listening instruction, therefore, is to help learners employ varied cognitive skills such as categorizing, comparing, synthesizing, hypothesizing, and testing, as well as learning strategies such as guessing, predicting, skimming, scanning, and looking for key words and clues in the context.

Table 1 summarizes the design of such a series of activities, from pre-listening through post-listening.

Table 1. Structured activities for dialogue "你的车找到了"

Summary	

Tasks and Goals	1. Pre-listening: (In the interpersonal mode) warm-up activities to
	  a. activate learners' relevant linguistic and background knowledge,
	  b. motivate learners' interest.
	2. Listening: (In the interpretive Mode)
	  a. encourage the use of cognitive skills,
	  b. induce learners to use certain specific strategies.
	3. Post-listening: (In the interpersonal Mode)
	  a. assess/confirm listening comprehension; learners negotiate meanings and clarify ideas,
	  b. guided composition for production; creatively apply what they already know to new learning,
	  c. group presentation.

Detailed Plan	

Step 1: Pre-listening
T/S interaction Interpersonal Mode
	1. Use questions for warm-up
	  a. 如果你的自行车丢了，你会做什么？
	  b. 谁可能把你的车找到？
	  c. 警察会问什么问题呢？
	2. Write down the key new words while listening to students' answers: (e.g., 丢, 自行车, 派出所, 警察).
	3. Present a picture of a Chinese police station with a Chinese police woman or man and a bike.

Step 2: Listening
S interaction w/ input Interpretive Mode
	1. Direction: listen for main ideas such as:
	  a. who is in the story?
	  b. why do they talk?
	  c. where are they?
	Remind students to guess the meaning in context and do not get stumped on a particular word
	2. Read listening comprehension questions on our handout first and listen for the second time. Then, write answers to questions.

Step 3: Post-listening S/S interaction Interpersonal Mode	Students interact and negotiate meaning by: 1. exchanging answer sheets with their partner and discussing the differences in their answers, 2. creating a new dialogue based on the input, 3. presenting the dialogue in class, 4. writing a narrative based on the input and submitting it as homework.

3. The relationship between input and output: The model of second language acquisition.

The development of listening and speaking skills reflects the processes of both first and second language acquisition (SLA). In a formal instructional setting for SLA, listening input is pedagogically designed to tailor its content, form, meaning, and function to the language development stages of learners. VanPatten (1995) proposed a model of SLA and use (figure 2) consisting of three processes and four concepts in an interactive relationship from instructional input to learner's output.

```
        I           II                      III
   Input → intake → developing system → output
   I = input processing.
   II = accommodation, restructuring.
   III = access, control, monitoring.
```

Figure 2. Model of second language acquisition and use (based on VanPatten 1995)

The model is highly applicable to teaching listening and speaking. One emphasis of the model is on meaning and comprehensibility of the input, and input processing. As scholars have stated (e.g., Long, 1990, Ellis, 2003, VanPatten, 2004), comprehensible input is the first step to the successful generation of language output. Comprehensible input, however, does not guarantee that input will become the learner's intake[2]. It is the learner who converts input into intake, and intake to output, who succeeds in developing strong listening and speaking abilities.

3.1. IMPLICATIONS OF THE MODEL OF SLA AND ITS RELEVANCE TO CFL LISTENING AND SPEAKING INSTRUCTION

Instruction can assist and enhance the listening and speaking processes. Well-designed learning activities need to accommodate intake and restructure the learners' language system by helping them access their linguistic repertoire on the one hand and monitoring their speaking output on the other. Examples of such activities are presented in Tables 1, 2, and 3 of this article. The instructor can strategically direct learners' attention to important features in the input, and facilitate form-meaning mappings that consequently lead to better intake and quality output. Instructors can design a variety of activities to facilitate listening comprehension by using visual images (以图助听), by designing activities that involve

---

[2]Intake refers to grammar knowledge that becomes part of a learner's competence after mediating between input and grammars.

taking notes (以笔助听) and listening by doing (以做助听), and by integrating speaking and listening in an interactive fashion (听说互动).

Visual aids help decrease the load of working memory and thus speed up input processing. They also promote interest in learning. Visual aids should vary in form and may be charts, tables, maps, schedules, or vivid or funny pictures from a web page. The choice of the form is determined by the content and difficulty level of the material. The image may have brief words in it so that learners compare and identify the relevant meaning, or can be an empty chart with a title that learners can fill in with key words from the input. Figure 3 is such an example.

8:00 a.m.
8:30 a.m.
10:30 a.m.
2:00 p.m.
4:00 p.m.
9:00 p.m.

Drawn by Miss Jiayao Pang

Figure 3. My schedule on Sunday

Taking notes while listening is an important skill that assists conversion from input to intake. Taking notes requires learners to use cognitive skills to look for cues and identify key information in the input. Notes taken can be numbers, connecting words to show sequences, layers of meanings, and relationships such as cause-effect pairs, conditions, and consequences. Notes might be words, such as nouns, key verbs with its nouns, time sequences, or clues in the context; or may even be a map or a floor plan. The form of the notes (Pinyin, characters, or English) should be flexible to accommodate individual learning styles and preferences, language proficiency levels, and goals of instruction.

Visual aids and taking notes make learning easier and help combine listening and speaking skills. For example, when learning locations and directions, students can draw a map while listening. Then they can exchange their maps in pairs or small groups, and compare differences among their drawings. Based on the input they have just heard and discussed, learners can work out a new description of a familiar location. It can be a favorite restaurant, a popular bookstore, or a quaint downtown street. The instructor can ask a few students to tell the class their descriptions individually while the rest of the class listens and draws the location based on the input. This activity that integrates listening and speaking (听说互动) is summarized in table 2.

This is an example of the output from a student:

Table 2.   Integrating listening and speaking "你知道这个地方吗?"

Goals of the Task Interpretive Interpersonal Presentational modes	Practice
	1. Listening strategies: note taking, identifying key words and information, guessing, inferring, synthesizing.
	2. Communicative skills: group discussion and negotiation of meaning based on their drawings.
	3. Speaking strategies: logical sequencing of the information, clarity.
Steps	1. Individual work: listen and take notes / draw. (The interpretive mode)
	2. Pair/group interaction: exchange and compare drawings. (The interpersonal mode)
	3. Individual work: use five sentences to create one's own description of a favorite place on campus or in town and how to locate it. (The presentational mode)
	4. Individuals report their descriptions to the class; other students listen, guess, and answer questions. (The presentational mode and the interpersonal mode.)
Cognitive skills and strategies practiced	1. For input processing: Listen for key words and information, grasp the gist, guess, listen for details by taking notes/drawing, tolerate unknowns, identify, and discover.
	2. For output: Logical sequencing based on the input, clarity, coherence, choosing interesting content.
Linguistic skills practiced	Understand meaning, and use forms accurately and appropriately:
	1. 1. S. 在 N. 的 location.
	2. N. 的 location 是 N.
	3. Location 有 N.
Activity form	1. Interactive between the learner and the input, and among learners.
	2. Communicative: learners interpret, express, and negotiate meaning about locations and directions.

"这个饭馆在 Calhound 街上。这个饭馆的旁边有一个加油站。这个饭馆的对面是 law school。这个饭馆的左边有 Wendy's。这个饭馆离45号公路不远。你知道这个饭馆吗？"

Listening by doing is another instructional strategy that facilitates the conversion from input to intake by focusing on comprehension. The method Total Physical Response (Asher 1982) is especially appropriate for material that takes time to process. In this method, learners are given time while listening to pay attention to the linguistic forms and react to meaning. Comprehension is reinforced through action. For example, the instructor can conveniently use props in the classroom to help learners understand the function of the "ba" construction (把字句) while they physically respond to the requests while listening:

"请把门关上／打开。" "请把灯关上／打开。"
"请把你的电话号写在黑板上。" "请把你的手机拿出来。"
"请把你的钱包拿出来。" "请把你的钱给我。"

The exercise can also be at the phrase level. For example, when teaching the verb complement, the instructor can ask learners to act on the input and pay attention to the word order and the language form:

"请你（们）走到教室前面来。" "走上来。"
"走过去，走到那儿去。" "走下去。" "开门出去。"
"往前走三步。" "往后退一步。"
"向左拐，往前走，停。走回来。"

It is fine if there are a few new words in the input (e.g., "退", "步" "向", "停"). Learners are encouraged to guess the meanings and to develop a tolerance for unknowns. A similar method can also be used in practicing locations and directions that are notoriously difficult to learn because of word order, preposition usage, and spatial conceptualization, which is abstract and culturally distinctive (Bowerman 1989, Wen 1994, 1995, and 1997a). Learners are asked to act on the statements to confirm their listening comprehension:

"你的笔在书上。" "你的笔在书里。" "你的书包在桌子上面。"
"你的手机在书包里面，不在书包外面。"
"你站在丽莎的后面，在斯蒂文的前面。"

After repeatedly hearing and acting on the statements, learners might be able to notice the word order and sentence structure of Chinese sentences and realize linguistic differences between Chinese and English, compare the input with their existing knowledge, and continuously restructure their interlanguage[3] system.

---

[3]An interlanguage is an independent linguistic system produced by a learner of a second language. It is developing towards the target language, and is also preserving some features of the learner's first language.

4. Integrating listening and speaking in communicative tasks: Task-based instruction

Task-based instruction is a teaching approach that integrates listening and speaking skills in one carefully designed task. In a simplified sense, a task is a means of motivating learners to actively use the language communicatively to achieve learning goals. One of the major underpinnings of task-based instruction is SLA theory, namely, that learning is autonomous and language may develop independently from instruction (e.g., Selinker 1972, Pienemann, 1987, Pienemann 1989, Wen 2006). Other underpinnings of the approach are theories of sociolinguistics that consider communicative competence and language use as fundamental to both language and language acquisition (Hymes 1971, Savignon 1983, Brown 1994), and from Halliday's theory of systemic-functional grammar (1975, 1978). Halliday takes a social semiotic approach to the function of the language, and investigates how meaning is constructed in relation to a speaker's intention, and understood within a context. He proposes that we use language as a means to achieve communicative goals, interpret information in context for purposeful use, and negotiate meanings interactively.

There are several implications of the underpinnings of task-based instruction to the teaching of CFL. Theories of language acquisition tell us that teaching must be learner-centered. In the classroom, learning tasks should be meaningful to learners, purposeful with specific outcomes that can be assessed, interactive by nature, and closely based on themes of daily life that reflect genuine communication. How are we to make these happen?

In the early days of task-based instruction, Prabhu (1987) proposed the "gap principle"; that is, that instruction creates an information, reasoning, or opinion gap within the input or among learners so that learners need to genuinely communicate in order to bridge the gap and accomplish the task. The task, "How to make "宫保鸡丁" and "蛋炒饭", as illustrated below, is such an example. In addition to input, Swain (1985, 1995) has posited that a learner's output is vital for language acquisition and the development of communicative competence. Learners need ample opportunities to produce "pushed output" that is not only fluent and accurate, but also with an appropriate sentence length and level of complexity.

In "gap" tasks, learners complete a task by consulting, gathering, and discussing the information with each other. During the process, learners are given opportunities to observe linguistic forms, make comparisons, and test their hypotheses by using the language meaningfully. For example, when reviewing the "ba" construction (把字句), students are divided into two A and B groups to receive different input and work in pairs to tell each other how to cook "宫保鸡丁" or "蛋炒饭". The task is designed in three phases with six steps: the pre-task phase for form-focused instruction, listening, and input processing; the in-task phase for

Table 3.   Interpersonal interaction: How to make "宫保鸡丁"and"蛋炒饭"

Phase	Steps
Pre-task 1. pre-listening 2. listening input Interpretive Mode	1. Linguistic preparation: practice the form, meaning, and function of 把字句, key words, and lexical chunks in the listening input. 2. Create information gap in input: Groups A and B listen to different tapes of how to make"宫保鸡丁"and"蛋炒饭"respectively. Students are informed that they will tell each other what they have heard afterwards.
In-task 3. interpersonal communication 4. negotiate meanings Interpersonal Mode	3. Students work in pairs to report to each other on how to make"宫保鸡丁"and"蛋炒饭" respectively. They negotiate meanings and clarify doubts. 4. They prepare what they obtained from the partner into a coherent narrative discourse. They are required to report to the class after their pair work.
Post-task 5. "pushed output" 6. discourse presentation Presentational Mode	5. The instructor selects a few students to report individually on what they learned from their partner. The rest of the students serve as judges for the report. 6. Home assignment: prepare a recipe for your favorite dish and send it to the class through email.

speaking and interpersonal communication; the post-task phase for assessment and follow-up language use in speaking or/and writing. Table 3 presents the steps in a structured fashion.

There are four features worth noting in the above task design. First, learners go through genuine communication. They must consult each other for necessary information so that they can do their next task of reporting what they have learned to the class. They must comprehend clearly and speak accurately to interact for meaning. Second, the series of activities is well-structured, with the previous activity feeding into the next activity. The activities start with form-focused instruction that guides learners to a range of possible language realizations, and end with the learning outcome of presenting a "recipe". Learners are provided with not only a good amount of exposure to listening input, but many opportunities to use the language for interpersonal communication. They are encouraged to speak with good quantity and quality. Third, the topic relates to daily life situations that promote interest and usefulness of the learning. Fourth, the assessment is conducted by the students themselves, which provides immediate feedback to facilitate their language processing and acquisition.

Task-based instruction provides myriad ways to integrate listening and speaking, and encourages learners to interact bi-directionally. Role-play presents "replication activities of the real world" (Willis 1990) in which learners use language and build up their communicative competence in a linguistically and culturally rich environment. Appendix II is such an example, in which a theme determines the context where learners play different roles to reach goals and produce outcomes. Tasks are not performed for simulation because learners tend to use language for acting and display. Instead, a task should be purposeful and require learners to interact to negotiate meanings, make suggestions, solve problems, and reach agreements. There is an objective to work toward in a task, and consequently learners obtain it through interaction.

Tasks should be diverse, and varied in in content, with the flexibility to meet learners' interests, learning styles, and proficiency levels. Interviews are easy to use and interesting to learners. It can be a job or a school entrance interview in which a student plays the role of an interviewee (students do so by turns), whereas others are all interviewers. It can be a news interview where learners go to interview two or three classmates or Chinese students on campus, and then report the results of their "news" or "survey" to the class. When teaching expressions of time and place, for example, students can work in groups to play the role of "detectives" to examine schedules of "suspected" students and report to the class the conclusion of their "investigation". When teaching locations and directions, the following tasks, for example, are easy to use and interesting. The difficulty level of the tasks below varies to fit the different proficiency backgrounds of learners.

1. Learning by discovering. The instructor informs students: "I have hidden over 20 items such as pens, notebooks, Chinese stamps, maps, apples, bananas, etc. in this classroom. Can you find them? You must use two sentences to describe the location of the item you have found, such as 这个笔记本在那把椅子的上头，桌子的下头，窗户的旁边. You must find a minimum of two items and then report to the class. This is a rewarding activity: you may keep one item for yourself!"

2. Learning by identifying. Play a guessing game: First, students prepare a short narrative about a well-known person (a president, a movie/sport star), or a popular place (a country, a state, a local restaurant, a favorite local street, a building on campus). Then, they tell the class individually, asking them if they can identify the name of the person or place, as illustrated in table 2.

3. Learning by interaction. Students are divided into two groups. Students in group A are given a campus map and work as "Campus Guides for new students". Students in group B are new to the campus and need to find their classrooms, bookstores, and campus service locations. Each "Campus Guide" needs to help at least two "new students."

4. Learning by doing. This is group work, with four students in a group. The directions are: "You are residential architects and work in teams. Two of you will design houses and the other two of you will design a community plan.

After finishing your drawings, tell each other about your design. For example, explain the location of different rooms in the house and locations of the school, post office, banks, and restaurants in the community. Then your group will work out a narrative to present to the class."

When implementing communicative task-based instruction in the classroom, the instructor needs to consider five "rules" to promote the ease of flow and success of the performance:

1. Build up the path. Start with comprehensible input and form-focused[4] instruction, so that learners are very familiar with the sentence structures and vocabularies to be used in performing the task;
2. Establish a clear purpose. Ensure that learners know what they are expected to do and how to contribute to the processes and the objectives;
3. State specific requirements for the output. Requirements may include length (e.g., how many sentences), language forms, and functions;
4. Specify a time frame. State the time period learners will use for each task. The range usually varies from 3–15 minutes in class;
5. End with learner output, such as a report or a presentation to the class. Students can take turns if the class size is large.

A well-structured task plan is the key to the success of learners' performance. The task of the instructor is to provide a highly interactive language environment with clear communicative goals, and to design the tasks that internally motivate learners. In this way, learners have the desire to actively participate and use the language to solve problems and make decisions. Motivation is significant in the learners' participation and strategy use (Wen 1997b). As illustrated above, tasks should be designed and organized according to students' interests, proficiency levels, learning content, and the size of the class. Tasks should be offered in different forms and in a variety of ways in order to bring a sense of innovation and creativity to the classroom.

NOTES

1. Input in this article refers to any language to which the learner is exposed.
2. Intake refers to grammar knowledge that becomes part of a learner's competence after mediating between input and grammars.
3. An interlanguage is an independent linguistic system produced by a learner of a second language. It is developing towards the target language, and is also preserving some features of the learner's first language.

---

[4]Form-focused instruction refers to instruction that focuses on language form, i.e. grammar structures. The form-focused instruction proposed in this article is implemented under the framework of Communicative Language Teaching.

4. Form-focused instruction refers to instruction that focuses on language form, i.e. grammar structures. The form-focused instruction proposed in this article is implemented under the framework of Communicative Language Teaching.

Appendix 1

你的车找到了（摘自《新实用汉语课本 2》刘珣等，2003）

女：喂，是马大为吗？

男：是啊，您是哪位？

女：我是东升派出所的警察，我姓刘。

男：刘小姐您好。找我有什么事儿吗？

女：我们想问一下，你是不是上个星期丢了一辆自行车？

男：对啊，就是上个星期六晚上丢的。

女：你的车是放在什么地方的？

男：那天我到城里去看朋友，车放在学院前边的公共汽车站了。

女：你的车是什么牌子的？什么颜色？

男：黑色的，永久牌。

女：你是哪天告诉派出所的？

男：我是星期天早上就告诉派出所了。

女：你的车已经找到了，你现在就可以到派出所来取。

男：真的？太好了！谢谢你们，我马上就去拿。

Appendix 2

Integrating the theme, context, language form, meaning, and function through role play

Theme	Context	Roles	Language form & meaning	Function
Reserve a hotel room	At the front desk of a hotel	Traveler / Hotel assistant	Unit price, money expressions: 一天多少钱？	Request, clarification, negotiation
Look for a job	Interview	Interviewee Interviewers	Past experience "-了","-过","了." S.是 emphasized V.的.	Self-introduction, explanation, convincing
Buy a house	At a sales office	Buyer Seller	Location and direction S.在 N.的 location. N.的 location 是 N. Location 有 N.	Consult, disagree, appraise

Theme	Context	Roles	Language form & meaning	Function
Buy a car	Car dealer's office	Buyer Seller	Comparison A 比 B adj (一点儿/ 得多/# 量词。 A 比 B 更 adj.	Comparison Identify, persuasion, clarification.
Reserve a ticket	On the phone	Buyer Seller	Time, place, money expressions 从 PI 到 PI 得票多少钱？	Introduction, recommendation, negotiation
Meet friends	At a party	Three people	Introduce friends A 对 B 有兴趣.	Greetings, compliment
Tourism	Conversation on a map	Tourist Guide	Narrative presentation, A 是 modifier 的 N. 之一。	Statement in discourse, suggestion

References

American Council on the Teaching of Foreign Languages. 1999. *Standards for foreign language learning in the 21st century.* Lawrence, KS: Allen Press, Inc.

Asher, James J. 1982. *Learning another language through actions.* Los Gatos, CA: Sky Oaks Productions.

Baddeley, A. D. 1986. *Working memory.* Oxford: Oxford University Press.

Baddeley, A., S. Gathercole, and C. Papagno. 1998. The phonological loop as a language learning device. *Psychological Review* 105 (1): 158–73.

Bowerman. 1989. Learning a semantic system: What role do cognitive predispositions play? In *The teachability of language,* ed. M. Rice and R. Schiefelbusch, 133–171. Baltimore: Brookes Publishing Company.

Bransford, J. D. and M. K. Johnson. 1982. Contextual prerequisites for understanding: Some investigations of comprehension and recall. *Journal of Verbal Language and Verbal Behavior* 11: 717–26.

Brown, H. D. 1994. *Principles of language learning and teaching.* 3rd edition. Englewood Cliffs, NJ: Prentice Hall.

Carrell, P. L. 1984. Evidence of a formal schema in second language comprehension. *Language Learning* 34: 87–111.

Clarke, M. A. and S. Silberstein. 1977. Toward a realization of psycholinguistic principles for the ESL reading class. *Language Learning* 27 (1): 135–154.

Cook, V. 2001. *Second Language learning and language teaching.* London: Arnold.

Ellis, R. 2003. *The study of second language acquisition.* Oxford: Oxford University Press.

Gathercole, S. E. and A. Baddeley. 1993. *Working memory and language.* Hove, UK: Erbaum.

Halliday, M. A. K. 1978. *Language as social semiotic.* London: Edward Arnold.

Halliday, M. A. K.1975. *Learning how to mean.* London: Edward Arnold.

胡波 2004 谈在听力训练中抓主要信息能力的培养，《云南师范大学学报》。

Hymes, D. H. 1971. *On communicative competence.* Philadelphia, PA: University of Pennsylvania Press.

刘珣, 张凯，刘社会，陈曦，左珊丹，施家炜 2003《新实用汉语课本 2》北京语言大学出版社.

Long, M. H. 1990. The least a second language acquisition theory needs to explain. *TESOL Quarterly* 24 (4): 649–66. Reprinted in *Readings on second language acquisition*, ed. H. D. Brown and S. Gonzo, 470–90. Englewood-Cliffs, NJ: Prentice Hall Regents, 1994.

Pienemann, M. 1987. Psychological constraints on the teachability of language. In *First and second language acquisition processes*, ed. C. W. Pfaff. Rowley, MA: Newbury House.

Pienemann, M. 1989. Is language teachable? Psycholinguistic experiments and hypotheses. *Applied Linguistics* 10: 52–79.

Prabhu, N. 1987. *Second language pedagogy*. Oxford: Oxford University Press.

Savignon, S. 1983. *Communicative competence: Theory and classroom practice*. Reading, MA: Addison Wesley.

Selinker, L. 1972. Interlanguage. *International Review of Applied Linguistics*. Vol. 10, 209–31.

Swain, M. 1985. Communicative competence: Some roles of comprehensible input and comprehensible output in its development. In *Input in second language acquisition*, ed. S. Gass and C. Madden. Rowley, MA: Newbury House.

Swain, M. 1995. Three functions of output in second language learning. In *Principles and practice in the study of language*, ed. G. Cook and B. Seidlehofer. Oxford: Oxford University Press

VanPatten, B. 1995. Cognitive aspects of input processing in second language acquisition. *Festschrift in honor of Tracy D. Terrell*, ed. P. Hashemipour, R. Maldonado, and M. van Naerssen. New York: McGraw-Hill.

VanPatten, B. 2004. Input Processing in SLA. In *Processing instruction: Theory, research, and commentary*, ed. B.VanPatten, 1–31. Mahwah, NJ: Erlbaum.

Wen, X. 1997a. Acquisition of Chinese aspect: An analysis of the interlanguage of learners of Chinese as a foreign language. *ITL Review of Applied Linguistics* 117–118: 1–26.

Wen. X. 1997b. Motivation and language learning with students of Chinese. *Foreign Language Annals* 30: 235–251.

Wen, X. 2006. Acquisition sequence o f three constructions: An analysis of the interlanguage of learners of Chinese as a foreign language. *Journal of Chinese Language Teachers Association* 41: 3.

Wen, X. 1994. Topic prominence in the acquisition of Chinese existential sentences by English-speakers. *International Journal of Psycholinguistics* 10 (2): 127–145. Center for Academic Societies, Osaka, Japan.

Wen, X. 1995. Second language acquisition of the Chinese particle *le. International Journal of Applied Linguistics* 5 (1): 45–62.

Willis, D. 1990. *The lexical syllabus: A new approach to language teaching*. London: Harper Collins / Cobuild.

Chapter 8

Technology in Chinese Language Teaching and Learning

Tianwei Xie

California State University, Long Beach

Tao-chung Yao

University of Hawaii at Manoa

Key Words

CALL, computer-aided language learning, learning Chinese, computer applications in teaching Chinese, web resources, technology

Introduction

Technology is used more and more extensively nowadays in all walks of life. Language educators have also been using technology to enhance their teaching.

The development of technology is reflected in the use of different types of technology over the past few decades. Language teachers have moved from using audiotapes to using audio CDs, and from videotapes to multimedia. This is also true for Chinese language learning and teaching. During the past decades, the extensive use of computers and the Internet in teaching languages is evidenced by a proliferation of web resources and multimedia software for learning (Bourgerie 2003; Xie 2007). Extensive use of computers in and out of the classroom has also been documented in research papers and articles. For example, Chun and Zhao (2006) state that "text-based online chat is a second language learning environment that holds some pedagogical potential, as it leads to higher rates of noticing."[1]

---

[1]"Noticing" means that students notice their problematic language production and the interactional feedback from their interlocutors during chat.

Computer Mediated Communication (CMC) has become a trend in foreign language teaching. MSN messenger, Yahoo messenger, Skype, AIM, and QQ have also been used for online tutoring and teaching (Godwin-Jones 2005).

Although some researchers disagree about the effectiveness of using technology in language education (http://www.nosignificantdifference.org), students seem to like technology. For example, Corbeil's research (2007) shows that students react more positively to using PowerPoint (PPT) in classrooms and consider it to be a more effective learning tool than textbooks. Other research shows that network-based group work carried out via emails, chats, and online discussions helps students increase their awareness of different aspects of the target language and increasingly focuses their attention on their own language learning process. This in turn increases students' confidence in using the language (Dooly 2007).

More and more teachers are becoming aware of the usefulness of computers and web resources in teaching. We can, for instance, use special software to prepare teaching materials more effectively than with simple word processing or typing alone. We can also use existing websites to supplement our teaching, or create our own websites and online exercises. However, Chinese language teachers are not always familiar with all the computer resources that are available, and often do not know how to locate them. This article intends to serve as a basic introduction to the role of technology, mainly computer technology, in teaching Chinese and how to utilize computer and Web resources.

This paper will discuss some important concepts and theoretical issues related to CALL (Computer-Assisted Language Learning) first, and then it will recommend some of the computer programs and websites that authors have found to be useful and effective. It is by no means intended to be an exhaustive study of general theoretical issues or any specific computer programs for learning Chinese for two reasons. First, computer technology develops so rapidly that some programs become out of date very soon while new ones appear almost every day. Second, the explosive growth of information has made it extremely difficult for anybody to cover too many aspects. Interested readers may refer to Yao (1996), Zhang (1998), and Bourgerie (2003) to understand the history of CALL for Chinese and to read reviews of various Chinese CALL software programs. The Chinese Language Teachers Association website also has a web page called "Online (CALL) Reviews" which provides online access to reviews of computer-assisted language learning (CALL) software and other computing-related reviews published in the *Journal of the Chinese Language Teachers Association* (JCLTA). The URL is: http://clta-us.org/reviews/reviews.htm.

Three stages of CALL

Educational technology has undergone great change during the past decades. At the earliest stages, technology used for language teaching and learning included gramophone records, tape recorders, slide projectors, radios, TVs and other electronic devices. Rapid development of computer technology, moreover, has been unprecedented in how it has revolutionized communication and its impact on teaching languages. The concept of CALL is now widely recognized as a positive force in foreign language education.

Some researchers have proposed that CALL has undergone three stages of development. Warschauer and Healey (1998) named these stages as "behaviouristic, communicative and integrative" stages. According to them, the first stage was characterized by using audio-lingual technology based on the structural linguistic view on language. The second stage featured interactive communication based on a cognitive approach to language acquisition. In the third stage, the focus moved to authentic discourse and fluent use of language in real situations. Bax (2003) has a somewhat different approach to defining these stages. He proposes that the three stages are: restricted CALL, open CALL and integrated CALL. He claims that during the first stage, computer programs were mostly for mechanical drills, with the students having minimal interaction with other students while teachers displayed an "exaggerated fear and/or awe" toward using computers. In the second stage of open CALL, the focus was placed on "linguistic skills development" where the students might interact with computers and other students occasionally. Finally, the third stage of integrated CALL featured computer mediated communication (CMC) and the students' interaction with others (students, teachers or native speakers). In this stage, the use of the computer becomes a normal part of teaching. Computers are accessible in "every classroom, on every desk, in every bag." That is to say, the use of computer technology is "normalized" (Bax 2003).

Theoretical Issues of Using Computers in Language Teaching

It is interesting that technologies used for language teaching have often been related to corresponding linguistic theories and that every type of language teaching has had technologies to support it (Warschauer and Meskill 2000). According to these theorists the audio tape was "the perfect medium for the audiolingual method." The appearance of computer software such as text-reconstruction, concordancing and multimedia programs[2] arrived in time to support cognitive approaches to language teaching. Computer-mediated communication (CMC) in classrooms and for long distance exchange provides teachers and learners with the opportunities to take sociocognitive approaches towards language teaching. The Internet has

---

[2]Text-reconstruction software is a type of program allowing students to fill in the blanks, rearranging the word order to make grammatically correct sentences. Concordance software allows users to search for instances of actual use of a specific word or phrase. Multimedia programs can simulate real language situations using image and sound.

also become a powerful tool for assisting sociocognitive approaches to language teaching.

Is Technology Effective?

One of the questions that language educators often ask is: Is technology (audiolingual or any high-tech device) really effective and useful in language teaching? Although the question is a yes/no question, there is no easy answer with 'yes' or 'no' as research evidence has not been able to give definitive answers. The web site http://nosignificantdifference.wcet.info/ has archived all articles published in academic journals from 1928 through 2007 and these articles document *no significant differences* (NSD) as well as *significant differences* (SD) in learning outcomes of long distance students' use or non-use of technology.[3]

No matter what the research results are, one way to argue is that using technology is at least as effective as the traditional classroom teaching because there is no significant difference. Therefore, teachers may use technology to supplement their teaching. The other way to argue is that since there is no significant difference, why bother to use technology? We would like to argue that even though the evidence in experimental studies does not reveal the significant difference in learning outcomes, there are some other factors that deserve attention: convenience and productivity, needs of globalization and normalization of computer use.

CONVENIENCE AND PRODUCTIVITY

By convenience and productivity it is meant that using technology greatly eases the job of teaching and learning. Sound files, for instance, can be easily stored and presented through computers, and images (pictures and movies) can be played anytime. Simulated situations for language learning can be easily created. Typing Chinese makes composing easier than before. Email and other computer-mediated communication allow students to exchange their writings with other students and even native speakers from target language communities. Teaching materials can be easily created, edited and revised. Documents can also be transmitted electronically to any other parties instantaneously. Computers have made teaching and learning much more convenient. We may use such a comparison: Chinese people used brush pens to write characters in the past. Later, pens replaced the brush although characters remained characters. But the convenience and ease of using pens to replace brushes is obvious. Now the tool for writing Chinese characters has changed again, with the keyboard becoming the tool of writing. This change has

---

[3]Interested readers may also refer to Thomas L. Russell's book, *The No Significant Difference Phenomenon* (2001) for details.

triggered another revolution in teaching Chinese and made Chinese writing and communication much easier.

NEEDS OF GLOBALIZATION AND LOCALIZATION

The world has become smaller. The term "globalization" may have various definitions but, without any doubt, globalization means more cross-linguistic and cross-cultural exchanges. People may use a common language, be it English or any other language, but learning languages of other nations has become an urgent issue. The business world has a slogan: "Think globally and look locally." As for language education, this can be interpreted as meaning that there is an increase for the need to learn a common language and local languages more effectively and quickly.

NORMALIZATION OF COMPUTER USE

Bax (2003) indicates that the use of technology will finally be normalized in our daily life. Normalization means that a certain tool or technology is no longer considered to be a tool, but a part of life. As Bax put it, "normalization is therefore the stage when a technology is invisible, hardly even recognized as a technology, taken for granted in everyday life" (Bax 2003). Nobody would say now that a pen and a book are technologies for language learning. Even the tape recorder is no longer considered high tech. The CD player and mp3 player now are replacing tape recorders. Computers are used more and more in all walks of life, so we can no longer imagine that foreign language education may stay away from this developmental trend.

Therefore, the question "should we use computers in language teaching?" has already become outdated. The appropriate question we may ask now is: "What technology is available and how do we use it effectively for teaching?" In what follows, we will try to provide some information and recommend some programs and web sites that we have found convenient to use, and productive for teaching Chinese. They may help teachers and students to meet the challenge of globalization and to better understand the use of computers.

1. Suggested Programs and Web Sites for Preparing Teaching Materials

Teachers nowadays are using computers on a daily basis to prepare materials related to teaching, such as syllabi, quizzes, and supplementary materials. Many of the materials require the teacher to type in Chinese. Teachers often need some tools to help them prepare teaching materials, with the most common being tools for converting between simplified and traditional characters, converting characters to pinyin, and typing pinyin with tone marks. Below are some useful tools for teachers to consider.

1A. TYPING CHINESE AND CONVERTING BETWEEN SIMPLIFIED AND TRADITIONAL CHARACTERS

Typing Chinese has become quite easy on newer computer models. For example, Windows XP or higher versions allow you to type Chinese in Unicode[4] with pinyin input and output in either traditional or simplified characters. Converting between simplified and traditional characters is also quite easy if you are using Microsoft Word (2000 or higher versions). The "Language Translation" function in the "Tools" menu will convert traditional characters to simplified characters or vice versa. At the same time, it translates some phrases used in Taiwan into phrases used on mainland China. For example, this program will "translate" 電腦 into 计算机. However, one can deactivate this function and leave 電腦 as 电脑. This function must be installed by purchasing Microsoft's additional "Proofing Tools" package. In addition to this type of conversion mechanism within Microsoft Word, there are several web sites that provide conversion services for free. Below are three examples.

1a1. Chinese-tools

(http://www.chinese-tools.com/tools/converter-tradsimp.html)

This is a website that allows users to type or paste a text in its text box. Click the button and the text will be converted and appear in a new window. It is simple and straightforward. This program is useful for converting small amounts of text.

1a2. Mandarintools

(http://www.mandarintools.com/zhcode.html)

The program does not convert the text online, but converts text files (.txt files only). Users need to prepare a text file, select the encoding of the source text file, then select the name of the source text file. Finally, users select the encoding to convert to and use the "Choose File" button on the bottom to select the name of the target file. This program is useful for batch conversion.

1a3. Adsotrans

(http://www.adsotrans.com)

This program offers several functions. It allows users to convert traditional characters to simplified, or vice versa. First you copy the text into the window, then select "Echo Chinese" under "Style." You also need to specify the encoding (both in and out). This program also allows you to convert a Chinese text to Pinyin or make a vocabulary list. (See more on Adsotrans under 1d2 below.)

Some commercial software producers have put all these functions in one product so users can easily do various types of conversion. KEY software is one of

---

[4]"Unicode" is a standard code for computer use to 'code' the writing systems of world languages.

these products. For further information, visit: http://www.cjkware.com/products. htm.

ChineseTA is another program that is designed to help teachers compile teaching materials. In addition to the above mentioned functions, ChineseTA can identify new words and characters, and calculate frequency of word and character usage. For more information, visit: http://www.svlanguage.com/

1B. TYPING AND CONVERTING TONE MARKS

When Unicode is used, typing Pinyin with tone marks becomes possible. However, most applications do not have an easy and direct input method for pinyin with tone marks. The most primitive way of inputting tone marks is to use the "Insert Symbol" function in Word, which is inconvenient and cumbersome. Some scholars have created easier ways of inputting pinyin with tone marks to look like this: Xiànzài kěyǐ hěn fāngbiàn de shūrù Pīnyīn. (现在可以很方便地输入拼音). There are three ways of doing it: Using an online input method, using a macro in Word, and using a Pinyin IME[5].

1b1. *Online input method*

An online input method is a program on the Internet which allows users to type pinyin followed by a number indicating the tone, e.g., zhong1guo2. The online program will automatically convert the number to an appropriate tone mark and place it over the correct vowel. Then one can copy and paste the pinyin string to other applications. There are several online programs of this type; we list a few here:

> http://www.chinese-tools.com/tools/pinyin-editor.html
> http://www.geocities.com/shixilun/pinyintextfield.html
> http://www.foolsworkshop.com/ptou/ (this program allows one to type pinyin with numbers first and then convert it to tone marks.)

1b2. *Using a macro[6] in Word*

Creating and using a macro file in Word is another way of inputting pinyin with tone marks. In Word, one can type pinyin followed by a number, e.g., pin1yin1 shu1ru4 fang1fa3, then run a macro program to convert the string to: pīnyīn shūrù fāngfǎ. The user must know how to create a macro file in Word. Instructions for creating a macro file are available at http://www.csulb.edu/~txie/PINYIN/pinyin. htm. Prof. Zhang Zhengsheng (San Diego State University) has created his own macro program. He uses the symbols -, /,\ and _ to represent the four tones. For

---

[5]IME means "input method editor." See below for explanation.
[6]A "macro" is a symbol, name, or key that represents a list of commands, actions, or keystrokes in computer applications. Once a macro is executed, a whole series of actions can be performed.

example, his macro program can convert pin-yin- shu-ru\ fang-fa_ to pīnyīn shūrù fāngfǎ. The source code for the macro program is available at:

http://www-rohan.sdsu.edu/dept/chinese/newtonemarkconversion.txt

1b3. Using a pinyin IME

Installing a pinyin IME is a recent and uncomplicated solution for typing pinyin with tones and can be accomplished through the use of a small program like Micro-soft's Chinese IME called Pinyinput. This program can be downloaded from http://www.chinese-forums.com/pinyinput-install.zip or http://www.mandarintools.com/download/pinyinput-install.zip

After the program is installed, the pinyin input bar will be listed as a Chinese input method. Selecting Pinyinput will activate it and a small icon [Pinyinput] will appear. One can just type pinyin with numbers, e.g. Pin1yin1 shu1ru4 fang1fa3 and the program will immediately convert the string to tone markers. For more information, see http://www.chinese-forums.com/showthread.php?t=13005.

1b4. Using Microsoft Word Asian Layout or Chinese fonts with Pinyin

Teachers sometimes need to use Pinyin to represent the pronunciation (above or below Chinese characters). There are two ways to do it.

(a)   *Using Microsoft Word Asian Layout function or Chinese Plus[7]*

Microsoft Word has a function to place Pinyin over the characters so that beginning students can better learn sound-symbol correspondence when they are learning Chinese characters. Choosing Format, Asian Layout, Phonetic Guide will convert characters and place Pinyin over these characters. Chinese Plus has a simi-lar function to convert characters to HanYuPinYin. The Pinyin with tones will be placed either over or below the characters. The size and position of Pinyin can be adjusted.

zěn yàng gěi hàn zì zhù yīn
怎 樣 給 漢 字 注 音

(b)   *Using special character-Pinyin fonts (e.g., Fangzheng Pinyin Ziku* 方正拼音字庫)

Some companies sell Chinese fonts with Pinyin. These fonts are combinations of characters and the corresponding Pinyin. Users don't have to type Pinyin — they just need to type characters and choose the special font for the characters. For example, the characters 怎样给汉字注音 will be displayed as:

---

[7]Chinese Plus is a product of Bider Technology of Singapore. Visit http:// http://www.biderworld.com.

zěn yàng gěi hàn zi zhù yīn
怎样给汉字注音

Both simplified and traditional character fonts are available. However, the size of Pinyin may not be changed because it is part of the graph and cannot be separated[8].

1C. FINDING CHINESE TEXTS AND OTHER TEACHING MATERIALS ON THE INTERNET

Language teachers often use examples to illustrate word usage. We can write examples, or we can find examples on the Internet using programs such as the concordancer developed by the Department of Linguistics and Modern English Language (LAMEL) at Lancaster University.

1c1. Concordancer

(http://bowland-files.lancs.ac.uk/corplang/cgi-bin/conc.pl) A concordancer is a computer program that retrieves a particular word or phrase in its immediate contexts. Using a concordancer allows teachers to find examples of word usage easily. For example, when an instructor needs some examples of using "讲究" when she is giving students examples of how this term can be used in different ways in different contexts, he/she can use the concordancer and find sentences like the ones below containing the word "讲究":

人们 越来越 讲究 v 生活 质量。
弟弟 妹妹 都 到 了 爱 漂亮 的 年纪，对 身上 的 衣着 很 讲究 v。
以前 人们 对 食物 营养 方法 不 讲究 v。

The concordancer will also indicate that the expression "讲究" is used as a verb in those sentences. The concordancer allows the user to search for sentences in 18 text categories, including news editorials, popular lore, science fiction, essays, and biographies.

1D. OTHER ONLINE TOOLS

There are some online programs that are very useful for teaching and learning Chinese. Some programs were developed by software companies and some were developed by Chinese learners. The learners clearly know what they need, so their programs are very pragmatic. However, due to limited funding resources, these programs are sometimes incomplete or not modified for further improvement.

---

[8]For more details, users can visit http://www.pinyinok.com/hanziku.htm.

One such an example is DimSum, a Chinese learning tool developed by Eric Peterson. DimSum is freeware which can be downloaded from http://www.mandarintools.com/dimsum.html. Once the program is installed, users can either type in a Chinese text or retrieve a text from web sites. There are many functions in DimSum, such as typing pinyin with tones, converting Chinese characters to pinyin, adding pinyin next to words, converting between traditional and simplified characters, etc. It also has a dictionary and flashcard-making function, with some characters being animated. Users can therefore see a stroke-by-stroke animation of characters being written. This is indeed a good learning tool for learners, but some functions are not fully implemented.

1d1. Online dictionaries

There are also electronic dictionaries available online. NJSTAR (njstar.com), Wenlin (wenlin.com) and Clavis Sinica (www.clavisinica.com) are three programs already familiar to many people. NJSTAR is basically a Chinese word processor with an e-dictionary, while the other two are basically e-dictionaries with limited word processing capabilities. These programs are very useful for students. The e-dictionaries that we would like to introduce in more detail are online dictionaries which are available over the Internet for free and which can be accessed through online searches. One of the dictionaries that we recommend is Dict.CN在线辞典 (http://dict.cn). This is an online dictionary that provides pronunciation, meaning, and sample sentences for words you look up. This feature is unique among online dictionaries. Users can save the words they have checked for future study, and online Chinese input and automatic translation are available. Traditional and simplified character versions are available.

1d2. Glossing engines

Glossing engines can "segment" and "annotate" Chinese texts and provide pop-up windows with the pronunciation and meaning of the words, which is useful for students doing online reading. There are several online glossing engines:

(a) *Adsotrans (http://www.adsotrans.com)*
This glossing engine not only annotates and glosses the text, but also provides more functions such as converting character text to pinyin text. (See 1a3 above)

(b) *Popjisyo (http://www.popjisyo.com/WebHint/Portal_e.aspx)*
Its pop-up window provides pronunciations in Mandarin, Cantonese, and Japanese.

(c) *Rikai (http://www.rikai.com/perl/HomePage.pl?Language=Zh)*
You put the text that you want to read in the window and press "Go." Then you just move the mouse over any Chinese word to see the pronunciation and definition.

(d)   *Chinese text annotator (http://online.eon.com.hk/annotate.html)*
This works in a similar manner to Rikai. You put the text into the box, then click the "Annotate" button. Then you just move the mouse over any Chinese word to see the pronunciation and definition.

The quality (accuracy) of segmentation and interpretation depends on the database the glossing engine uses, and there is no way for users to change anything in the dictionary. Some words may not be properly segmented and interpreted, and some words simply cannot be annotated because there is no such entry in the online dictionary. However, we have recently seen an online program that allows users to edit the word interpretations. The program requires registration and it can be accessed at http://www.wordchamp.com/lingua2/Home.do.

Although the above information is geared primarily to help Chinese language teachers, students might also find these websites useful. Teachers might want to introduce one or two of the sites listed above to their students.

2. Suggested Resources Available on the Internet

There are hundreds, if not thousands, of websites designed to help students learn Chinese. How to pick out the most useful websites is a real challenge. In the following pages, therefore, we will introduce some websites that Chinese language teachers might find useful.

One of the most popular sites where Chinese teachers can seek online resources is Tianwei Xie's "Learning Chinese Online" (http://www.csulb.edu/~txie/online. htm or http://learningchineseonline.net). This site is the most complete and the most frequently updated website for guiding people to useful websites for learning Chinese. The menu covers just about everything that a Chinese language student and teacher need to know, including grammar, characters, dictionaries, online schools, etc. We strongly encourage the reader to visit this website regularly for newly added entries.

2A. LISTENING

The listening materials available online cover different levels, serving beginners as well as advanced learners. Most of them are stand-alone lessons. But there are also some sound files that go with certain Chinese language textbooks. For example, sound files are available from the University of British Columbia in both WMA and MP3 formats for *A Primer for Advanced Beginners of Chinese* by Duanduan Li et. al. (2003) New York: Columbia University Press. (http://www2.asia.ubc.ca/faculty/li/audio/daxueyuwen.htm)

In the following section, we have selected a few sites to allow the readers to sample what is available online. Teachers may want to use some of the materials listed below as supplementary materials. The most effective way to use them is for the teacher to go over the materials first and select the ones corresponding to the topics and objectives covered by the course that the instructor is currently teaching. The teacher can prepare a chart listing which video segment corresponds to which lesson, so the student can listen to the video on a certain topic when the topic is taught in class.

2a1. Chinese Recordings (unspecified author)

(http://www.obegong.com/class1.php?lang=en)

This site has lessons for students to listen to, with topics including home, travel, law, etc. It also allows you to record and play back your speech if you have RPAppletmp3.jar on your computer. Sound files only, no video. The materials presented on this site are most suitable for beginning and intermediate level students.

2a2. Chinese Video Exercises (by Mingliang Hu)

(http://camel2.conncoll.edu/academics/departments/chinese/mhu/videos2/index/index.html)

This site provides video segments of short conversations covering topics related to daily life. It also has online exercises that give instant feedback. The materials presented on this site are most suitable for beginning and intermediate level students.

2a3. Cultural Interviews with Chinese-Speaking Professionals (by Orlando R. Kelm, Haidan Wang and Jeanette Chen)

(http://www.laits.utexas.edu/orkelm/chinese/index.html)

This is a collection of video clips of interviews with professionals on various topics, including "ability vs. connections", "Hierarchy and Social Status" and "talking business vs. socializing." The materials are suitable for advanced learners. Chinese language classes can use this site to prepare students to engage in classroom conversations or debates. No online exercises.

2a4. My Chinese Lessons (unspecified author)

(http://www.mychineseclass.com/)

This site offers free listening exercises and video clips online. The screen displays colorful drawings with animation when the sentences are read. You may obtain free membership and listen to the lessons online. However, if you want to download the transcripts and the vocabulary list, you have to pay a fee. This site offers a wide range of materials, from beginning to advanced levels.

2a5. Podcasting or webcasting

Podcasting was first introduced several years ago and started to take off as a learning tool shortly thereafter. By the time teachers read this article podcasting may not be so new anymore. According to Wikipedia, a podcast is a digital media file, or a series of such files, that is distributed over the Internet on portable media players and personal computers. In other words, a podcast is a collection of files (usually audio but may include video) residing at a unique web feed address. People can "subscribe" to it so when new "episodes" become available in the podcast, they will be automatically downloaded to that user's computer (http://en.wikipedia.org/wiki/Podcast).

Webcasting can be very useful for conversational classes while using podcasting as a supplementary homework assignment is also worth trying. Teachers might also ask students to listen to the dialogue, checking their comprehension, teaching new words, then discussing it in class or even writing a blog entry about it (i.e., less mechanical type exercises and more communicative ones, especially for more advanced students.)

Some popular podcasting sites:

(a)   *Chinesepod.com (by chinepod.com in Shanghai, China)*
(http://chinesepod.com)
Chinesepod.com offers listening materials for all levels ranging from "newbie" lessons to advanced ones. Listening to the basic podcasting is free but users pay fees for additional services such as obtaining transcripts of dialogues, exercises, online tutoring, etc.

(b)   *Serge Melnyk's Chinese Lessons with Serge Melnyk*
(http://www.melnyks.com/)
The site offers theme-based and progressive lessons from beginning to advanced levels. The student may take the lessons with downloaded programs on his iPod or Mp3 player and study anytime and at any place.

(c)   *iMandarinPod (by a team in Tianjin, China)*
(http://www.imandarinpod.com/hoola/)
This podcasting site offers online Chinese classes, with audio for the text displayed on the screen with the teacher explaining the text on the screen in detail. It also provides a learning guide in pdf format to help the learner understand the lesson better.

2a6. Voice Web (by Beijing Infoquick Sinovoice Speech Technology Corp)

(http://www.sinovoice.com.cn/e-voice.asp)

This website will read texts aloud in several languages, including Mandarin Chinese and English. If you want to listen to a Chinese text, you can type the Chinese text into the box, or simply cut and paste any Chinese text into the box, set the pitch and volume to your preference, then click "submit." The sound quality is pretty close to that of natural speech.

In addition to what was described above, it is worth noting that the recent development of YouTube (http://youtube.com/) will be a very useful source for language learning. Some language learners or teachers take advantage of this new streaming technology[9] and create many video clips for language learning. These video clips can be very good supplementary materials for listening.

2B. READING

There are many websites that can be used to help learners to read Chinese. They range from the most basic ones which only provide raw reading materials, such as "A Chinese Text Sampler" by David Porter (http://www-personal.umich.edu/~dporter/sampler /sampler.html), to more sophisticated ones that come with exercises and feedback. There are also sites geared to preschoolers, such as "Chinese Language for Preschoolers" (http://members.tripod.com/~StudyChinese/textbook.htm) and sites that anybody can use.

In the interest of space, we will only introduce four sites below.

2b1. *Progressive Reading (by the University of Southern California)*

(http://www.usc.edu/dept/ealc/chinese/Level/1.htm)

We selected this site because of its pedagogical value. The same reading text appears several times but at various difficulty levels. The student can therefore start from the beginning level and than gradually move up to higher levels. Each reading text comes with questions for the student to check comprehension. The teacher might want to remind the student not to look up the new words when moving to the higher level, but try to guess the meanings of those new words.

2b2. *Chinese Reading World (by Helen Shen)*

(http://www.uiowa.edu/~chnsrdng/index.html)

The reading materials are divided into three levels: beginning, intermediate and advanced. Each level has eighty reading pieces. This is an ongoing project, with readings continuously being added. Each reading piece comes with audio file and reading comprehension questions. The reading materials cover a wide range of topics, from "Self Introduction" to "Panda Story," and from "Chengdu Tea House" to "Being a Volunteer in the United States." When using this site to supplement a regular course, the teacher should identify the web lessons relevant to course materials, and ask the students to read them at the appropriate times.

2b3. *LangNet (by National Foreign Language Resource Center)*

(http://128.8.10.217/)

LangNet is a state-of-the-art online language learning system that offers free mini- language lessons to foreign language faculty, administrators, and students at U.S. institutions. Chinese is one of the thirty-plus languages being offered. Each lesson (Learning Objects) starts with an overview, followed by a series of activities.

---

[9]Streaming technology means that sound or image files such as sound, movie or video files can be played at the same time when they are downloaded. Therefore, users don't have to wait until the material is downloaded before it can be viewed or listened to.

The materials are graded according to the ACTFL Proficiency Guidelines and arranged according to five topic areas: culture/society, economics/politics, science/technology, defense/security, and ecology/geography. You need to contact the National Foreign Language Center at the University of Maryland (c/o LangNet Administrator, Patapsco Building, Suite 1110, 201 Paint Branch Parkway, College Park, MD 20740) to obtain access.

2b4. Read Chinese!

(http://www.nflc.org/)

This is a state-of-the-art website developed by the University of Maryland's National Foreign Language Center (NFLC). It offers reading lessons arranged as Learning Objects similar to the texts cited above in LangNet. Although this site is intended to help high school students to read Chinese, it is also accessible to students in lower level courses at colleges and universities and to the public at large. The instructional materials are available via the Internet without costs. CD-ROMs are available to schools that prefer an alternative to the online version. For ordering information call the main NFLC line at (301) 405–9828.

One of the challenges always faced by Chinese teachers when teaching reading is to select authentic texts that are interesting to the students, yet are level-appropriate and pedagogically designed so as not to overwhelm and frustrate the student. As an example, a teacher might want to create a lesson whereby students learn to read street signs in Chinese that convey warnings or admonishments. After an in-class lesson, each student could perform one of the exercises in Read Chinese! dealing with street signs for homework over the next few days, then report and explain to the class three new signs that they learned from these exercises

2C. SPEAKING

While it is relatively easy to find listening and reading materials online, it is very hard to find websites that can help students improve their speaking skills. This is primarily because the computer cannot easily check students' speaking performance and offer specific feedback. We will introduce a couple of sites that are designed to help the student practice speaking.

2c1. Chinese Learn Online (by chineselearnonline.com)

(http://www.chineselearnonline.com/about/)

This site offers online Chinese lessons with sound files where the student can listen to the dialogues. This website has a new feature called "Pong Audio Forum" whereby the online teacher will ask some questions and the student has an opportunity to answer the questions through online chat. The students then can compare their own answers with those given by the teacher and other students.

2c2. Learn Chinese (by Tianwei Xie)

(http://www.clearchinese.com/learn-chinese/index.htm) "Learn Chinese" is available on ClearChinese.com. It has a "Practice" section that asks the student to say something in Chinese. The student can click the "answer" button to compare his answer with that given by the teacher.

Both "Chinese Learn Online" and "Learn Chinese" ask the students to check their own speaking against the model answer. Since the computer technology is not yet sophisticated enough to check open-ended answers, this is a viable way to allow the student to practice speaking at home.

2c3. Online Speaking Homework

Instructors sometime may require students to do some voice homework. In the past, teachers would ask students to record their voice homework on cassette tapes and hand them in. Now it is possible to do voice homework over the Internet. One of the examples of using online voice technology is YackPack (http://www.yackpack.com/). Some teachers use this online voice chat room for students to post their voice homework and talk to each other (Sun 2007).

2c4. Wimba voice email (by wimba.com)

(http://www.horizonwimba.com/demos/voiceemail.php)

It is very easy for both instructors and students to use Wimba's voice email system online. Users don't have to download and install any software. They just go to the Wimba site (see URL above) and use it. It is a demo version, but it functions well. Students can record their voice and send it to their instructor's email address. When the instructors receive the voice message, they can either listen to the message or save the message for future use. There are some other voice email programs, but this one is easy to use and doesn't require any installation.

2D. WRITING

In today's world, typing Chinese on the computer is a necessary skill that everyone who writes in Chinese should possess. When we write to our Chinese friends, we type Chinese in the e-mail message. In fact, the first AP® Chinese test which took place in May 2007 was done completely on the Internet whereby the student was required to type in the answers to the writing section. In addition to teaching students how to write Chinese characters on paper, Chinese language teachers should also train their students to type Chinese on the computer.

2d1. Using blogs

It is worth noting that blogs (short for "web logs") have been recently used more and more often by language learners. Students can write anything and share their writing with their friends. To encourage students to write Chinese outside of the class, some teachers have created their own blogs. For example, Xiao Yang (University of California at Davis) created a blog called 萧老师的中文教室 (http://xiaolaoshi.livejournal.com/friends) when she was teaching at the University of Hawaii. According to Xiao, students enjoy writing on the blog, and because the blog is for the public to view, students are more careful not to make any mistakes when they write. For a list of blogs for learning Chinese, see John Pasden and John Biesnecker's website (http://www.chinabloglist.org/csl/).

It is interesting to note that most blog sites for learning Chinese were created by learners rather than teachers. Xie (2007) has listed some blog sites dealing with teaching and learning Chinese.

2d2. Using course management software

Many universities and public schools are using Blackboard or WebCT (http://www.blackboard.com and http://www.webct.com)[10]. These are two popular course management software programs which allow teachers to store and deliver course materials without too much computer knowledge. The two programs are very similar. The programs that teachers and students can use include discussion forum and chat for asynchronous and synchronous communication. These functions are good for collaborative learning. Readers can refer to Zhang and Mu (2003) and Xie (2002) for more information on these topics.

2d3. Collaborative learning tools

(http://docs.google.com)

Another way to make writing interesting is through "collaborative learning," which can take place online through Google docs (http://www.docs.google.com), a free service offered by Google. When one student starts a project of writing a dialogue or an essay, he/she may invite other students and/or instructors to be his/her collaborators who are able to view and edit the document that the first student created. They can work at different times or at the same time (real time). Each one will see that the document is being edited by other parties, and any changes or modifications are recorded as a "history" of revisions. In this way, students can write something collaboratively, while instructors may also add comments or corrections at any time. A relatively easier online program is http://writeboard.com which allows one student to start writing. Then the first student can invite other students to join, review and edit the same text. It does not require registration but it allows one to edit plain text only and does not have any formatting functions.

2E. CHINESE CHARACTERS

Learning how to write Chinese characters has been considered to be a big hurdle for many Chinese language learners. Thanks to computer technology, learning Chinese characters has become a little bit easier.

2e1. Learning characters using animated characters

One of the most difficult tasks in learning Chinese is to learn how to write characters. Characters must be written stroke by stroke according to a particular sequence.

---

[10]BlackBoad and WebCT are merged now.

The traditional way for textbook writers to present the stroke order was to make a chart by hand showing the stroke order:

Unfortunately, it was time consuming to create this type of chart for hundreds and hundreds of characters. However, technology has made it possible now to produce such a stroke sequence picture automatically (see "Making stroke order chart" below). What is more amazing is that computer software can create the animation of characters and show the process of writing a character stroke by stroke while also providing the pronunciation in Pinyin, and the meaning in English, while also showing possible words or phrases containing this character. There are two products of this type that have similar and unique functions. The first product is called eStroke and it can be downloaded at http://eon.com.hk/estroke/. The second product is Chinese Writing Master http://www.cchar.com/. Users just type in a character or drag any character from the Internet to the box, and the animation will be displayed immediately.

The software eStroke mentioned above not only shows the animation of writing characters stroke by stroke, but also saves the animation as a .gif file. Instructors may take advantage of this function to make animated characters for demonstration in the classroom or to put the animated characters in their web pages. When eStroke is activated, right click and select "Export to Animated Gif," then choose a character. When the animation is finished, the .gif file is also saved. One can include this .gif file in a web page. If users select the "Create sequence" function, the writing of the character stroke by stroke will be saved as a picture with the word's stroke order:

Exercises for learning stroke order in traditional first-year textbooks are usually found in workbooks or other exercise formats whereby students have an example character displayed to them, with each stroke numbered in the order in which the strokes should be written. Students, then, will follow the stroke order to write the character, thus ensuring that they develop "muscle memory" for writing characters accurately and with the strokes in the proper order. Teachers can use animated character writing programs as an adjunct for the learner to check his written work by drawing the character anew as the computer draws it stroke by stroke on the computer screen, thus giving the learner a more visually compelling graphic sequence, either to learn to write new characters, or to serve as a way to check whether they have mastered the writing of characters they have already learned.

2e2. Websites tailored to textbooks

Some websites that teach Chinese characters using animation are tailored to certain textbooks. For example, the users of the textbook *Integrated Chinese* can learn how to write the Chinese characters taught in this book by going to this website prepared by Audrey Li and her team at the University of Southern California (http://www.usc.edu/dept/ealc/chinese/character/). The computer will draw each character stoke by stroke for the student to view and copy. It also displays the radical of each character in pink color to let the student know what radical group this character belongs to. Also, see Character animation for *New Practical Chinese Reader* offered by YellowBridge (http://www.yellowbridge.com/general/invoke. php?http://www.hanyu.com.cn/En/htm_newlesson/cc-01.htm).

2e3. Electronic flash cards

Learning how to write Chinese characters properly is not an easy task. Memorizing the Chinese characters that one has learned is equally difficult. Before the computer era, students used flash cards to help them learn new words. Now they can use electronic flashcards. Below are two examples:

2e4. Online Chinese Flashcards (by YellowBridge)

(http://www.yellowbridge.com/language/flashcards.html)
This site offers online Chinese flashcards that go with more than ten textbooks. Flashcards are divided into many "decks" corresponding to each textbook chapter or wordlist so that they match the user's lesson plan. This site also offers flashcards for commonly used characters in Hong Kong and Taiwan, as well as HSK vocabulary items.

2e5. FlashcardsExchange (by an unknown author)

(http://www.flashcardexchange.com/)
This site is a huge flashcard library containing 11,212,344 flash cards for the world languages including Chinese. The Chinese flash cards made by teachers and students can be found at http://www.flashcardexchange.com/tag/Chinese. Teachers and students can create a free account there and develop their inventory of flash cards.

2F. PRONUNCIATION

There are many websites designed to introduce Chinese pronunciation. We will only mention two here:

Chinese Pronunciation (by New Concept Mandarin Limited, Hong Kong)
(http://www.newconceptmandarin.com/support/Intro_Pinyin.asp)

Standard Mandarin (by Joel Hansen)
(http://www.standardmandarin.com/)

2G. TEXT-TO-SPEECH SOFTWARE

Text-to-speech (TTS) programs "read" aloud any text, whether Chinese or English. The quality of earlier technology was not very good because the voice did not sound like a human voice. The recent development of text-to-speech technology is very fascinating, so now the intonation of sentences is more natural and the sound is like a human voice. What is more amazing is that the computer software can automatically "recognize" the correct pronunciation of certain Chinese characters in context such as "行"(xíng, háng) as in 行人xíngrén and 銀行 yínháng, "重" (zhòng, chóng) as in 重量 zhòngliàng 重慶 Chóngqìng.

Text-to-speech programs can be used by instructors in the classroom, so now it is even more convenient for students to listen to any text they have found without having to wait until their instructors make voice recordings for them. There are several commercial programs such as KeyTip (http://www.cjkware.com/download.html) and Speech Plus 一聲通 (http://www.biderworld.com/) and YellowBridge Talker (http://yellowbridge.com/talker/) for this purpose.

3. Computerized Testing Formats

Assessment is an integral part of a language program. Tests are used to check the student's progress and achievement. Some Chinese language tests are now available on the web. We will introduce a few of them below.

3A. COMPUTERIZED TESTS

3a1. AP® Chinese test

Many high school students take AP® courses and AP® tests before they enter college (see Chi, this volume). The first AP® Chinese exam administered in May 2007 was an iBT (Internet Based Test) which covers the four language skills of listening, reading, speaking and writing. A sample test is available online at:

> http://www.starttest2.com/5.0.0.0/starttest.aspx?cmd=demo&program=ap&type=consumer&target=order&limit=all&test=xxxx

3a2. Chinese Horizon: Placement Test (By Chinese Placement Test Online)

(http://www.chinesehorizon.com/placementTest.cfm)

This site offers a free placement test and is available to anyone. The test was designed by the company to evaluate students' proficiency and place them in an appropriate level for online learning and it is not related to other standardized test such as SAT, HSK, etc.

3B. PREPARE YOUR OWN COMPUTERIZED TESTS

Creating quizzes, tests and exams is a routine job for a language teacher. Some commercial test authoring software like Questionmark and online quiz "makers" can help teachers. One of the online test makers that many teachers have used is Quia Web at http://www.quia.com/. Instructors can easily create activities, quizzes, games, Web pages, surveys, etc. The preformatted test templates include multiple choice questions, true or false questions, short essay questions, fill in the blank exercises and other formats. Both voice and picture files can be used for questions. Voice files can be used for listening comprehension exercises and pictures can be used for any other purposes. The quiz/test can be automatically or manually graded and the results can be saved. Statistical analysis is also provided.

Concluding Remarks

We have only listed some resources for teaching and learning Chinese that we feel are helpful in conducting daily teaching activities. It is impossible and unrealistic for us to exhaust all programs and web sites. Whether these programs or resources really work for teachers depends on how they use them. It is also our belief that teachers do not have to learn and use all these programs at one time. A more realistic way is to ask the question: "What kind of technology may be available if I want to accomplish a certain task?" For example, if someone wants to take advantage of technology to teach characters, he/she can search over the Internet and see if there are any programs that will help. Consulting with experts and experienced colleagues is another effective way to locate appropriate computer resources. This will save lots of time and one doesn't have to "look for a needle in a haystack." Using technology, then, is not a fad, but should be viewed as a means to accomplish more convenient and effective teaching.

There is one more aspect of using technology that deserves our attention: the ephemeral nature of the web resources (Harter and Kim 1996). This means that online teaching and learning materials, like all other online data, change rapidly. According to research, 20–50 percent of online materials will change or disappear within two or three years. Chinese teachers must be aware of this fact and should continue to stay abreast of newly emerging technologies and resources for teaching Chinese. Therefore, this article is also "ephemeral" and its contents will be and should be updated in the near future.

References

Banados, E. 2006. A blended-learning pedagogical model for teaching and learning EFL successfully through an online interactive multimedia environment. *CALICO Journal* 23 (3): 533–550.

Bax, S. 2003. CALL — past, present and future. *System* 31: 13–28.

Bourgerie, D. S. 2003. Computer assisted language learning for Chinese: A survey and annotated bibliography. *Journal of Chinese Language Teachers Association* 38 (2): 17–47.

Chan, Marjorie K. M. 2002. Concordancers and concordances: Tools for Chinese language teaching and research. *Journal of Chinese Language Teachers Association* 37 (2): 1–58.

Chun, L. and Y. Zhao. 2006. Noticing and text-based chat. *Language Learning & Technology* 10 (3): 102–120.

Corbeil, G. 2007. Can PowerPoint Presentations effectively replace textbooks and blackboards for teaching grammar? Do students find them an effective learning tool? *CALICO Journal* 24 (3).

Dooly, Melinda. 2007. Joining forces: Promoting metalinguistic awareness through computer-supported collaborative learning. *Language Awareness* 16 (1): 57–74.

Godwin-Jones, R. 2005. Skype and podcasting: Disruptive technologies for language learning. *Language Learning & Technology* 9 (3): 9–12. Retrieved May 2007 from http://llt.msu.edu/vol9num3/emerging/default.html.

Godwin-Jones, R. 2007. Tools and trends in self-paced language instruction. *Language Learning & Technology* 11 (2): 10–17.

Harter, Stephen P., & Hak Joon Kim. (1996). Electronic journals and scholarly communication: A citation and reference study. *Information Research* 2 (1). Retrieved January 31, 2008 from: http://InformationR.net/ir/2-1/paper9a.html.

Li, Duanduan, et al. 2007. *A primer for advanced beginners of Chinese*. New York: Columbia University Press.

Russell, Thomas L. 2001. *The no significant difference phenomenon*. 5th edition. IDECC (the International Distance Education Certification Center).

Moore, M. 1973. Toward a theory of independent learning and teaching. *Journal of Higher Education* 44 (12): 661–679.

Sun, Lo. 2007. Stay connected: The use of YackPack audio forum to enhance communication and oral exchanges. ACTFL Annual Convention and World Languages Expo Presentation. Accessed February 2008 at http://www2.ups.edu/faculty/perry/yackpack.ppt

Warschauer, M., and D. Healey. 1998. Computers and language learning: An overview. *Language Teaching* 31: 57–71.

Warschauer, M., and C. Meskill. 2000. Technology and second language teaching. In *Handbook of understanding second language education*, ed. J. Rosenthal, 303–318. Mahwah, New Jersey: Lawrence Erlbaum.

Xie, T. 2001. e-Generation's Chinese language teachers: Meet the new challenges. *Journal of Chinese Language Teachers Association* 36 (3), 2001.

Xie, T. 2002. Using Internet relay chat in teaching Chinese. *CALICO Journal* 19 (3), 513–524.

Xie, T. 2007. Blog, wiki, podcasting and learning Chinese language. *Journal of Chinese Language Teachers Association* 42 (1).

Yao, T. 1996. A review of some current computer-assisted language learning (CALL) for Chinese. In *Chinese language pedagogy: Current perspectives of the emerging field*, ed. Scott McGinnis, 255–284. Columbus, Ohio: Foreign Language Publications.

Zhang, D., and A. Mu. 2003. Use of online chat in a WebCT-enhanced elementary Chinese language class. In *Proceedings of world conference on e-learning in corporate, government, healthcare, and higher education 2003*, ed. G. Richards, 1265–1271. Chesapeake, VA: AACE.

Zhang, Z. 1998. CALL for Chinese: Issues and practice. *Journal of Chinese Language Teachers Association* (33)1: 51–82.

Challenges and Strategies for the American Classroom

Chapter 9

Teaching Chinese as a Heritage Language

Keys to Success

Yun Xiao

Bryant University

As Americans are becoming increasingly concerned with national security and economic competition in a global society, a series of changes has taken place in the United States. One of these changes is the recognition of heritage languages (HL) as a national resource, among which Chinese, hitherto a less commonly-taught language, has been designated as a critical language by the U.S. government and is getting unprecedented attention from the media as a rising language. To our Chinese teaching community, this new recognition has brought abundant opportunities and challenges. On the one hand, more and more students come to the language classroom to learn Chinese, half of whom are estimated to have a family background in Chinese language and culture and are hence referred to as Chinese heritage language (CHL) learners. On the other hand, the rapid influx of CHL learners has challenged Chinese language classrooms, which have been traditionally geared to "foreign" language learners, i.e., English speakers with no previous knowledge of the language. As noted by Brecht and Ingold (1998), the United States has traditionally placed little value on language skills other than English, and the formal education system is not designed to help students develop foreign language skills for professional purposes. Consequently, language teachers are often frustrated that they know little about HL students and that the curriculum, pedagogical approaches, and teaching materials available to them do not quite fit this group. To succeed as a teacher of Chinese in a foreign/immigrant language setting, we need to understand the social context of Chinese HL education, the unique characteristics of HL learning, and the challenges and promises HL learners bring to the language classroom. For this purpose, this chapter will start with a brief review of CHL education in the United States, discuss the various aspects of CHL learning and its associated contextual factors, and explore the keys to success in our CHL classrooms.

CHL Education in the United States

Enrollment figures in 2005 revealed that there were, nationwide, around 24,000 students of Chinese in secondary schools and 160,000 in Chinese community HL schools (McGinnis 2005). This indicates that Chinese language teaching has been operating in both mainstream and community HL schools and that there are six times more students in the latter than in the former. Apparently, Chinese community HL schools have played a much more important role than the mainstream schools in CHL maintenance and development.

With a history of more than one century in this country, Chinese community HL schools started in the 1840s when the first wave of immigration of Chinese laborers reached the West Coast and were, unfortunately, situated in a prevailing racially discriminatory environment. There were very few employment opportunities for the frontier Chinese immigrants, and the only hope for them was to build some fortune in America and then return to China. To prepare for their children's adult lives back in China, parents started HL schools in Chinatowns and made Chinese language and cultural training a must for second-generation Chinese, who as children attended a few more hours of class on Chinese culture following the end of their public-school day (Liu 2002). Largely a grassroots community effort, these schools did not have a shared history with the mainstream education system, nor any form of interaction with or substantial support from the government. Although the recent Chinese immigrant environment, in response to improvements in U.S.-China relations, has undergone positive changes since then, the CHL school system remains basically the same.

As grassroots ventures, the Chinese community HL schools have operated in makeshift classrooms and survived on meager donations and/or tuition. Dedicated toward the goal of maintaining their heritage language and culture and building an ethnic network, enthusiastic parents and volunteers formed the administrative body and made decisions about curriculum design, student placement, teaching materials, orthographic form, and which "Chinese" to teach: Mandarin, Cantonese, or other Chinese dialects. Studies show that the majority of the American-born Chinese children and young arrivals attend these schools starting at age three but typically drop out once they enter grade school (Xiao 2008b). It is here that their Chinese studies involuntarily come to a halt because most of the K–12 schools in this country do not have Chinese programs. A survey by the College Board in 2004 showed that there were 2,400 secondary schools in the United States which intended to offer Chinese programs but could not, due to a lack of certified Chinese teachers (Asia Society Report, Stewart and Wang 2005). The results were confirmed by a follow-up College Board survey in 2005, which showed that out of the 50 U.S. states only 33 states had established Chinese programs in elementary and secondary schools, with a total of 313 in the entire nation, ranging from 56 (Massachusetts) to 1 (Utah). Compared with the major foreign languages such as Spanish and French, Chinese enrollment was trivial. The 2000 U.S. Census showed that K–12 Chinese accounted for less than 1.3 percent of the total foreign language enrollment in the United States, while Spanish alone accounted for 68.7 percent of the total (Wiley 2005, 599), in spite of the fact that Chinese has grown to be the third most frequently spoken language in the United States, after only English and Spanish.

However, with the rise of China as a major force in the global economy, an awareness of the need for professionals with advanced Chinese language proficiency is rapidly increasing, and so is the effort to develop CHL programs. This effort is becoming more coherent and interactive as the Chinese community schools become united and government initiatives abound. For the first time since the establishment of the pioneer Chinese community schools in the mid-nineteenth century, two organizations were formed to lead and unify the approximately 600 Chinese community HL schools across the country. They are NCACLS (the National Council of Associations of Chinese Language Schools) organized by Taiwan and Hong Kong communities, and CSAUS (the Chinese School Association in the United States) organized by the People's Republic of China (PRC) communities. Although these organizations are not government-funded, they serve as advocacy agencies and are intent on increasing public awareness of CHL issues. The leaders of these organizations are reaching out to the Chinese community, mainstream schools, and government organizations, while also making their voices heard at conference meetings largely dominated in the past decades by professors and researchers.

With this concerted effort at various levels, the federal government has introduced a number of top-down initiatives in recent years. For instance, the Foreign Language Assistance Program, which provides grants to establish, improve, or expand innovative foreign language programs for elementary and secondary school students, has declared Chinese as a critical language entitled to funding priority (http://www.ed.gov/news/pressreleases/2007/06/06152007.html). And the National Security Education Program has established a number of Chinese Flagship Programs such as those at Brigham Young University, Ohio State University, and the K–16 Chinese Pipeline Flagship Program at the University of Oregon in partnership with the Portland Public Schools (http://casls.uoregon.edu/flagship) (see Spring, this volume). These flagship programs provide a model for articulation and immersion/content-based pedagogy to advance students' Chinese proficiency. Encouraged by the Chinese Flagship Programs, more and more schools are experimenting with Chinese immersion programs. One example is the Pioneer

Valley Chinese Immersion Charter School established in 2007 in Hadley/Amherst, Massachusetts, a gigantic step in a state where bilingual education was officially eliminated through general voting in 2002. In all of these new programs, CHL learners constitute a significant portion of the student population.

On the research front, CHL learning and teaching have become a new field of inquiry. Besides a large number of studies reported in various journals and books, several prominent journals have dedicated special issues to CHL inquiry, such as *Heritage Language Journal* (Volume 4, 2006 http://www.heritagelanguages.org) and *Language Policy* (Volume 6, 2007 http://www.ingentaconnect.com/content/klu/lpol). And *The Journal of Chinese Applied Linguistics*, a brand-new journal sponsored by the Confucius Institute at the University of Iowa and focused on CHL teaching and learning as one of its essential components, is forthcoming. In addition, a number of research monographs with a focus on CHL issues have emerged, such as *Culturally Contested Pedagogy: Battles of Literacy and Schooling Between Mainstream Teachers and Asian Immigrant Parents* (Li 2006); *Heritage Development: Focus on East Asian Immigrants* (Kondo-Brown 2006); and *Chinese as a Heritage Language: Fostering Rooted World Citizenry* (He and Xiao, 2008).

CHL Learning

Although Chinese as a heritage language has only recently been included in the academic research agenda, CHL researchers have already spearheaded and revealed interesting findings on how CHL can be acquired, maintained, and developed through the experience of assimilation and acculturation in an English-speaking country. Drawing on such findings, this section will discuss the major characteristics of the CHL learner and learner language, as well as the various contextual factors associated with them.

THE CHL LEARNER

Following Valdés (2001, 38), a heritage language learner is defined broadly as a language student who is raised in a home where a non-English language is spoken. Heritage language learners speak and hear the HL spoken at home and in their immediate communities, but do not receive formal instruction in their HL in the mainstream schools. Instead, their literacy is built on English as a second language, and they are, like anyone with an immigrant background, subject to social and psychological assimilation and acculturation forces. Researchers report that in a dominant English-speaking culture, the immigrant HL typically deteriorates, erodes, or is lost (Wong Fillmore 1991; Li 2003), because when HL learners enter mainstream schools, there is "an abrupt shift" from the HL to the dominant language (Bougie, et al. 2003, 349) accompanied by an intense disconnection between home and school literacy practices (McCarthey 1997). To gain acceptance,

HL learners typically drop their home language and make English their primary language (Pease-Alvarez et. al. 1991; Li 2003, 2006). As a result, they arrive at the foreign language classroom not entirely as first-language speakers or second-langauge speakers of their heritage language (Lynch 2003) and bring with them a set of linguistic ambiguities and skewed language skills which are typically absent in the genuine foreign language learner.

CHL LEARNER LANGUAGE

Recent data derived from varied research studies show that the HL learner has a head start in the learner's home language but develops along a path different from L1A learners (i.e., children acquiring a first language in their home country) and L2A learners (i.e., children or adults acquiring a second language in a host country) after going through an English-only mainstreaming process (Shin 2006), as illustrated below:

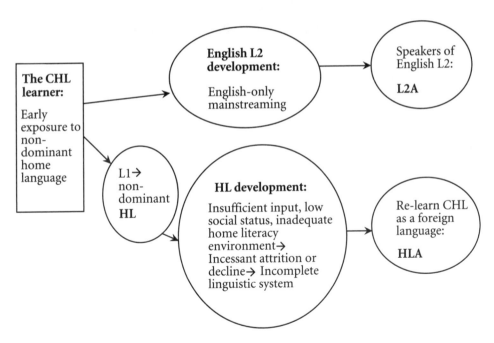

Figure: CHL developmental path (modified from Xiao, 2008a)

This figure provides a road map for the development of CHL learner language. As shown in the figure, CHL learners, like L1 children, have childhood exposure to their home language, but they involuntarily switch to the dominant language and go through an English-only mainstreaming process at a young age. Consequently, their HL learning evolves along a path different from children who acquire Chinese as a L1 in China or Taiwan, or learners who acquire Chinese as a L2 in China or Taiwan.

WHAT DOES THIS MEAN FOR CHL TEACHERS?

To CHL teachers, this means that the CHL curriculum, teaching materials, and pedagogy approaches should be different from those used for Chinese as a L1 or Chinese as a L2 learners. Given the fact that CHL is a new territory and there is not much to "hang on," we need to explore the essentials or "keys" to success. First, we need to understand, theoretically and pedagogically, the various factors associated with the CHL learning and literacy development upon an already existing HL spoken language base. Secondly, we need to know our students well — their home background, their prior Chinese proficiency, their motivations and challenges. Finally, we need to set up the HL program, place students in appropriate levels, and develop level- and culturally-suitable instructional materials. In the following sections, I will discuss these essentials or "keys" with more details and make some concrete suggestions.

Keys to Success in Teaching Heritage Learners

UNDERSTANDING FACTORS ASSOCIATED WITH CHL LEARNING AND LITERACY DEVELOPMENT

CHL language development has been found to be associated with various factors, such as insufficient HL input, multilevel social contacts, and immigrant home environments.

First, as shown in the figure above, the CHL learners' L1 input beyond their childhood exposure is typically insufficient, especially after they start grade school. Its development solely depends on the availability of informal learning, such as studies in weekend community Chinese language schools or literacy activities at home, which are usually neither adequate nor fruitful. Through a survey that involved 127 Chinese heritage language learners in three American universities, Xiao (2008b) found that, compared with speakers of the mainstream dominant language, the CHL learners' home literacy environment most often did not provide HL reading materials or literacy activities that fostered sustained growth in Chinese literacy. Likewise, Chinese community schools did not possess substantial resources to improve learners' HL literacy. By examining CHL literacy development among school-age students, Koda et. al. (2008) found that, in weekend Chinese schools, the quantity of the input available to children was heavily restricted. In her four-year extensive study of Chinese HL schools, Wang reported that "there was no sense of progress or achievement. Students basically stay at the same level, unable to move forward in their HL proficiency or literacy" (2004, 368).

Another factor is that CHL learners experience multi-level social contacts, which result in enormous linguistic disparity and dialectal diversity (Hendryx, 2008). Chances are that CHL learners do not understand each other or their Mandarin-speaking instructor, or a fluent Cantonese-speaking learner has to start from the novice level because he cannot pronounce Mandarin sounds and tones, although he may be fairly advanced in reading or writing. Furthermore, while some HL learners may spend more time in their native country, others leave their native country at a young age. Some may return regularly to a region where Chinese is spoken on a regular basis, and others may not. And some may spend considerable time in community Chinese language schools, while others do not.

Finally, situated in an immigrant context, the CHL learner language is influenced by a number of variables, such as the learner's birthplace, age of arrival, length of English immersion, family socio-economic status, and parents' view of HL role in their children's adult life. It has been found that China-born children typically outperform their U.S.-born counterparts of the same age group in Chinese learning tasks (Jia and Bayley 2008). The likely reason is that the China-born children have prior exposure to input in larger quantity and better quality in their native country. In addition, for first-generation immigrants, age of arrival in the United States and length of exposure to English are also significant factors for CHL development (Jia, 2008). Specifically, those who were exposed to English at a younger age and immersed in it for a longer time had a lower level of CHL proficiency, while those arriving in the United States at an older age had a higher level of CHL proficiency. Moreover, those who had a richer family literacy environment tended more often to retain their Chinese studies at college than those who did not (Xiao 2008b). Furthermore, contrary to the popular expectation that children from families of higher socio-economic status do better in school, it is the children from lower income families that demonstrate higher CHL proficiency in the Chinese immigrant context (Jia, 2008). The likely reason is, as suggested by Jia, that lower family income is more associated with lower educational levels and poorer English ability on the part of the parents and grandparents; thus, the use of HL is vital and indispensable in those families.

The parents' view of the role of HL in their children's life also exerts a significant impact on CHL maintenance and development. Unlike the frontier Chinese immigrants who did not see future success for their children in the United States but hoped to return to China, contemporary Chinese immigrant parents envision abundant opportunities for their children in their host country and assume the responsibility of preparing their children for success in American mainstream society. Thus, their children's English proficiency and school work become their highest priority, since these parents view fluency in English and success at school as the keys to securing a college degree and obtaining a decent job. Consequently, their home HL literacy environment is inadequate, and their children's studies in Chinese HL schools typically stop when the children enter kindergarten or grade school.

UNDERSTANDING LEARNERS AND VALUING THEIR EXISTING HL KNOWLEDGE

As discussed above, with an immigrant family background, CHL learners are typically marked with varied ethnic identities and skewed linguistic skills. Recent

CHL data show that in their growth CHL learners experience a unique process of forming and transforming their HL identity and re-creating their own identity (He, 2008). They perceive their own cultural identities differently and show a high degree of variability in this regard. While some identify themselves with Chinese culture, others identify with both Chinese and American cultures, with only American culture, or, worse, with neither culture. Moreover, some of them often feel marginalized: "Those in America see me as Chinese, while those in China see me as an American" (Dai and Zhang 2008).

The strength of an individual's ethnic identity has been found to go hand in hand with his or her motivation for HL learning. Jia (2008) found that CHL learners who experience ethnic ambivalence tend to have a negative attitude towards their HL maintenance and that those who feel a stronger sense of Chinese cultural identity show a positive attitude toward their HL learning. It is not uncommon for learners to drop their Chinese studies at a young age but pick them up again later in life when they realize the need to connect with their ethnic community or to regain their cultural pride. An illuminating example is Mr. Yang, a CHL learner who discontinued his Chinese studies shortly after arriving in the United States as a kindergartener, but resumed them as a young adult and eventually gained advanced Chinese proficiency. He realized that as a Chinese man, knowing Chinese was about reconnecting with his Chinese identity, which he had neglected for a long time (Santos 2007).

Linguistically, CHL learners are marked with skewed linguistic abilities. They typically have better listening and speaking abilities than their non-HL counterparts but do not likewise have better literacy skills, due to the fact that their primary literacy is, like their non-HL counterparts, built on L2 English in the United States. Moreover, their pronunciation and vocabulary may reflect non-Mandarin dialects. Or they may be highly proficient in expressing everyday topics but lack the vocabulary or usages used in formal social situations. However, with their rudimentary prior knowledge, when they come to the formal Chinese classrooms, HL learners typically start with unrealistically high expectations and end up frustrated and disappointed. In her eight years of teaching at the college level, the writer had the privilege of working with both HL and non-HL students. She observed that a number of CHL students started with the plan of earning an easy A and ended up working hard for a B or C. One of her students who had studied in Chinese HL schools on the East Coast for nine years signed up for an advanced class in Spring 2007. At the beginning of the semester, he confidently bragged about his nine years of studying Chinese in the community CHL schools, where his mother was the principal and monitored the school curriculum closely. However, as the class moved on, he found it extremely difficult, especially in reading and writing, and finally lost all interest in learning Chinese. If he had been placed in a class appropriate to his level and experience, he might have been able to stay in the course and succeed.

This said, ample evidence from CHL classroom research has shown that CHL learners arrive in the Chinese classroom with significant prior listening/speaking abilities and grammar knowledge (Xiao 2004). Studies on children learning Chinese in the United States also found that CHL children outperformed their non-heritage counterparts in various aspects of the language, such as better use of the particle 了 and faster learning of Chinese characters (Jia and Bayley 2008; Koda et. al. 2008). Previous studies from both language acquisition and neurolinguistic perspectives also showed that early exposure to a language has positive effects on subsequent learning (Au and Romo 1997; Stowe and Sabourin 2005). Given the fact that Chinese is one of the most difficult foreign languages for English speakers, i.e., it takes as much as three times the instructional hours for an English speaker to develop the same level of proficiency in Chinese as in Spanish and French, the CHL learners' prior Chinese abilities are a godsend and should by all means be cherished and cultivated.

SETTING UP THE HL PROGRAM

Wherever the enrollments warrant it, a separate CHL program alongside a CFL program is recommended (and should be fought for). The successful setup of such a programs depends on appropriate placement, which should be 有的放矢, that is, built on reliable assessment. Although there are many different ways to do so, a pre-program survey and a well-designed proficiency test will be helpful in this process.

PRE-PROGRAM SURVEY

A pre-program survey is an important part of the assessment process that aims to find out the students' home backgrounds, Chinese experience, and learning motivations. Questions can be asked such as what language/dialect (i.e., Mandarin, Cantonese, Hakkah, Xiang, Min, etc.) is spoken at home, who speak(s) it, where the learner was born, how old the learner was when arriving in the United States, whether the learner went to Chinese community school, if yes how long did he/she study there, where else did the learner study Chinese, what motivated him/her to learn Chinese, etc. (See Appendix 1 for a sample.)

PROFICIENCY/PLACEMENT TESTING

Once the initial information about the learners' background is obtained, we can further assess the learner's oral and written Chinese proficiency, the results of which can determine the areas that need the most work, knowledge that can be built upon and, more generally, help us understand the characteristics and possible ranges of each heritage student's proficiency (http://www.international.ucla. edu/article.asp?parentid=24734#intro). Oral proficiency can be assessed by an oral interview or recording of a speech sample combined with a test for listening, or by a certified tester as advocated by ACTFL (American Council on the Teaching of Foreign Languages, http://www.actfl.org/i4a/pages/index.cfm?pageid=3348). Written proficiency can be assessed by a written test of both reading and writing for students who are literate. So far, there have been a number of Chinese oral and written proficiency tests developed in recent years, which have been widely field-tested and adopted. I am recommending a few below:

1. Student Achievement Test (SAT®) in Chinese by ETS (Educational Testing Services). http://www.collegeboard.com/student/testing/sat/lc_two/chinese/chinese.html?chinese

2. Hanyu Shuiping Kaoshi (HSK) by the People's Republic of China Ministry of Education, in conjunction with Beijing Language and Culture University. http://www.hsk.org.cn/english/Default.aspx

3. Oral Proficiency Interview (OPI) in Chinese by ACTFL. http://www.languagetesting.com/corp_opi.htm

4. Standards-Based Measurement of Proficiency (STAMP) by Language Learning Solutions (LLS). http://www.stamptest.net/stamp0708/stamptest

5. Chinese Computerized Adaptive Listening Comprehensive Test by Chuanren Ke and Zizi Zhang; OSU Chinese Flagship Program. http://chineseflagship.osu.edu/current_students/assessment.html

6. Online Chinese Computerized Adaptive Reading Comprehensive Test; OSU Chinese Flagship Program. http://chineseflagship.osu.edu/current_students/assessment.html

7. Online Computer Aided Vocabulary Assessment; OSU Chinese Flagship Program. http://chineseflagship.osu.edu/current_students/assessment.html

PLACEMENT

With the results of the pre-program survey and the proficiency tests, we are ready to place the learners. Depending on the available enrollments, students can be placed in dual tracks (HL vs. non-HL) or 3-fold tracks (HL I vs. HL II vs. non-HL) or classes that must combine all different learners due to limitations in scheduling and/or resources. Dual tracking means that the students are divided into two groups — HL vs. non-HL; 3-fold tracking means that students are first divided into HL and non-HL groups, with the HL group further divided by their home dialects. For instance, the University of California at Davis has run a very successful Chinese program which places Mandarin speakers, Cantonese speakers, and true beginners (non-HL) into three separate tracks due to the fact that there are an equally large number of Mandarin and Cantonese speakers in their Chinese language program.

The benefit of dual- or 3-fold-track placement is that students' needs are more converged and the curriculum can be more focused. And the tension typical of the mixed classes, such as non-HL students being intimidated while HL students feel bored, can be largely avoided. Such advantages become even more acute if the HL group can be further separated on the basis of their home language background. However, the downside of such separate tracking is that students miss the benefits of the otherwise multilingual and multicultural classroom environment, a characteristic of the mixed classroom. In a mixed class, students bring in multiple linguistic and cultural proficiencies, which can largely benefit each other if the teacher takes an appropriate pedagogical approach such as collaborative or interactive learning.

DEVELOPING LEVEL- AND CULTURALLY-APPROPRIATE HL INSTRUCTIONAL MATERIALS

Given the fact that Chinese is taught as a foreign language (i.e., not a tool for societal communication) in the United States, the CHL curriculum should follow the ACTFL (http://www.actfl.org) guidelines and the National Foreign Language Standards for its pedagogical framework (See Everson, The Importance of Standards, this volume). Here are some specific recommendations, adapted from the Curriculum Guidelines for Heritage Language Classrooms at the University of California, 2003. (http://www.international.ucla.edu/article.asp?parentid=24734#intro)

1. Materials for beginning HL students can start at a higher level and move at a faster pace than materials for beginning non-HL learners.

Because of their prior exposure to the language, many heritage speakers are capable of covering material more quickly than non-HL learners. Early in the program, they can also be exposed to higher-level discourse and register, as well as to more advanced vocabulary and sentence structure.

2. Materials for HL students should be appropriate to students' level of cognition and their age.

HL students' language development often lags behind their cognitive development. For college-age students, elementary school materials from the target culture are cognitively inappropriate. Introductory foreign language textbooks are equally unsuitable because HL students are not typical foreign language learners. Using middle school texts from the target country/region such as China or Taiwan in a variety of subjects, including mathematics, the natural sciences, social sciences, and literature, may not be appropriate, either. We also see many different versions of 寓言典故，文学名著 imported from China or Taiwan, but few can be used without modification.

3. Materials for HL students should include a significant and authentic cultural component.

One important reason that HL students study their heritage language is that they want to strengthen their connection with their home culture, so HL instruction should help students acquire greater cultural literacy by including materials composed of Chinese history, literature, philosophy, art, calligraphy, films, artistic entertainment, etc.

4. Materials for HL students should be sociolinguistically appropriate.

While HL students often do well with informal, spoken language, they may still lack knowledge of sociolinguistic rules, which include register, politeness markers, honorifics, and the vocabulary and expressions used in more formal contexts by educated native speakers.

5. Materials for HL students should be more content-based.

Content-based materials, for example, those focused on target media and business, incorporate the eventual uses of the target language in specialized contexts and take into account the interests and needs of the learners.

Compared with the major foreign languages such as Spanish and French in this country, CHL materials which meet the above guidelines are in short supply and, therefore, in urgent need. In reality, most of the Chinese language programs — at both universities and secondary schools — have been using the same textbooks for non-HL and HL learners, only at an accelerated speed for the latter. The good news is that CHL educators are committed to filling this gap. So far, there are a growing number of quality course materials designed for CHL learners at various levels, such as:

FOR BEGINNING LEVEL

1. *Flying with Chinese* (Wang, et. al., 2007–2008, Panpac/Cheng & Tsui Company).

    Flying with Chinese is a K–6 series created by a team of K–12 world language educators. It is specially designed for mainstream Chinese programs and is easy to accelerate for HL learners.
2. *Oh, China: Elementary Reader of Modern Chinese for Advanced Beginners* by Princeton University Press (Chou, et al., 1999)
3. *A Primer for Advanced Beginners of Chinese, Volume 1* by Columbia University Press (Li, et al., 2003)

    These materials are well-written and focused on developing learners' reading proficiency and some oral skills as well. They are appropriate for students in high school and college.

FOR INTERMEDIATE LEVEL

1. *Masterworks Chinese Companion: Expressive Literacy through Reading and Composition* (Anderson, 2004, Cheng & Tsui Company). This book is designed to help heritage students at the high school and college levels develop reading and writing skills.

2. *How Far Away Is the Sun? Cheng & Tsui Readings in Chinese Culture Series, Volume 2.* (Huang and Ao, 2007, Cheng & Tsui Company).

3. *The Moon Is Always Beautiful: Cheng & Tsui Readings in Chinese Culture Series, Volume 3.* (Huang and Ao, 2008, Cheng & Tsui Company).

   The *Cheng & Tsui Readings in Chinese Culture Series* (Volumes 1–5) is a series of graded readers spanning from the beginning through advanced levels and consisting of original essays on topics related to China and Chinese culture.

FOR ALL LEVELS

Tales & Traditions: Readings in Chinese Literature Series 《新编中文课外阅读丛书》

   Volumes 1–4 by Xiao, et. al., (Volume 1, 2007; Volume 2, 2008. Cheng & Tsui Company). This book series presents stories and anecdotes that are part of the Chinese literary canon and essential for cultural fluency. They include sayings from classical philosophers, folk tales, legends, excerpts from great works of literature, and more. All stories are adapted to a level appropriate for learners of Chinese, from beginning level in Volume 1 through the advanced level in Volume 4. With its blend of language learning and culture, this series is recommended as supplementary reading for both HL and non-HL learners, but especially for HL learners.

Summary

The Chinese language teaching community has just started to understand HL learning and HL learners, and begun to develop an appropriate pedagogy for them. The goal of having five percent of American high students learning Chinese by the year of 2015 is very exciting. Together we will make this goal a reality. The Chinese teaching community should continue to seek national recognition, reach out for resources and support, explore new approaches, and work closely with the Chinese community and parents.

Questions for Discussion

1. How many students learn Chinese in your school? How many of them have a Chinese family background? How are the students placed? In your view, what is the best way to place them? Why?

2. In your view, what are the primary challenges your students face in acquiring the targeted proficiency in Chinese?

3. Based on your own foreign language learning and teaching experience, what is the best way to improve CHL learners' reading and writing proficiency?

References

Anderson, Qin-Hong. 2004. *Masterworks Chinese companion: Expressive literacy through reading and composition.* Boston: Cheng & Tsui Company.

Bley-Vroman, Robert. 1990. The logical problem of foreign language learning. *Linguistic Analysis* 20: 3–49.

Bougie, Evelyne, Stephen C. Wright, and Donald M. Taylor. 2003. Early heritage-language education and the abrupt shift to a dominant-language classroom: Impact on the personal and collective esteem of Inuit children in Arctic Quebec. *International Journal of Bilingual Education and Bilingualism* 6 (5): 349–373.

Brecht, Richard D. and Catherine W. Ingold. 1998. Tapping a national resource: Heritage languages in the United States. *ERIC Digest.* Washington D.C.: ERIC Clearinghouse on Languages and Linguistics. EDO-FL-98–12.

Dai, Jin-huei Enya and Zhang Lihua. 2008. What are the CHL learners inheriting: *Habitus* of the CHL learners. In *Chinese as a heritage language: Fostering rooted world citizenry,* ed. Agnes Weiyun He and Yun Xiao, 35–50. Honolulu, HI: University of Hawaii National Foreign Language Resource Center.

Draper, Jamie B. and June H. Hicks. 2000. Where we've been; what we've learned. In *Teaching heritage language learners: Voices from the classroom,* ed. John B. Webb and Barbara L. Miller. ACTFL Series 2000.

Duff, Patricia A. and Duanduan Li. 2008. Issues in Chinese heritage language education and research at the post-secondary level. In *Chinese as a heritage language: Fostering rooted world citizenry,* ed. Agnes Weiyun He and Yun Xiao, 13–36. Honolulu, HI: University of Hawaii National Foreign Language Resource Center.

Feuerverger, Grace. 1991. University students' perceptions of heritage language learning and ethnic identity maintenance. *Canadian Modern Language Review* 47 (4): 660–677.

He, Agnes Weiyun. (2008). Chinese as a heritage language: An introduction. In *Chinese as a heritage language: Fostering rooted world citizenry,* ed. Agnes Weiyun He and Yun Xiao, 1–12. Honolulu, HI: University of Hawaii National Foreign Language Resource Center.

He, Agnes Weiyun and Yun Xiao, eds. 2008. *Chinese as a heritage language: Fostering rooted world citizenry.* Honolulu, HI: University of Hawaii National Foreign Language Resource Center.

Hendryx, Jason D. 2008. The Chinese heritage language learners' existing linguistic knowledge and abilities. In *Chinese as a heritage language: Fostering rooted world citizenry,* ed. Agnes Weiyun He and Yun Xiao, 53–66. Honolulu, HI: University of Hawaii National Foreign Language Resource Center.

Jia, Gisela. 2008. Heritage language maintenance and attrition among first generation Chinese immigrants in New York City. In *Chinese as a heritage language: Fostering rooted world citizenry,* ed. Agnes Weiyun He and Yun Xiao, 189–204. Honolulu, HI: University of Hawaii National Foreign Language Resource Center.

Jia, Li and Bayley, Robert. (2008). The (re)acquisition of perfective aspect marking by Chinese heritage language learners. In *Chinese as a heritage language: Fostering rooted world citizenry,* ed. Agnes Weiyun He and Yun Xiao, 189–204. Honolulu, HI: University of Hawaii National Foreign Language Resource Center. 201–220.

Koda, Keiko, Chan Lu and Yanhui Zhang. 2008. Effects of print input on morphological awareness among Chinese heritage language learners. In *Chinese as a heritage language: Fostering rooted world citizenry,* ed. Agnes Weiyun He and Yun Xiao, 125–136. Honolulu, HI: University of Hawaii National Foreign Language Resource Center.

Kondo-Brown, Kimi, ed. 2006. *Heritage language development: Focus on East Asian immigrants*. Amsterdam/Philadelphia: John Benjamins Publishing Company.

Li, Guofang. 2003. Literacy, culture, and politics of schooling: Counternarratives of a Chinese Canadian family. *Anthropology & Education Quarterly* 34 (2): 182–204.

Li, Guofang. 2006. *Culturally contested pedagogy: Battles of literacy and schooling between mainstream teachers and Asian immigrant parents*. New York: State University of New York Press.

Liu, Haiming. 2002. Historical connections between the Chinese trans-pacific family and U.S.-China relations. In *The expanding roles of Chinese Americans in U.S.-China relations*, ed. Peter H. Kowehn and Xiao-huang Yin. Armonk, New York: M.E. Sharpe.

Lynch, Andrew. 2003. The relationship between second and heritage language acquisition: Notes on research and theory building. *Heritage Language Journal*, http://www.heritagelanguages.org.

McCarthey, S. J. 1997. Connecting home and school literacy practices in classroom with diverse population. *Journal of Literacy Research*, 29 (2): 145–182.

McGinnis, Scott. 2005. Statistics on Chinese Language Enrollment. Chinese Language Teachers Association website, http://clta.osu.edu/flyers/enrollment_stats.htm.

Ming, Tao and Hong-yin Tao. 2008. Developing a Chinese heritage language corpus: Issues and a preliminary report. In *Chinese as a heritage language: Fostering rooted world citizenry*, ed. Agnes Weiyun He and Yun Xiao, 167–188. Honolulu, HI: University of Hawaii National Foreign Language Resource Center.

Pease-Alvarez, L., Garcia, E. E. and P. Espinosa. 1991. Effective instruction for language-minority students: An early childhood case study. *Early Childhood Research Quarterly* 6: 347–361.

Santos, Fernanda. 2007. "Students search for the words to go with their cultural pride." New York Times, May 7, 2007, http://www.nytimes.com/2007/05/07/nyregion/07heritage.html.

Shin, Sarah J. 2006. High-stakes testing and heritage language maintenance. In *Heritage language development: Focus on East Asian immigrants*, ed. Kimi Kondo-Brown, 127–144. Amsterdam/Philadelphia: John Benjamins Publishing Company.

Stewart, Vivien, and Shuhan Wang. 2005. *Expanding Chinese-language capacity in the United States: What would it take to have 5 percent of high school students learning Chinese by 2015?* New York: Asia Society's Education Division, www.askasia.org.

Valdés, Guadalupe. 2001. Heritage language students: Profiles and possibilities. In *Heritage languages in America: Preserving a national resource*, ed. Joy Kreeft Peyton, Donald A. Ranard, and Scott McGinnis, 37–80. McHenry, IL: Center for Applied Linguistics.

Wang, Shuhan. 2004. Biliteracy resource eco-system of intergenerational language and culture transmission: An ethnographic study of a Chinese-American community. University of Pennsylvania unpublished dissertation.

Wiley, Terrence G. 2005. The reemergence of heritage and community language policy in the U.S. national spotlight. *The Modern Language Journal* 89 (4): 594–601.

Wong Fillmore, Lily. 1991. When learning a second language means losing the first. *Early Childhood Research Quarterly* 6: 323–346.

Xiao, Yun. 2004. L2 acquisition of Chinese topic-prominent constructions. *Journal of the Chinese Language Teachers Association* 39 (3): 65–84.

———. 2006. Heritage learners in foreign language classroom: Home background knowledge and language development. *The Heritage Language Journal* 4 (1): 47–57, http://www.heritagelanguages.org.

———. 2008a. Charting the CHL developmental path. In *Chinese as a heritage language: Fostering rooted world citizenry*, ed. Agnes Weiyun He and Yun Xiao, 151–66. Honolulu, HI: University of Hawaii National Foreign Language Resource Center.

———. 2008b. Home literacy environment in Chinese as a heritage language. In *Chinese as a heritage language: Fostering rooted world citizenry*, ed. Agnes Weiyun He and Yun Xiao, 259–266. Honolulu, HI: University of Hawaii, National Foreign Language Resource Center.

Appendix 1: Pre-Program Survey

CHINESE LANGUAGE COURSE QUESTIONNAIRE

Chinese Course No. _____ Year & Semester _____

Student's Name (English): _____ Gender: _____

(Chinese Character or *pinyin*, if applicable) _____

Local address _____

e-mail address _____

Phone no. _____ (H) _____ (O)

Student Status (indicate as applicable):

The last four digits of your social security number _____

Undergraduate class of (year): _____

Graduate student (indicate school, department, degree sought, and year): _____

_____

_____

Employer _____

What is your motivation for taking this course? (if more than one, please rank priorities):

college language requirement ____

need for academic research ____

family background ____

expected need in future career ____

general cultural or linguistic interest ____

other (please specify) _____

Where were you born? _____ If you were born in a foreign country, how old were you when you arrived in the United States? _____

Did you attend weekend Chinese community school(s)? _____

If yes, how long? _____ And when did you stopped going? _____

What is your primary language? _____

Other languages previously learned (indicate poor, fair, good excellent for the four skills):

language	years learned	place learned
_____	_____	_____
_____	_____	_____
_____	_____	_____

Language	Listening	Speaking	Reading	Writing
_____	_____	_____	_____	_____
_____	_____	_____	_____	_____
_____	_____	_____	_____	_____
_____	_____	_____	_____	_____

What Chinese dialect is spoken in your home? _____

Who speaks it? _____

Other exposure to East Asian culture (time and location of travel, residence, etc.)

_____

_____

Is there anything else about yourself that relates to your study of Chinese and you would like to share with your instructors? _____

_____

_____

Chapter 10

Linking Curriculum, Assessment, and Professional Development

Challenges of a K–16 Articulated Program

Madeline K. Spring

Arizona State University

In the United States, language learning is often sporadic and unfocused. The lack of functional language skills hampers economic growth, national security, and social stability. Recognizing this, in the wake of the 9/11 attacks, the federal government took a number of initiatives to remedy the situation. One of these is The Language Flagship, an initiative of the National Security Education Program. In 2006, The Language Flagship chose a partnership between the University of Oregon and Portland Public Schools to be the nation's first K–16 Flagship. The goal of this program is to produce Superior level Mandarin language users.

Most traditional language programs lead to Novice or, sometimes, Intermediate proficiency, so clearly the Oregon Chinese Flagship needed to think differently about how to structure a language program. The first radical departure from common practice was to design a program for students who begin learning the language in kindergarten and continue through the college years. Merely following traditional practices for a longer period of time, however, was not enough. This article describes the innovative curricular and instructional practices being developed in the Oregon Chinese Language Flagship with special attention to the implications for teachers interested in adopting some of these practices.[1]

An Overview of The Language Flagship and the Oregon K–16 Chinese Flagship Program

The Language Flagship was developed to address the urgent and growing need for Americans with professional levels of competency in languages critical to national security. Targeting advanced language training in Arabic, Korean, Chinese, Persian, Hindi, Urdu, and a variety of Eurasian languages, The Language Flagship offers a partnership between the federal government and leading U.S. institutions of higher education to implement a national system of programs designed to produce advanced language competency (i.e., Interagency Language Roundtable [ILR] Level 3 and/or the American Council on the Teaching of Foreign Languages [ACTFL] Superior level.)[2] Beginning in 2002, The Language Flagship has established programs that offer instruction in the United States and further instruction and professional externships at select sites abroad. Currently there are five Flagship programs in Chinese, housed at Brigham Young University, Ohio State University, the University of Mississippi, the University of Oregon, and a new Flagship Partner Program at Arizona State University. At present, only the Oregon program, which received the Flagship grant in fall 2005 and admitted its first cohort of Flagship Scholars at the University of Oregon in Fall 2006, takes as its mission providing students with an articulated K–16 curriculum. This effort is the first in the nation and will serve as a national model for future programs. The Language Flagship is an impetus for changing how languages are taught in the United States. One of the key features of this project is replicability, i.e., the ease with which a program can serve as a model for creating other programs in Chinese or other languages.[3]

The partnership between Portland Public Schools (PPS) and the University of Oregon (UO) is unique in that it offers all students, regardless of language or cultural background, an opportunity to reach advanced Mandarin proficiency necessary to communicate at a professional level in the field of their choice.

---

[1] I would like to acknowledge Carl Falsgraf, Director of the Center for Applied Second Language Studies (CASLS) and Project Director of the Oregon Chinese Flagship for helpful comments on an earlier draft of this chapter.

[2] The ILR, which was a modification and refinement of the proficiency categories originally developed by the Foreign Service Institute (FSI) in the early 1950s, is often used along with ACTFL guidelines when referring to proficiency levels of foreign language learners. For a detailed description of the ILR and ACTFL proficiency guidelines, see Hadley (2001, p. 16–18). See also http://www.actfl.org/i4a/pages/index.cfm?pageid=4236 and http://www.actfltraining.org/ilr_speaking_descriptors.cfm.

[3] More details about The Language Flagship and the Chinese Flagship in Oregon can be found at http://www.thelanguageflagship.org/ and http://casls.uoregon.edu/ORflagship/. For information on the other Chinese Flagship Programs, see http://chineseflagship.byu.edu/, chineseflagship.osu.edu/, http://www.olemiss.edu/depts/modern_languages/NFLP.html and http://chinaflagship.silc.asu.edu/.

This partnership brings together educators who are committed to creating innovative learning environments for students of Chinese from kindergarten through the postsecondary level. Ultimately these students will be well prepared for the challenge of interacting professionally in Chinese.

The Chinese Immersion Programs at Portland Public Schools (PPS)

Drawing on extensive experience in their Japanese and Spanish immersion programs, PPS established a Mandarin immersion program at Woodstock Elementary School in 1998.[4] The success of this program, in which students spend half of the school day learning in Chinese and the other half learning in English, is largely due to administrative and parental support coupled with the dynamic expertise of a highly talented teaching staff. The PPS Chinese Language Flagship continues for students in the sixth grade at Hosford Middle School, with two class periods a day (social studies and Mandarin language arts) devoted to instruction in Chinese. The high school components of the Chinese immersion programs are currently being developed at two sites. Chemistry and humanities courses are taught in Chinese at Franklin High School as part of their Chinese Heritage Program situated in the World Languages Institute. In 2007 Cleveland High School, which will implement a Chinese immersion curriculum in 2008–09, offered a special Chinese language development class and a China Research Residency preparation course held at Hosford.[5]

Parent involvement and community support is another significant part of the PPS Mandarin immersion program. In 2000 parents of children in the program at Woodstock formed a nonprofit organization, called Shu Ren of Portland, to support the Mandarin program through networking, advocacy, volunteerism, and fund-raising. At that time there were about 73 students in the program, all of whom had begun Chinese in kindergarten. The role of the Shu Ren organization has been important as the program has grown and as the number of teachers involved with the program has increased (currently there are four immersion teachers at the elementary school level and five teachers involved with Chinese middle and high school programs). As with all innovative K–12 initiatives, the PPS Mandarin

---

[4]For more information on various models for immersion foreign language programs in K–12, see Met (1993), Lenker and Rhodes (2007), and Howard et. al (2005). An informative discussion of the pros and cons of immersion education by Fortune and Tedick (2007) can be found on the Portland Public Schools website for bilingual/immersion programs at http://inside.esl.pps.k12.or.us/.docs/pg/11940.

[5]For information on the history of the Chinese Immersion Program in Portland, see the website developed by Shu Ren of Portland, a non-profit organization made up of parents whose children are in the Mandarin Immersion Program of Portland Public Schools, http://www.shurenofportland.org/history.html. In the 2006/2007 school year, about 200 children were participating in the Woodstock program, and about 45 students were at Hosford Middle School. The high school program for these students will be launched at Cleveland High School in 2008.

Immersion program from the outset has recognized the need for administrators, teachers, and parents to work together to ensure that the students have the highest quality educational experience possible and that the objectives of the program are clearly defined and met. Shu Ren of Portland works closely with teachers on many critical issues, such as exploring ways that parents, most of whom have no background in Chinese, can support their children outside the classroom, and understanding what are reasonable expectations of language proficiency for students in various stages of the program. Their enthusiastic involvement in supporting both the academic and experiential components of the program is highly valued by the Chinese teachers and school administrators. A parental organization of this type can be a great boost to all teachers of Chinese, regardless of whether the program is immersion or not.

In addition to the Chinese immersion programs at Hosford, Cleveland, and Franklin, each school offers beginning level Mandarin classes, which students may take as electives or in some cases to fulfill foreign language requirements. Successful students in these language courses may well elect to find other paths (e.g., intensive summer programs, or language camps in China or the U.S., online language instruction, etc.) that will lead more quickly to intermediate-high or advanced-level language proficiency and thus qualify them to apply to the Flagship program at the University of Oregon or elsewhere. As administrators of the Flagship programs frequently note, students can achieve high levels of proficiency through multiple avenues; the Chinese Immersion Programs at PPS are simply one option.

The Chinese Flagship Program at the University of Oregon

The University of Oregon recruits talented high school seniors or transfer students with intermediate-high to advanced-level proficiency in Mandarin. These students, who are committed to developing superior-level Chinese fluency for use in future careers, come from a variety of backgrounds. As was noted above, participation in the PPS Chinese immersion programs is **not** a prerequisite for admission to the UO program, which is administered through the Center for Applied Second Language Studies (CASLS). Indeed students from all over the country apply to participate in this competitive, honors-level program that offers a broad range of challenging and innovative courses and learning opportunities. Student applications undergo a rigorous review process, that includes consideration of academic performance and potential, proficiency level in Mandarin, and other factors that indicate a strong commitment to personal and educational growth.[6] Top candidates are awarded generous scholarships.

---

[6]Language proficiency level is determined by multiple measures, including Standards-based Measure of Proficiency (STAMP) and online assessment using abased on benchmarks consistent with the ACTFL Performance Guidelines, and individual interviews.

Students can choose their major from over a hundred different programs at the University of Oregon. During their first and second years at the university, they take two Flagship courses each term, the nature of which may vary, depending on the student's proficiency level in Mandarin. Generally speaking, most students take one content class and one Chinese Flagship Language Strategies class. However, some students with higher level language skills may be recommended to take two content courses, whereas students who need to concentrate specifically on intensive language development, will be required to take a combination of Flagship and regular Chinese courses offered through the Department of East Asian Languages and Literatures. The content classes, which usually satisfy general education requirements in the humanities, social sciences, or natural sciences, are regular university courses taught entirely in Chinese by native or near-native speakers. Some of the courses offered so far in the program are Mind and Brain: Psychology of the East, Modern Chinese History, Sustainable Development in China, and The City in Modern Chinese Literature and Film. There are two levels of Language Strategies courses, each of which provides explicit instruction in the vocabulary, discourse structures, and strategic approaches to the material presented in the content courses. Each course is specifically designed to improve students' ability to read and write in various prose styles (i.e., expository, instructional, descriptive, and argumentative). Individualized and interest-based projects allow students to focus on issues that affect their area of studies and boost their translation, reading, and researching strategies skills.[7]

During their freshman and sophomore years, Flagship students live and take some of their classes in the University of Oregon's International House. An on-site Chinese Flagship program assistant works with Flagship staff to coordinate structured study groups, social and cultural activities, guest lectures, and dinners with faculty and graduate students who do research in China-related fields. This enriched residence hall experience fosters a sense of community and also offers opportunities for students and faculty to interact in Chinese beyond the classroom.

In their junior year Flagship students travel to China, where they enroll for two semesters in regular Nanjing University classes in subjects that match their interests and major fields of study. Students can apply language skills and expertise through the various volunteer and internship opportunities available in Nanjing and in a subsequent summer internship program run through the Qingdao Flagship Center. Using the information collected in China during their junior year, students return to the UO campus in their senior year to participate in a capstone class that results in a final project and/or senior thesis, written and presented formally in Chinese. Students' language proficiency at that time is also assessed through multiple assessment measures, including the *Hanyu shuiping kaoshi*, the Defense Language Proficiency Test, and an ACTFL-Oral Proficiency Interview

---

[7]For more details about these and other Flagship courses offered at UO, see http://casls.uoregon.edu/uoflagship/curriculum3.php.

(OPI) administered by external examiners. In addition to language assessment, personalized career counseling and introductions to prospective employers is an integral part of each student's senior year.

Special Challenges for Teachers in the Oregon K–16 Program

As is apparent in the preceding overview of the program, the Oregon Language Flagship is quite different from traditional Chinese language programs. Pedagogical approaches and decisions at every step of the way present new challenges to teachers, administrators, and, ultimately, to students.

Three key challenges face the Oregon Chinese Language Flagship in its current early stages. These same challenges will face **all** teachers trying to enhance student performance through improved articulation, more effective curriculum, and innovative instructional practices, and thus are not limited to a program that adopts the Language Flagship model.

Challenge #1.   To create a framework for curricular articulation linked to demonstrable language proficiency as determined via multiple assessment measures.

Challenge #2.   To develop age-appropriate teaching strategies for students at all levels.

Challenge #3.   To provide multiple opportunities for experiential learning that occurs beyond the classroom environment.

As educators and pioneers in the field of Chinese pedagogy, Flagship teachers are developing innovative approaches to content-based language instruction that will have a positive influence on the field. These issues will likely be common to almost any program aiming at high proficiency levels through intensive and sustained exposure to and instruction in a second language.

Challenge #1. To create a framework for curricular articulation linked to demonstrable language proficiency as determined via multiple assessment measures.

The well-noted need for articulation in language programs is by no means unique to the Oregon Flagship, nor is it particular to the field of Chinese pedagogy (e.g., The College Board 1996; Swaffar 1990; McGinnis 1999; Spring 2005). The recent surge in interest in developing AP® Chinese (see Chi, this volume) and in creating and sustaining a range of other programs in Chinese on the K–12 level (e.g., immersion, Foreign Language in Elementary Schools [FLES] programs, etc.)

has brought to the forefront how critical it is that students and teachers follow a systematic approach that moves learners to higher levels of language proficiency sooner.

What makes the Flagship program different is that articulation is central to the mission of the program and that articulation must extend all the way from kindergarten through college. Teachers and students in the program must have clear guidelines that will plot how students will achieve superior-level language proficiency by the time they have completed the university-level Flagship program. This degree of accountability is rare in language programs. Often teachers focus mainly on the immediate course or course sequence they are teaching and are relatively unaware of instructional practices and decisions that occur in courses that precede or follow theirs. A certain amount of "curricular propriety" frequently ensues, which may impede objective discussions of how instructor-generated materials can best align with long term curricular goals and state or national standards. The Oregon Chinese Flagship insists that instructional frameworks, curricular materials, and assessments are embedded in the core of the program and that teachers work as a team to develop, explain, and disseminate their standards so that future programs of this type in any language can reduplicate them.

The nature of the Oregon Flagship program requires long-term tracking of individual students by multiple instructors. In addition to national assessments and online portfolios, which will be mentioned later in this chapter, teachers need to have specific, performance-based guidelines for determining what kind of language students at different levels of the language learning continuum can actually produce. The language curriculum project grew out of the need to develop direct links between context and explicit language instruction that go beyond the syllabus of any single teacher or any type of school environment (e.g., primary school, middle school, etc.).

THE CHINESE LANGUAGE CURRICULUM PROJECT: DEVELOPING A LANGUAGE CURRICULUM FRAMEWORK

As part of the Oregon Chinese Language Flagship, Portland Public Schools, in collaboration with faculty from the University of Oregon, is currently developing an articulated K–12 Chinese language curriculum framework that sets proficiency-based outcomes at each grade level and for the subsequent post-secondary Flagship courses at UO.[8] This curriculum framework provides a clear roadmap for grade-specific language objectives that are contextualized according to thematic topics.

---

[8]The curriculum project is expected to be completed by Spring 2008 and will shortly thereafter be posted on the PPS Flagship website (http://casls.uoregon.edu/ppsflagship/curriculum.php) for easy access by language educators, parents, and others interested in learning more about the explicit language goals of PPS' Chinese immersion programs. A sample of the project is included in Appendix 4.

The framework allows teachers and programs to achieve alignment in curricular development and assessment, which will result in more informed and effective classroom instruction.

The goal of the Language Curriculum Development Project is as follows:

> To create a comprehensive, articulated K–12 Chinese language curriculum framework that will provide teachers with a clear set of language expectations by grade level. The online document will include functions, grammar, vocabulary, reading, writing, and other important aspects of the language program. The curriculum will be compatible with the State of Oregon second-language standards and benchmarks.

Despite the fact that the Chinese immersion program at PPS had been in place for some years, teachers had yet to define an explicit, articulated language curriculum. This is common in immersion programs, where teachers often focus primarily on state-mandated content standards, and may previously not have time for or access to formal training in Teaching Chinese as a Second Language. Research on immersion programs in the United States has highlighted the need to couple subject matter instruction with explicit language instruction. Contrary to the expectations of early adopters of immersion education, students in these programs do **not** necessarily learn the mechanics of a language simply because it is the medium of instruction. Rather, they need to have an awareness of linguistic structures and forms in order to ensure linguistic accuracy (Met and Lorenz 1997; Swain 1985). Planning for effective and accurate language acquisition is particularly critical in the Oregon Chinese Flagship because the goal is Superior proficiency, which requires a high degree of accuracy, especially in the productive skills.

The benefits of establishing a language curriculum that is independent of the standard curriculum are enormous. Teachers will turn to such a resource in setting long- and short-term goals, regardless of shifting content standards, new textbook adoptions, changes in teaching staff, or other decisions that may be dictated by school districts or other factors beyond their control. In addition, given that immersion programs generally give greater attention to academic language rather than social and informal discourse, teachers need a mechanism to determine whether their students will truly become proficient language users who have mastery of a range of registers and linguistic functions. This is especially important in a non-cognate language such as Chinese where these discourse styles differ greatly from English. Thus, by presenting both academic and social language, the framework helps define the special and overall proficiency goals for the Chinese immersion program. It simplifies planning of units and lessons, focuses the medium of instruction, facilitates assessment, and brings better accountability. Since this framework is independent from the standard curriculum, teachers can use it to understand the broader implications of instructional strategies that will lead to seamless articulation, be it from grade to grade, from school to school, or from K–12 to the post-secondary level. Another benefit of this framework is that it assures clearer transition for transfer students. This is important because not all students who want to participate in the Chinese Immersion program will have begun Chinese at the kindergarten level. Some will have transferred from other schools, or have other language experiences that allow them to join the program at a level that better matches their linguistic and cognitive abilities.

Although the final version of the curriculum project is not yet completed, it may be helpful to offer here a short description of what it entails. As mentioned above, one aspect of the project is to define language functions (e.g., responding to an invitation, expressing agreement, asking for clarification, etc.) and align these with language forms (e.g., vocabulary, formulaic expressions, sentence patterns, etc.) that allow a person to perform a language function. Students at different levels are able to express the same function with greatly varying levels of sophistication. For example, a second grade student can be expected to accept an invitation to a birthday party by simply saying "*hao* 好," whereas a high school student at grade 11 may respond to a similar invitation using considerably more complex language that expresses why s/he can or cannot attend. Thus "making and responding to invitations" is identified as a Novice-Mid level function, whereas "expressing obligation/necessity/cause and effect" falls under the category that describes a speaker at the Intermediate-Mid level.[9]

The curriculum project offers teachers at each grade a handy reference for language functions and forms that are aligned with grade-specific themes and are contextualized, with communicative tasks and objectives and sample vocabulary clearly delineated. The functions in the curriculum project are also referenced to topics and language benchmarks, which are, in turn, tied to specific measures of assessment (see the ensuing discussion on assessment). See Appendix 4 for a sample of how these various components of language and subject matter instruction are aligned in the Mandarin Immersion Curriculum Framework for the students in the first grade.

Explicit attention to classroom interactions that provide multiple opportunities for students to show mastery of language forms, and functions in their oral and written communication is important for teachers in the Oregon Chinese Flagship. One issue that the curriculum project brought to teachers' attention was that students often are not given enough chance to produce extended samples of complex language. Frequently students in foreign language classes are only asked questions that simply require one or two word answers (whereas the teacher produces most of the longer, complex utterances). Under these circumstances, even the most

---

[9]For the complete listing of Chinese oral and literacy benchmarks (that are directly linked both to the curriculum project and also the NOELLA and STAMP assessments mentioned below), see http://casls.uoregon.edu/chineseOralBenchmarks.php.

comprehensive curriculum framework linked to the most reliable measures of proficiency-based assessment will prove meaningless. One practical tip for teachers to avoid this common pitfall is to distinguish consciously between types of questions they ask. As some SLA researchers have noted, there are two broad categories of question types, namely, 1) "display" questions, which expect answers already predetermined and known by the teacher, and 2) "referential" questions, which allow open-ended answers based on new information determined by the student (Kumaravadivelu, 2003). Studies based on actual classroom practice have shown that almost 79 percent of questions in foreign language classrooms are "display" rather than "referential" questions (Long and Sato 1983). In addition, as one might expect, these studies proved that students' responses to referential questions were indeed more complicated in terms of use of vocabulary, level of grammatical difficulty, and length of utterance, and as such, provide more meaningful learning opportunities (Brock 1986; Thornbury 1996). The PPS-UO curriculum framework has proved to be a good impetus to remind teachers to incorporate both display and referential questions in designing lesson plans. As such, teachers using this framework profit from a kind of "embedded" professional development that is integral to successful implementation of the curriculum.

MATERIALS

In addition to the curriculum framework on the K–12 level, teachers in the Flagship need to adjust their orientation from relying on a single textbook or set of books to using a variety of materials more creatively and effectively. Textbooks inherently carry limitations. As several researchers have noted, it might be useful for teachers to consider the textbook simply as one type of source material from which they can create their own interactive curricular and pedagogical approaches (Prabhu 1987, p. 94; Kumaravadivelu 2003, p. 46). In the Chinese Flagship the need to look beyond a particular set of textbooks is essential, since the program requires pedagogical resources that meet the double demands of subject matter instruction and age-appropriate language objectives. The lack of suitable curricular materials becomes especially problematic when students move to the middle school program. Often texts that match linguistic levels are not sufficiently engaging or cognitively challenging for young teens, whereas content-rich materials are written in an academic style that is far beyond the level of these students. Instructors need professional guidance either through mentorship or professional development workshops to learn about creative and effective approaches to adaptation of curricular materials, and they need release time explicitly for curriculum development.

As students approach the higher ends of the language proficiency spectrum, the lack of resources that present discipline-specific knowledge in language that is accessible to those whose native language is not Chinese becomes even more apparent. At the university level most Chinese language textbooks target students in the novice to intermediate-high range. Rarely do Chinese programs teach significant numbers of students beyond the third or fourth-year level and seldom do they offer courses delivered in Chinese in subjects that are not in the regular domain of a language and literature department. In other words, one may occasionally find Business Chinese or Modern Chinese literature offered in such programs but seldom are there general education courses in other subjects taught in Chinese. Textbooks used in Chinese universities are geared to a specific audience; though appropriate in some Flagship courses, these materials may need to be broken down into smaller segments and teachers may need to equip students with specific learning strategies to use these materials most effectively.

Defining materials and linking linguistic proficiency explicitly to performance benchmarks, as described above in the Chinese Language Curriculum Framework project are key components of the Flagship program. Naturally, the next question that arises involves assessment. How can teachers and learners know whether students are actually performing at appropriate levels and what kind of feedback can they get that will guide them in achieving the program's goals?

ASSESSMENT

The importance of connecting curricular decisions to issues of assessment cannot be overemphasized. Assessment drives curriculum. More specifically, student performance, as measured by multiple assessments, is the goal and organizing principle of good curricula (Wiggins & McTighe, 2001). After all, any curricular decisions are irrelevant if they are not tied closely to multiple, objective measures of evaluating student performance. As many researchers have noted elsewhere, this is especially important in a program that requires long-term tracking of students' progress (e.g., Asia Society 2006; Bligh 1982; Kubler 2006; Malone, Rifkin, Christian and Johnson 2005). For this reason, Portland Public School and the University of Oregon are aligning curricular materials with benchmarks and standards that are geared to a set of benchmarks that are the core of the formative assessments created by teams of educators nationwide.

To facilitate efficient and practical summative assessment, The Oregon Chinese Flagship utilizes two online assessments. The National Online Early Language Learning Assessment (NOELLA) is the first affordable, universally accessible, and empirically verified assessment of proficiency for early language learners (grades 3–6). NOELLA provides a summative measure of young students' performances accurately and reliably in all four skills. In 2006, educators involved with the Oregon Chinese Language Flagship at PPS and UO, along with experienced master teachers in primary and secondary schools from across the country, participated in writer's workshops to set benchmarks and create test materials that are currently being piloted nationwide.[10]

---

[10]For more information on NOELLA, see http://noella.uoregon.edu/noella/do/login.

For students in grade 7 and above the Oregon Chinese Flagship Program uses the Standards-based Measurement of Proficiency (STAMP). A criterion-referenced test that is textbook- and curriculum-neutral, STAMP provides educators, parents, and students with a clear and comprehensive evaluation of students' level of competency in reading, writing, listening comprehension, and speaking. This assessment tool is being used by students beginning in the seventh grade and as part of the application process for all students interested in becoming Flagship scholars at the university level.[11]

Three other measures of oral proficiency are also being used to track student performance in the Chinese immersion program in PPS in grades K–8. These interactive listening and speaking assessments, developed by the Center for Applied Linguistics, are the Early Language Listening and Oral Proficiency Assessment (ELLOPA) for Grades PreK–2, the Student Oral Proficiency Assessment (SOPA) for Grades 2–8, and the CAL Oral Proficiency Exam (COPE) for Grades 5–8.[12] PPS Immersion teachers participate in extensive training sessions to learn how to administer and rate students' oral language using these innovative assessment tools.

In addition to the online proficiency tests outlined above, the Oregon Chinese Flagship, along with the Flagship programs in all languages, are currently moving to implement a comprehensive, online portfolio system that will provide students, educators, and potential employers with profiles of learners as they progress in their language careers. Among the materials that will be amassed in digital form are the following: 1) a language biography, detailing programs a student has participated in, types of curricular materials used, etc., 2) video/audio language samples, such as formal presentations, debates, spontaneous interviews, etc., 3) writing samples in Chinese and English that show students' familiarity with different genres and of text types, 4) resumes in Chinese and English, 5) self-assessment essays in Chinese and English, 6) official documents, such as transcripts, certificates, diplomas, and 7) language test scores, with an indication of whether tests are proficiency or achievement based. Clearly this is an ambitious effort and of course such portfolios will vary depending on educational settings or student/teacher needs and expectations. Nevertheless, this model has tremendous implications for providing students with a detailed record of their language careers. Such documentation implicitly alleviates the need for placement testing or reliance on single test scores that often give faulty impressions of language proficiency. As such, electronic language portfolios are certainly one aspect of the Flagship model that educators in all settings should seriously consider implementing.

---

[11]For more information about STAMP, see http://casls.uoregon.edu/stamp2.php and http://www.onlinells.com.

[12]Information of these language proficiency assessment instruments can be found at http://www.cal.org/topics/ta/sopa_ellopa.html.

Challenge #2. To develop age-appropriate teaching strategies for students on all levels.

The next challenge that faces educators in The Language Flagship moves beyond curriculum and assessment. Given the high expectations for student success in the Flagship program, teachers must be continuously conscious of providing instruction for students as they progress through the various stages of language learning (novice→intermediate→-advanced→superior) and similarly as they develop cognitively (i.e., as students in primary school→secondary school→university). Flagship instructors use a variety of implicit and explicit types of feedback and error correction to motivate and encourage all students to become highly motivated life-long language learners.

A number of studies, drawing on the work of Lev Vygotsky (1896–1934), emphasize that instructors must pay careful attention to the mental and social processes of students' developmental stages. Vygotsky stressed that researchers should closely consider students' potential, rather than simply focusing on students' immediate linguistic performances (Lantoff & Appel 1994; Donato 1994; Gillette 1994). This premise leads to two important pedagogical issues for which Flagship teachers must develop explicit strategies as they work with students throughout the K–16 continuum.

The first teaching strategy that teachers in immersion programs (and in all second language programs, for that matter) must consider is how to approach error correction. Marysia Johnson, in her study on the philosophical constructs of SLA, reminds educators that, "learning cannot occur if too much assistance is provided or if a problem-solving task is too easy" (2004, p. 141). Of course this principle is important for **all** language teachers. Flagship teachers especially need to be aware of the danger of over-correcting or preventing students from finding multiple ways to find answers to linguistic and content-based questions. The ways that teachers handle error correction directly relate to their own pedagogical beliefs, which inevitably affect student perceptions and attitudes. Those less tangible, affective issues are critical, and lead to the second important teaching strategy that Flagship teachers must consider, namely how to encourage and maintain student motivation. There is little doubt that, in addition to challenging students linguistically and cognitively, eliciting student interest and long-term motivation are integral elements of immersion programs. These programs are only sustainable when consecutive cohorts of students progress intact from the early years of primary school to subsequent language immersion in secondary schools. Student retention, always a concern in language classes, is even more critical in these programs, given their high visibility, need for support from the community, and local and national requirements for administrative accountability.

Historically, immersion programs face the greatest challenges in student motivation (which directly relates to retention or the lack thereof) at the middle school and high school levels. As Montone and Loeb noted in a report on two-way immersion programs in secondary schools, "Adolescents are pulled by many bio-logical and social forces. On the one hand, they are developing their individuality, while on the other hand, they can be extremely susceptible to peer pressure and the fear of being perceived as different from the 'in' group" (2000, p. 6). When par-ticipating in an immersion program precludes these students' ability to take elec-tives or being in the same classes as their friends, they may no longer be motivated to continue with the program, regardless of pressure by parents and teachers.[13]

Motivating and inspiring students via course materials that are academically challenging, cognitively appropriate, and at a suitable linguistic level is a complex and lofty objective. One pathway to achieve this ambitious goal, which in essence is the underpinning for the Oregon Language Flagship, is to instill students with metacognitive learning strategies.[14] Beginning in kindergarten and first grade, stu-dents are exposed to a variety of teaching strategies, which combine teacher-fronted activities with those that maximize the use of group dynamics (e.g., peer modeling, role playing, singing songs, playing games, etc.). This breadth of pedagogical activities is maintained, albeit with age appropriate considerations, throughout the students' academic careers. By way of illustration, below are descriptions of two teaching scenarios from opposite ends of the K–16 spectrum. The connecting element is that both lessons share the objective of motivating students and empowering them with strategies to direct their own learning process.

SAMPLE TEACHING PLAN #1

Level: Grade 1
Long term objectives:

1. To increase students' proficiency level in Chinese through acquisition of vocabulary, language functions and forms that prepare them for the mastery of nutritional, scientific, and mathematical concepts that, in conjunction with literacy benchmarks, are delineated in state and national standards for students in Grade 3.
2. To stimulate and maintain student motivation for learning Chinese through various forms of multi-sensory activities.

Unit/lesson objective: Students will be able to identify 30+ words for fruits and vegetables that will be integral for pre-nutrition and pre-science exploratory segments. They will be able to use these terms appropriately to express simple mathematic operations and personal likes/dislikes, etc., and will use specific

---

[13]For an informative discussion of how individual learner characteristics, such as age, motivation, attitude, cognitive style, etc. effect language learning, see Larsen-Freeman (2001).
[14]For further information on the importance of learning strategies and metalinguistic awareness, see Chamot (2001) and Wenden (2001).

language and linguistic functions to demonstrate their understanding of these terms and how to use them.[15]

Explicit linguistic focus: *Language functions:* greeting, self-introduction; *linguistic forms* identified in the Chinese Language Curriculum (e.g., 你叫什么名字？我叫红萝卜。)

Procedure:

Step 1. Each student is assigned the name of one fruit or vegetable that s/he is responsible for knowing how to pronounce correctly and recognize the *hanzi* for that term.

Step 2. Students are given multiple opportunities via structured input activities to hear, read, and say their own word and the words of their classmates, as they play games, act out stories, sing songs, draw pictures, and participate in other individual and group events.

Step 3. The use of peer modeling ("*xiao laoshi*") is embedded in the instructional plan.

Step 4. Teacher-fronted activities focus on preparing students to incorporate the explicit language learned in this unit in future lessons on science, nutrition, mathematics, and other general course work content.

SAMPLE TEACHING PLAN #2

Level: First-year college students in the Language Flagship at the University of Oregon ("Grade 13").

Long term objectives:

1. To improve academic writing so students will succeed when taking regular, content courses with Chinese students at Nanjing University.

2. To equip students with meta-awareness of their Chinese writing skills and develop strategies for self-improvement.

Unit/lesson objective: Students will be able to synthesize and express their reflections and analytical interpretation of materials that were the subject of class lectures, discussions, and readings. Through individualized writing modules, they will have multiple opportunities to revise their writing through guided self-correction, and will learn writing techniques that will transfer to future writing tasks.

Procedure: Students are assigned weekly essays (approximately 500 characters in length) that are connected to readings and discussion sessions in a Flagship general

---

[15]Approximately one month of instructional time is devoted to this unit. The focus is mainly on oral production; mastery of writing these words in Chinese is emphasized in second grade, by which point students have already incorporated the words into their active vocabulary.

education course (e.g., course in literature, history, art, psychology, sociology, etc.). Students have multiple opportunities for feedback from instructors and for self-correction:

Step 1. Members of the Flagship teaching staff (who are generally Graduate Teaching Fellows [GTFs] offer minimum corrections on drafts of students' writings (based on a unified grading code that indicates commonly made types of errors).[16]

Step 2. Students revise essays and meet individually with a GTF to discuss specific linguistic issues such as word choice, paragraph organization, etc.

Step 3. Students present the final version of paper to the faculty member responsible for teaching the content course, who evaluates the academic content of the essay.[17]

This brief sample of teaching plans focused on primary school students as well as those at the university is presented here as an illustration of the need for instruction from K–16 to match the learner's cognitive and emotional development, while motivating students to sustain interest in Chinese. In structuring curricula and teaching strategies for students who start Mandarin at early ages and continue throughout adulthood, it may be useful to refer to the distinction social and educational psychologists make between intrinsic and extrinsic motivation (Deci and Ryan 1991, 1992). Clearly it is one thing for parents of kindergarten-age children to enroll them in the Woodstock Chinese immersion program, but quite another when it comes to university students who are striving to function professionally in their chosen field of expertise. Those students can no longer rely on

---

[16]See Appendix 2 for the correction code that Flagship teachers (and students) developed at UO at the beginning of the academic year based on the most predictable errors in writing Chinese. The code is given here as a sample; teachers should feel free to devise a correction code that is appropriate to their own articulated program. The benefits of using a correction code are surprisingly numerous. Since students and teachers both have access to the same code and since it is used consistently from one level to the next, regardless of instructor, students approach self-correction as a positive part of the learning process. Furthermore, teachers who previously devoted countless hours to the often-unappreciated task of providing copious, detailed corrections are now free to look at students' writing more objectively. Later in the process, teachers may choose to make a limited number of comments or suggestions about structural features of the entire writing assignment and also focus on the content and manner of exposition. A correction code offers learners and educators a helpful first step to indicate common errors. In addition to using such a code, teachers should also consider more holistic approaches to assessing writing. See Appendix 3 for a sample writing assessment rubric, developed by Professors R. Davis, P. Ellister, and L. de González for the Spanish program at the University of Oregon. Using this rubric, teachers can highlight specific sections of the text that either exceed standards or fall below standard, providing students with clear, objective feedback on how to improve their writing.

[17]For an in-depth explanation of how this process works, see Appendix 1.

teachers and parents to determine learning objectives; rather, they will need to have an internalized sense of incentive that drives them forward. As Leo van Lier notes in his discussion of motivation, autonomy, and achievement, "Having established the need to see intrinsic and extrinsic motivation as two independent forces which increasingly fuse in an individual's actions, we next have to consider how extrinsic motivation can be used to marshal the productive forces of intrinsic motivation (1996, p. 111). As teachers build their repertoire of teaching strategies, they will profit by keeping this important goal in mind. Hopefully this snapshot view of specific teaching objectives in the Flagship-articulated curriculum provides some insight into how teachers can move from first focusing on extrinsic motivation of their students at the early years, to gradually guiding them to develop intrinsic motivation and individualized learning strategies that will result in superior levels of language expertise.

Challenge #3. To provide multiple opportunities for experiential education that occurs beyond the classroom environment

Experiential learning practices, in which students engage in real and meaningful life experiences requiring them to use their language and cultural skills, are an important part of the Oregon Language Flagship for students at all levels. For example, elementary-age students are encouraged to participate in a new summer immersion camp; middle school students have an opportunity to participate in a two-week research residency program in China in May 2008 (as part of the regular school year); and plans for a short-term China Summer Institute or Immersion Camp at the high school level are currently being explored. In addition, students in the K–12 Chinese immersion program are strongly encouraged to participate in community-based language learning experiences and other activities, like after school Chinese clubs or email "pen pal" exchanges with students in China, that offer opportunities for using language skills beyond the classroom setting.[18] Too often, experiential learning opportunities are seen as chances to just chat in another language. In real life, we always communicate for some purpose, not just to use language for the sake of using it. Similarly, experiential learning programs must be structured so that students have a concrete purpose for communicating. The eighth grade research residency is a good example. Unlike many overseas opportunities

---

[18]Currently at Hosford Middle School there is a Mandarin Club that meets after school three times a week. This gives students in the Grades 6-Chinese Immersion Program an opportunity to play games and learn songs in Chinese, do homework, and work on other projects, in a Mandarin-speaking environment that is beyond the traditional classroom setting. Approximately twenty-five students participate consistently in these club meetings.

for students that consist of visiting famous places and, perhaps a few uncomfortable interactions with Chinese students with whom they are to "become friends, "ostensibly to meet and talk (about what?), the research residency is carefully embedded in the regular academic curriculum. At the beginning of the school year each student identifies an individual inquiry project about an aspect of contemporary Chinese culture or society of particular interest. Possible topics are wide-ranging, depending on individual student interest. They might include environmental issues, trends in pop culture, or students' attitudes toward competition in sports and/or academics. In all cases, students will develop a research plan that requires extensive preparation and involves a component that is dependent on data that can only be obtained in China (e.g., interviews with students, conducting surveys and questionnaires, etc). By tailoring the project to fit students' interests, language is used for a practical, meaningful purpose, and students' motivation for learning is enhanced by a clear and immediate need. Another unique and crucial element of the research residency is a one-week home stay, which will help students negotiate Chinese culture and society independently by using the language and culture skills they have previously learned in classroom settings.[19]

At the university level, students also have a number of options for experiential learning. Through formal and informal social and professional interactions with peers at the university and in the local community in the Eugene-Portland area, as well as structured involvement through supervised internships in Nanjing and Qingdao, Flagship scholars are encouraged to become active participants in Chinese culture. In addition a new mentorship program called Aspiring Educators is being developed. One aspect of this initiative focuses on writing exchanges between specific cohorts of the K–16 Flagship students. This program offers opportunities for middle school students to write brief stories for students in K–2, high school students to write texts for middle school students, and UO Flagship students to create some more complex essays for high school students. This is one more way that the Language Flagship connects classroom experiences with local and global communities as a means to enhance and support language and cultural proficiency.

Challenges Ahead: Strengthening and Sustaining a Collaborative Culture

Articulation is not just a matter of coordinating standards and curriculum, but of clear and consistent communication among teachers and administrators responsible for the program at all levels. Many of the issues central to the development and sustainability of the Oregon Chinese Language Flagship are similar in the Portland Public School district and at the University of Oregon.

---

[19]For an in-depth explanation of the China Research Residency, see http://casls.uoregon.edu/ppsflagship/chinatrip.php.

Working with existing departments and centers, developing support from administration, maximizing resources, and providing support to students and teachers are all high priority and require careful planning and concerted, ongoing efforts by dedicated staff. The idea of team building is integral to every aspect of the program, be it technology, public relations, or even the selection of classroom materials. In addition to frequent formal meetings between people working on the PPS and UO Flagship initiatives, explicit connections between the PPS and UO Flagship teams have been built into the program. For example, the PPS Immersion Administrator works with UO committees to screen applications from incoming UO Flagship scholars, the UO Academic Director works with PPS Chinese teachers on the curriculum project, and both partners have pooled resources to hire a media specialist to coordinate public relations efforts on behalf of the program. In addition, all Flagship personnel are keenly aware of the need to recruit and train highly qualified teachers and other education specialists and are working together to develop programs, such as those resulting in state certification for K–12 teachers and summer workshops to support and strengthen the teaching staff at the university program. These kinds of joint efforts may not seem that remarkable, yet it is this commitment to working together that forms the fabric of successful articulation. As such it must not be overlooked.

As the Oregon Chinese Language Flagship moves forward, a number of areas of improvement have been identified. Creating programs that maintain student, teacher, administrators, and community enthusiasm and commitment is not easy and is not a one-time effort. Coordinating a diverse group of teachers and accommodating the special needs of different schools and programs is fundamental to the success of the program and requires flexibility, patience, and long-term planning. Finding qualified students to be Flagship Scholars on the post-secondary level has involved concerted recruitment efforts. National and international interest in the Oregon Language Flagship has been overwhelming, and educators from PPS and UO have striven to address the growing demand for leadership in K–16 articulated language programs through presentations at conferences, workshops, and written documentation for scholarly and non-scholarly venues. In addition, the Flagship teams are involved in statewide efforts to bring greater awareness to the importance of Chinese in the global context and to work with local and statewide China-related business initiatives as well as local Chinese communities and organizations.

Adapting the Flagship Model to Fit Different Educational Settings

PROMOTING THE DIFFUSION OF INNOVATION GRANT PROGRAM

In 2007, The Language Flagship announced a new initiative to broaden its mission of designing, supporting, and implementing a new paradigm for advanced language education in the United States. Promoting the Diffusion of Innovation Grant Program encourages strategic partnerships between institutions, organizations, or individuals and existing Flagship Centers offers opportunities for foreign language educators throughout the country to create programs that relate to the goals of The Language Flagship.[20] Arizona State University (ASU), one of three institutions that were awarded this grant, is currently developing an intensive, undergraduate-level two-year program that is a hybrid of the Flagship programs at the University of Oregon and Brigham Young University. Like those programs, the ASU Flagship Partner Program is designed to produce graduates with dual strengths in professional-level Mandarin language proficiency and in their chosen career domains. This undergraduate program, which admits its first cohort of students in Fall 2008, offers advanced-level content courses taught exclusively in Mandarin for one year at ASU and another year in China. Typically, these students will spend one semester taking regular university-level courses in their major field of study at Nanjing University and one semester in an internship program administered through the Qingdao Flagship Center.[21]

THE ARIZONA STATE UNIVERSITY (ASU) CHINESE FLAGSHIP PARTNER PROGRAM

Student Recruitment

Students applying to the ASU program should have intermediate-high or advanced-level proficiency in Mandarin, (which usually is achieved after completion of a university-level third- or fourth-year course). Among the multiple paths a student might follow to attain this degree of proficiency are the following:

1. A combination of study in K–12 programs AND university Chinese programs
2. Study at Heritage schools (possibly combined with university coursework)
3. Study in ASU's Chinese language program (academic year) AND intensive summer study run through the Flagship Center at Qingdao University, at ASU's Intensive Chinese Program at Sichuan University, or at other intensive language programs)
4. Intensive summer (see above) and appropriate yearlong language programs in China or Taiwan.

The benefit of this multi-option model is that it allows a wide range of students clear choices for different pathways to reaching higher level of Chinese that will qualify them for participation in The Language Flagship. Like the model in the partnership between Portland Public Schools and the University of Oregon, the

---

[20]For more details about the Flagship Centers and the Promoting the Diffusion of Innovation Grant Program, see http://www.thelanguageflagship.org/.

[21]The specific features of the ASU program are outlined at http://chinaflagship.silc.asu.edu/.

ASU program reaches out to K–12 programs and Chinese Heritage Schools to motivate and offer guidance to students who plan to attend a specific university that houses the Language Flagship. Unlike the Oregon Flagship, however, first year university students will generally not be eligible to participate in the ASU Flagship program.

Academic Curriculum: Pre-requisites and Course Offerings

One of the lessons learned early on in The Language Flagships is that simply having advanced language skills does not necessarily lead a student to achieve a superior level proficiency. In order to be prepared for sophisticated ways of functioning in different cultural settings, students need to discover how their linguistic and cognitive abilities intersect. Background knowledge, based on explicit instruction in and exposure to China's rich social, literary, and historical culture is, along with intellectual curiosity, essential for students striving for superior-level ability in Chinese. From their experience with the first cohort in the Oregon Flagship, instructors realized that there is often a gap between first-year college students' general awareness of China and China-related subjects (e.g., Chinese history, political science, current events, literature, culture, philosophy, etc.) and traditional upper-division university students who have reached a higher level of Chinese language through coursework in Departments of Chinese Language and Literature/Culture or Asian Studies Programs. This gap is not surprising, since the curricula in high schools are generally Eurocentric and do not expose young people to these topics. In contrast, most students in upper-division language classes at the college level have taken one or more China-related courses (taught in English) that led them to become independently motivated learners of social and cultural issues pertaining to China.

The ASU Flagship program is addressing potential disparities between language proficiency in Chinese and exposure to academic study of key aspects of Chinese civilization by instating a cultural literacy requirement, for incoming Flagship students. The first part of this requirement is successful completion of a college level course (taught in English) on a China-related subject, such as history, literature, economics, political science, geography, etc. Samples of work from this type of course (e.g., a term paper, course project, PowerPoint presentation) will be part of each student's application. The second part of the cultural literary requirement is a semester or more of college-level Classical (or Literary) Chinese 文言文.

A brief explanation about the connection between Literary Chinese and Modern Chinese may be useful. According to the national ACTFL guidelines, one characteristic of a superior-level reader is being "able to read with almost complete comprehension and at normal speed expository prose on unfamiliar subjects and a variety of literary texts."[22] In addition, a reader at this level is able to comprehend

---

[22]See   http://www.sil.org/lingualinks/languagelearning/OtherResources/ACTFLProficiencyGuidelines/contents.htm.

"grammatical patterns and vocabulary ordinarily encountered in academic/ professional reading." Texts written in Classical Chinese figure prominently in Chinese literature and history, and most academic and professional readings include structures and vocabulary that are drawn from the literary language. Students in China, Taiwan, and other Chinese educational settings normally begin their study of literary Chinese in middle school and continue learning to read works of this type through their freshman year of college. Classical Chinese is also part of the college entrance examination in China and Taiwan. Although it may not be feasible for American students to attain the same degree of familiarity with Literary Chinese as their Chinese counterparts, it is quite reasonable to require that they have a grasp of the fundamentals of that language so they can succeed in advanced level coursework at ASU and Nanjing University. Since ASU, which has a particularly strong group of faculty working in pre-modern Chinese literature, culture, and religion, and who have broad experience teaching Literary Chinese, already offers a year of Literary Chinese, students can readily avail themselves of this resource. Furthermore, these courses also count toward requirements in both the regular and Flagship-track BA major in Chinese.

Housed in the School of International Letters & Cultures (SILC), the ASU Flagship Partner Program is currently in the process of establishing a Chinese Flagship Track within its Chinese BA major. This will offer students the option to earn a double major, i.e., the major in their domain area (such as economics architecture, journalism, etc.) and a major in Chinese (Flagship Track).[23] By providing an academic home for Flagship in a large school (rather than a department) that, by definition, supports a trans-disciplinary approach to education, the ASU program has increased flexibility in designing the curriculum, hiring and training faculty, and assigning credits for coursework across the ASU campus and abroad.

Beginning Fall 2008 Flagship Scholars will enroll in four Flagship courses per semester, which will be chosen from the following tentative list: Chinese for Professional Purposes I and II, Modern Chinese History, Bridging Science, Technology, and Humanities in China, The History of Chinese Medicine, Chinese Religions, Urban Life and Culture in Premodern China, and the History of the Chinese Language. Like students in the other Chinese Flagships, ASU Flagship Scholars will participate in multiple measures of proficiency-based assessment, and their progress will be tracked through the online portfolio system. The writing modules, outlined earlier in this chapter will also be a part of the program, and the opportunities for individual tutorial sessions that focus on domain specific study are

---

[23]SILC developed out of out of the former Department of Languages and Literatures in response to changing educational needs. In addition to its very extensive traditional strengths in languages, literatures and cultures, SILC also emphasizes making interesting new trans-disciplinary opportunities available to undergraduate and graduate student alike. For more information on SILC and the Chinese degree options, see http://www.asu.edu/clas/silc.

currently being explored. As with the other Chinese Flagship programs, ASU students will participate in a yearlong overseas program, which offers direct enrollment at Nanjing University and an Internship in Qingdao.

Applying Aspects of The Language Flagship Models to Non-Flagship Programs

As we have seen in detail regarding the Oregon and ASU Flagship Programs, there is an array of paths to bring students to a higher level of proficiency in Mandarin. Each Flagship program has built on the strengths of the educational institutions that are involved; it would be naïve to suggest that additional institutions could adopt any single model wholesale. Educators should keep in mind that although many aspects of the Flagship programs described in this chapter have been made possible through grant funding, a number of the principles outlined here do not require financial assistance and can be applied or adapted in other educational settings. The Language Flagship offers a model; instructors are encouraged to see how they can apply parts of the model in their own classes. For example, teachers in most programs do not have the luxury of offering individual sessions to students (or having teaching assistants who can do so) as delineated in the writing modules described above, but they certainly can use a writing code and assessment rubric as constructive ways to allow students multiple opportunities to improve their writing through self-correction. Middle school or high school teachers may not have the resources to send students to China for a residency type of program, but they definitely could embed some of the pedagogical concepts outlined in a student-centered research project that makes use of the Internet and possible resources in their own community or a "virtual" online community. Whereas creating an entire curriculum of content courses taught in Chinese may seem prohibitive to many university faculty, the idea of one single advanced course or a section of one course on topics such as Business Chinese, Chinese film, or Chinese culture, would probably be met with departmental and administrative enthusiasm. Courses like these are especially attractive since they can appeal to a student population that hitherto has remained largely disengaged from or overlooked by traditional Chinese language and literature departments. Students with higher levels of language proficiency, be they Chinese heritage learners, students returning from study abroad programs, or graduate students in China-related programs, are often excited about the prospect of taking university-level courses in Chinese that allow them to apply their language skills in new, meaningful ways. This approach to interspersing a Flagship type of course in the regular curriculum is an easy first step in allowing faculty and administrators to experiment with offering this different curricular option before committing to a more intensive Flagship curriculum. Drawing on institutional strengths and instructional expertise that are already in place, whether in a regular Chinese curriculum or in non-language academic units like Asian Studies, Schools of Business or Engineering, Centers for Global Studies, is an excellent strategy to use when designing new Flagship programs.

A final reminder to educators involved with **any** kind of articulated curriculum development is that objective assessment and professional development for teachers are key to building and sustaining effective language programs — be they immersion or not. When teachers are actively engaged in determining learning objectives through collaboration with colleagues who teach Chinese at a range of levels, they have exciting opportunities to look beyond what takes place in their individual classes and consider broader programmatic goals and challenges. Similarly, as instructors work together to decide upon both formal and informal measures of assessment, they can better focus on what students are actually able to accomplish in the program and what pedagogical approaches are best suited to ensuring student success.

Discussion Questions

1. Discuss how assessment and curriculum are linked in the K–16 Oregon Flagship. How can these same instructional approaches be used in other types of programs?

2. Many of the features in the Flagship program described in this chapter apply to any program for Chinese. Consider how each of the following topics might be adapted in a non-Flagship setting:
   a. Multiple measures of proficiency-based assessment and electronic learner portfolios
   b. Development and adaptation of age-appropriate curricula
   c. Explicit instruction in language learning strategies
   d. Student motivation through multiple means of experiential learning
   e. Strategic implementation of error correction
   f. Instructional approaches to asking questions and other techniques for allowing students, to speak in Chinese using longer, more complex language
   g. Teacher collaboration on curricular development and other pedagogical decisions

3. If you were going to develop or strengthen a Chinese language program in a K–12 setting or in a Chinese Heritage School, how might you apply the models used by the Portland Public School Chinese programs?

4. Why do you think the Research Residency is such a motivating force for immersion students? How could a project like this be adapted in different educational settings? In what ways could online and community resources be used to simulate the type of in-country experience that is described here?

5. Consider how you approach grading students' written work. What objective indicators do you have that show students' writing abilities improve as a result of your feedback? How might pedagogical tools such as a writing code

and assessment rubric allow students develop learning strategies that will empower and motivate them to improve their writing proficiency?

References

Asia Society. 2006. *Creating a Chinese language program in your school.* New York City: Asia Society.

Bligh, D., ed. 1982. *Professionalism and flexibility in learning.* Guildford, Surrey, England: Society for Research into Higher Education.

Breen, M., ed. 2001. *Learner contributions to language learning: New directions in research.* Singapore: Pearson Education Limited.

Brock, C. 1986. The effects of referential questions on ESL discourse. *TESOL Quarterly* 20 (1): 47–59.

Chamot, A. U. 2001. The role of learning strategies in second language acquisition. In *Learner contributions to language learning: New directions in research,* ed. M. Breen, 25–43. Singapore: Pearson Education Limited.

Deci, E. L., and R. M. Ryan. 1991. A motivational approach to self: Integration in personality. In *Nebraska Symposium on Motivation: Vol. 38. Perspectives on motivation,* ed. R. A. Dienstbier, 237–88. Lincoln: University of Nebraska Press.

Deci, E. L., and R. M. Ryan. 1992. The initiation and regulation of intrinsically motivated learning and achievement. In *Achievement and motivation: A social-developmental perspective,* ed. A. K. Boggiano & T. S. Pittman, 9–36. Cambridge: Cambridge University Press.

Donato, R. 1994. Collective scaffolding in second language learning. In *Vygotskian approaches to second language research,* ed. J. P. Lantoff and G. Appel, 33–56. Norwood, NJ: Ablex Publishing Corporation.

Falsgraf, C., and M. Spring. 2007. Innovations in language learning: The Oregon Chinese flagship model. *Journal of the National Council of Less Commonly Taught Languages* 4: 1–16.

Fortune, T. W., and D. J. Tedick. 2007. Immersion benefits and challenges: Does one size fit all?" CAIS Conference, San Francisco, March 18, 2007.

Gillette, B. 1994. The role of learner goals in L2 success. In *Vygotskian approaches to second language research,* ed. Lantoff & Appel, 195–213. Norwood, NJ: Ablex Publishing Corporation.

Hadley, A. O. 2001. *Teaching language in context.* 3rd edition. Boston: Heinle and Heinle.

Howard, E. R., J. Sugarman, D. Christian, K. J. Lindholm-Leary, and D. Rogers. 2007. *Guiding principles for dual language education.* 2nd edition. Washington, D.C.: Center for Applied Linguistics.

Johnson, M. 2004. *A philosophy of second language acquisition.* New Haven: Yale University Press.

Johnson, R. K., and M. Swain. 1997. *Immersion education: International perspectives.* Cambridge: Cambridge University Press.

Kubler, C. C. (Ed.). 2006. *NFLC guide for basic Chinese language programs.* 2nd ed. Columbus, Ohio: OSU UniPrint.

Kumaravadivelu, B. 2003. *Beyond methods: Macrostrategies for language teaching.* New Haven: Yale University Press.

Lantoff, J. P., and G. Appel. 1994. Theoretical framework: An introduction to Vygotskian perspectives on second language research. In *Vygotskian approaches to second language research,* ed. Lantoff & Appel, 1–32. Norwood, NJ: Ablex Publishing Corporation.

Larsen-Freeman, D. 2001. Individual cognitive/affective learner contributions and differential success in second language acquisition. In *Learner contributions to language learning: New directions in research*, ed. M. Breen, 12–24. Singapore: Pearson Education Limited.

Lenker, A., and N. Rhodes. 2007. Foreign language immersion programs: Features and trends over 35 years. Online *CAL Digest*. Retrieved October 28, 2007 from http://www.cal.org/resources/digest/flimmersion.html.

Long, M., and C. Sato. 1983. Classroom foreigner talk discourse: Forms and functions of teachers' questions. In *Classroom-oriented research in second language acquisition*, ed. H. Seliger and M. Long, 268–85. Rowley, MA: Newbury House.

Malone, M. E., B. Rifkin, D. Christian and D. E. Johnson. 2005. Attaining high levels of proficiency: Challenges for foreign language education in the United States. *Online CAL Digest*. Retrieved October 28, 2007 from http://www.cal.org/resources/digest/attain.html.

McGinnis, S. 1999. Articulation. In *Mapping the course of the Chinese language field* (CLTA Monograph Series, vol. III), ed. M. Chu, 331–44. Kalamazoo: CLTA Inc.

Met, M. 1993. Foreign language immersion programs. Retrieved October 28, 2007 from http://www.cal.org/resources/digest/met00001.html.

Met, M., and E. B. Lorenz. 1997. Lessons from U.S. immersion programs: Two decades of experience. In *Immersion education: International perspectives*, ed. R.K. Johnson and M. Swain, 243–264. Cambridge: Cambridge University Press.

Montone, C. L., and M. I. Loeb. 2000. Implementing two-way immersion programs in secondary schools. *Educational Practice Report* 5. Center for Research on Education, Diversity & Excellence, Santa Cruz, CA and Washington, DC. Also available online at http://www.cal.org/crede/pubs/edpractice/EPR5.htm.

Prabhu, N. S. 1987. *Second language pedagogy*. Oxford: Oxford University Press.

Spring, M. 2005. Curriculum articulation and professional development: Where do they intersect? In *International symposium proceedings: Operational strategies and pedagogy for Chinese language programs in the 21ˢᵗ century*, ed. S. Teng, 42–47. Taipei: National Taiwan Normal University.

———. (June 2007). Flying the flag for Chinese. *Language Magazine* 6 (10): 20–23.

Swaffar, J. K. 1990. Articulating learning in high school and college programs: Holistic theory in the foreign language curriculum. In *Shifting the instructional focus to the learner*, ed. S. Magnan, 27–54. Middlebury, VT: Northeast Conference on the Teaching of Foreign Languages.

Swain, M. 1985. Communicative competence: Some roles of comprehensible input and comprehensible output in its development. In *Input in second language acquisition*, ed. S. Gass and C. Madden, 235–53. Boston, MA: Heinle & Heinle.

The College Board. 1996. *Articulation and achievement: Connecting standards, performance, and assessment in foreign language*. New York: College Entrance Examination Board.

Thornbury, S. 1996. Teachers research teacher talk. *ELT Journal* 50: 279–88.

Van Lier, L. 1996. *Interaction in the language curriculum: Awareness, autonomy, and authenticity*. Boston: Addison Wesley Publishing Company.

Wenden, A. L. 2001. Metacognitive knowledge in SLA: the neglected variable. In *Learner contributions to language learning: New directions in research*, ed. M. Breen, 44–64. Singapore: Pearson Education Limited.

Wiggins, G., and J. McTighe. 2001. *Understanding by design*. Upper Saddle River, NJ: Prentice Hall, Inc.

Appendix 1

FLOW CHART FOR WRITING MODULES

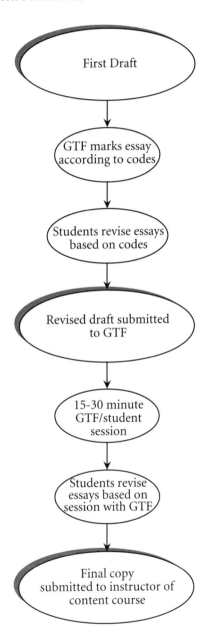

Appendix 2

SAMPLE CORRECTION CODE FOR WRITING MODULES

Developed at the University of Oregon

1. Same sound wrong character: ☐

   Example: 轻而│一│举

   Should be: 轻而易举

2. Character written wrong: ○

   Example: 中国的 ⊂乘⊃ 孩子

   Should be: 中国的乖孩子.

3. Word order: _____wo

   Example: 在全班同学中热烈地引起了讨论 wo

   Should be: 在全班同学中引起了热烈的讨论.

4. English transfer: _____Eng

   Example: 我有一小白色电脑 Eng

   Should be: 我有一个白色的小电脑

5. All kinds of grammar mistakes: 〜〜〜〜

   Example: 这件汗衫又大又是白色的.

   Should be: 这件汗衫很大，是白色的.

6. Doesn't make sense: _____?

   Example: 打孩子是我也不明白文言文？

7. Word choice: △△△△

   Example: 他的祖父 △死△ △了△ 以后。

   Should be: 他的祖父去世以后。

8. Unnecessary word/phrases: ——

   Example: 这本书和那本书是一样那么好

   Should be: 这本书和那本书是一样好

9. Missing word or phrase: ⌄‾

   Example: 我在中国学⌄。

   Should be: 我在中国学中文。

Appendix 3

SAMPLE WRITING ASSESSMENT RUBRIC

Developed by Professors R. Davis, P. Ellister, and L. de González for the Spanish program at the University of Oregon

Exceeds standard			Meets standard	Below standard	
A+	A	B	C	D	F
includes required information +3 features below	includes required information + 2 features below	includes required information + 1 feature below	includes all required information	includes most of required information	only partial or no required information
no or almost no errors	only a few minor errors	minor errors or infrequent; major errors (not repeated)	some major/minor errors	many errors	many major errors
mastery of topic, reader is impressed	shows control of topic, enjoyable to read	solid, but not exceptional control of topic, comprehensible	basic ideas expressed, comprehensible content	some incomplete ideas, partially comprehensible	many incomplete ideas, largely incomprehensible

To receive a B or higher, students should do one or more of the following:

- Go beyond basic chapter vocabulary and incorporate the expressions and vocabulary used in class.
- Provide extensive personal detail on the assigned task (not random material) OR significant cultural content.
- Demonstrate excellence in composition: organization, use of transition words, complex/compound sentences, etc.

Appendix 4

PPS Mandarin Immersion Curriculum Framework: First Grade

	A	B	C	
3	Theme	Context	Communicative Tasks & Objectives	Language Functions
	Self/Family	Classroom or other various sites Introducing main and some extended family members Daily routine	Can introduce oneself, providing detailed personal information (age, name, identity, grade, gender) Can introduce some extended family members and differentiate paternal from maternal (grandparents, uncles, aunts) Can briefly describe one's daily routine (get up, get dressed, brush teeth, etc.)	1. Introduction 2. Describing
	Friendship	Working together Playing together Making friends	Can use daily greetings Can express basic courtesy (compliments, apologies, gratitude) Can use basic questions to gather personal information from friends	1. Greeting/Courtesy 2. Asking questions 3. Describing 4. Encouragement
	School environment	School; classroom; playground	Understand basic commands Understand a student's basic responsibilities Can briefly describe a student basic daily routine	1. Permission 2. Ability 3. Describing
	Hobbies	Talking with friends and classmates Birthdays; holidays	Can briefly describe personal hobbies and interests Can describe basic abilities Can differentiate likes and dislikes	1. Likes/Dislikes 2. Ability
	Math/Time	Classroom; store, home and other sites	Can count up to 100 2. Can count by 2s to 50; 3. Can count by 5s to 100	1. Count 2. Adding/Subtracting 3. Calendar

D	E
Language Forms	(Sample) Vocabulary
1. 我叫…;我是男生（女生），不是女生（男生）；我六岁了； 2. 我的家有…个人；我是一年级的学生； 3. 爸爸的哥哥（弟弟，姐妹）叫…； 4. 我天天…	一年级，穿衣，穿鞋，穿裤子，穿袜子，穿裙子，戴帽子，吃饭，睡觉，刷牙，洗脸， 美国人，中国人，男生，女生，家，哥哥，姐姐，弟弟，妹妹，外婆，外公，公公，婆婆，伯伯，叔叔，姑姑，阿姨，起身，
1. 你们好；早上好，下午好，晚安；谢谢；再见；对不起；很好；请 2. 你叫什么名字？你几岁了？你的家有几个人？你喜欢什么？ 3. 我们一同…；我们都…； 4. 加油！	我们，你，你们，很好， 大家，一同，一起，都，笑嘻嘻，笑哈哈；快乐， 玩，看电视，玩游戏
1. 可以…，不可以…；要…，不要…；举手说话； 2. 我会…； 3. (…地方)有…，还有…；	不说话，，坐下，听讲，听写，排队，慢慢走，不要跑，读书，做功课，交功课,蜡笔，铅笔，剪刀，纸，橡皮，中文，英文 同学，老师，校长，学校，教室，礼堂，食堂，操场，书包，读书，写字，做功课，还有，上课，下课，讲故事
我爱…；我会…；我喜欢…，不喜欢…；	跳舞，玩游戏机， 唱歌，打球，玩球，玩游戏，看电视，听故事，画画，做操，跑步，
1. 数一数；数到100；两个两个地数；五个五个地数 2. 今天（昨天，明天）是星期一，…；	十，二十，三十，四十，五十，六十，七十，八十，九十，一百；星期一，星期二，星期三，星期四，星期五，星期六，星期日；早上，中午，下午

	A	B	C	
4	Holidays & Celebrations	School; classroom; home and other sites	Can name some basic objects and concepts related to Chinese holidays Can say some basic holiday greetings Can sing some basic songs related to Chinese holidays	1. Greetings 2. Describing
	Nature & Environment	Seasons; physical world	Can name some common objects in nature Can briefly describe weather changes with some basic details Can comfortably describe and differentiate basic colors Can name most farm animals and some wild animals	1. Describing 2. Comparison
	Body parts & clothing	When demonstrating body parts When describing clothing	Can name at least 20 common body parts; Can briefly describe their basic functions Can describe basic wear	1. Ability 2. Describing

D	E
1. 恭喜发财！新年快乐！ 2. 今天是…	穿新衣，发红包，放鞭炮， 包饺子，中国新年，吃月饼， 看月亮，挂灯笼，十二生肖，雪人， 新衣服，
1. 下雪了，很热（冷); …地方有…，还有…；没有… 2. …像…;	红色，绿色，黄色，蓝色，橙色， 紫色，白色，黑色，咖啡色， 粉红色，灰色，熊，熊猫，龙， 长颈鹿，… 春天，夏天，秋天，冬天 下雨，下雪，天晴，
（手）有什么用？（手）可以…; 我们用(手)…; 穿(衣，裤，鞋);	脚，手指头，脚指头，头发，脸， 脖子，舌头，肚子，屁股，手臂， 腿，眉毛；

Understanding the Culture of American Schools, and Managing the Successful Chinese Language Classroom

Leslie Schrier

University of Iowa

Part 1: Goals and Perspectives of American Education

Entering into an American high school as a foreign language teacher can be a very intimidating experience, not only for the international teacher but for American born teachers as well. The teachers most likely to be comfortable with the experience are those who are very familiar with the local community and the culture of that particular school district. The intent of this chapter is to outline the assumptions that are the basis of American schooling in general and to address specifically how these assumptions might influence the teaching of Chinese in the schools. In the first part of the chapter the goals of American education will be explained via examples from America's educational history and current national policies. In the second part of the chapter issues related to managing a foreign language classroom will be presented and illustrated for the novice Chinese language teacher.

All Schools are Different

The unique and celebrated quality of American schooling is that it is particular to the region, city or town that surrounds it. Historically, American schools were founded and financially supported by the citizens of the community. Most importantly, the immediate instructional needs that the community decided on became the curricular focus of the schools (e.g., Labaree 2004). Even today, the above elements are the foundations for public schooling in the United States.

The curriculum, the instructional plan of the schools, and the extracurricular activities, which include all forms of engagement for students from interest clubs such as those playing chess to athletics are unique to each community within the United States. The structure of American schools is tied to the American Dream, which is a very powerful concept. The premise of the American Dream is to encourage each person who lives in the United States to pursue success, and it creates the framework within which everyone can do it. It holds each person responsible for achieving his or her own dreams, while generating shared values and behaviors needed to persuade Americans that they have a real chance to achieve them. The educational system so envisioned under the premise of the American Dream, holds out a vision of both individual success and the collective good of all (Hochschild & Scovronick 2003).

Open Access

For the purposes of this chapter there will a discussion of six goals or premises which form the foundation of public schooling in the United States. The first premise, of the American education system, is open access to education. This premise is based on the idea that as many people as possible should have access to as much education as possible. This alone distinguishes the United States system, since in the majority of other countries the objective is as much to screen people out, as it is to keep them in. The U.S. system has few standardized examinations whose results systematically prevent students from going on to higher levels of study, as is true of the British system, for example. There are some well-known standardized tests, such as the SAT, ACT, TOEFL, GRE, and GMAT, but results of these tests are just one among several factors considered in college admissions decisions (for a definition of these terms, see Labaree 2004).

Throughout elementary, secondary and sometimes in postsecondary institutions, the American system tries to accommodate students even if their academic aspirations and aptitudes are not high, even if they have a physical and in some cases mental disability, and even if their native language is not English.

The idea that as many people as possible should have as much education as possible is, of course, an outcome of Americans' assumptions about equality among people, which is part of the American Dream. These assumptions do not mean, however, that everyone has an equal opportunity to enter Harvard, Stanford, or other highly competitive postsecondary institutions. Admission to such institutions is generally restricted to the most academically able. The other, 80 percent of the population has a wide variety of very attractive postsecondary institutions from which to select.

As of March 2000, more than 98 percent of all Americans aged 25 or older had completed at least five years of elementary school (in the American system, elementary school usually lasts from ages 5 to 10, middle school or junior high, from ages 11 to 13, and high school, from ages 14 to 18). Eighty-four percent of those 25 or older had completed four years of high school or beyond, and 26 percent had completed a bachelor's degree or more (National Center for Educational Statistics 2000). Compare this with the United Nations Educational Scientific and Cultural Organization (UNESCO) data and the number of tertiary (that is postsecondary) students per 100,000 inhabitants was 5.34 percent in 2006. In no other country was the number of postsecondary students above 5 percent per 100,000. Spain was the closest with 4.25 percent tertiary students per 100,000 inhabitants and Ethiopia the lowest with .0074 percent (www.unesco.org/academia/schooling). UNESCO did not survey Asian countries.

Naturally, an educational system that retains as many people as the American system does, is likely to enroll a broader range of students than a system that seeks to educate only the few who seem especially suited for academic work. In the American system, academic rigor tends to come later than in most other systems. In many instances American students do not face demanding educational requirements until they seek a graduate (that is, post baccalaureate) degree. In contrast, many other systems place heavy demands on students as early as their primary years-though college may be far less demanding as in the case of Japan (e.g., Shimahara & Sakai 1995).

WHAT DOES THIS MEAN FOR THE CHINESE TEACHER?

Universal access to education means that foreign language teachers will have students from a variety of socio-economic backgrounds in their classes. Further, these students will have different educational goals; some will be highly academically motivated and some will not; some will be highly conscious of the social realities of education and some will not, but most will have a variety of reasons for studying Chinese. It is up to the teachers to discover what the motivations for studying Chinese are and to design a curriculum that meets the needs of their particular student body. Only when there is a good match between the students' needs and goals for study and instruction will meaningful Chinese language learning take place. Do not assume all of the students enrolled to study Chinese will be equally motivated to succeed.

The Ideal of Universal Literacy

The second premise underlying the American educational system is that of producing a society that is 100 percent literate. All states in the United States (remember that in America, education is governed by state and local authorities, not by the national government, as will be explained below) have compulsory attendance laws that require young people to attend school until a specified age (16 in the majority of states, 17 or 18 in others). The goal of 100 percent literacy has yet to be achieved, and may never be achieved, but it remains the stated goal (NCLB 2000).

WHAT DOES THIS MEAN FOR THE CHINESE TEACHER?

For the Chinese teacher this means that it is quite possible to have students in the elementary levels of foreign language instruction who do not have a complete ability to read in English (or their first language). When introducing the Chinese characters, teachers should remember that this lack of first language literacy might have a negative effect on the student's success in reading Chinese (see Everson, Literacy Development in Chinese as a Foreign Language, this volume).

Local control

The third premise of the American educational system is based on the ideal of local control. The United States has no national ministry of education. There is a U.S. Department of Education, but it has no power over individual schools[1]. State departments of education have some influence over the curriculum of primary and secondary schools whether they are public (that is, supported by taxes) or private (supported by tuition and other non-governmental sources). Local bodies, however, bear the main responsibility for guiding educational institutions. Public primary and secondary schools are under the general directions of bodies that are usually called boards of education or school boards. Members of these school boards' are elected by the public to represent the community. These school boards hire and fire administrators, oversee the curriculum of the schools in their jurisdiction, and review teacher performance. A school district may be no larger than one city or county. Additionally, each state has many school districts for example the small rural state of Iowa has over 500 school districts.

How a school district functions can be of great concern in local politics. A well-run district with safe and clean schools, graduating students who are able to attend universities and technical schools, can enhance the value of housing in its area, and thus increase the amount of tax revenue available to carry out its operations. Conversely, a poorly run district may cause growth in the area to be far less than surrounding areas, or even create a decline in a population and hence not

---

[1]The US Department of Education has the ability to increase or decrease federal funding for only one aspect of education within local control and that relates to subsidizing meals (breakfast, snacks, and lunch) for economically disadvantaged youth. The funding for meals can be dependent on the districts' or individual schools' performance on standardized examinations; however, the federal government does not frequently enforce this policy.

generate enough tax revenue to support the needs of the schools. In addition to the various schools it operates and the numerous support facilities they require for their operation, such as school bus yards, laundries, warehouses, and kitchens, some very large school districts even have medical clinics, television stations, and some have fully functioning campus police departments. Additionally, it is not unusual to find public libraries or recreational programs operated by a school system. Still it is important to remember at all levels of education, standards are set and maintained by regional accrediting associations that the schools subscribe to, not by the United States government.

WHAT DOES THIS MEAN FOR THE CHINESE TEACHER?

Few if any countries have educational systems as thoroughly decentralized as that found in the United States. Many Chinese teachers have difficulty comprehending the fact that so much control over educational matters rests at the local level and that there is no national body empowered to override local decisions.

Frequently for example, all decisions regarding textbook selection, extra-curricular activities (such as going to see a Chinese exhibit at a museum) and participation in national examinations such as Advance Placement exams, must be presented to the local school board, either by the teacher or the teacher's immediate superior. Hence, it is very important for Chinese teachers to understand what the local goal for foreign language instruction is, because it is at the local level where funding for sustaining foreign language programs lies. Without local support, programs can be terminated.

Parental Involvement

The fourth premise for many primary and secondary schools is the idealization of parental involvement in children's education. Schools encourage parents to become acquainted with the facilities and with their children's teachers, to talk to their children about what happens in school, and to confer and work together with the teachers should a child encounter any difficulty that interferes with his or her academic progress or social adjustment (more on this in the second part of the chapter).

Schools often have "back-to-school nights" at the beginning of the school year to give parents the opportunity to visit the school, meet the teachers, and learn about the curriculum. Throughout the academic year, schools send printed information and have updated webpages on the Internet so parents are informed about school activities. Periodic parent-teacher conferences are intended to give parents the opportunity to talk with their children's teachers.

Parents normally expect to help their children with homework, keep track of their children's assignments and important school-related deadlines, and attend athletic competitions, music performances, and theatrical productions in which they participate. Parents may even be asked to chaperone their children's field trips or volunteer in some other way. This call for parental involvement may seem odd to international teachers where education is considered the teachers' business, not a process in which parents have a special and very active role.

WHAT DOES THIS MEAN FOR THE CHINESE TEACHER?

The novice Chinese teacher should make a special effort to present an open and willing partnership with the parents of the students in the Chinese program (see Part II for examples). This connection is helpful in gaining support for the program from the people who have the most influence on the success or failure of foreign language programs, the parents.

Productive versus Receptive Learning

The fifth premise of American schooling is the assumption Americans make about the basic nature of knowledge and learning. The premise is that only a certain part of all that is potentially knowable is already known (Kliebard, 1989). Scholars and students, mainly advanced scholars and graduate students work at the "frontiers of knowledge" to discover new information or to conceive innovative ways of understanding or interpreting what is already known. Learning at all levels is thus considered not just a process of memorizing as much as one can of a more or less fixed body of knowledge that already exists in books and in scholars' minds. Learning is viewed as an enterprise of exploration, experimentation, analysis, and synthesis, processes that students engage in along with their teachers and professors. The ideal educational situation is, therefore, one in which students are learning the skills of analysis and synthesis and are applying those skills to the process of discovering knowledge for themselves, a very independent process. Another way of saying this is that Americans tend to view education as a productive activity, whereas people raised in many other societies conceive of education process as a receptive activity (e.g., Kohls 2001; Kohls & Knight 1994).

WHAT DOES THIS MEAN FOR THE CHINESE TEACHER?

This view of the educational process reflects the value Americans place on individualism and equality, namely, the propensity to "question authority." Students at all levels are encouraged to think for themselves, which can entail questioning or even challenging a teacher. For Americans, questioning a teacher or other authority figure is normally viewed as a good thing, showing that the student is developing critical thinking skills. For people from many other societies, such as China, however, this behavior may be viewed negatively and be seen as disrespectful of older people, people in authority, or even tradition itself.

Novice Chinese teachers need mentoring which helps them confront the challenges placed before them by parents, students, and others in the school community. Proper communication with these groups will determine how supportive they will be towards the demanding nature of learning the Chinese language. It is important for the new foreign language teachers to respond competently and warmly to the questions asked of them, to encourage learning in a productive manner and not merely in a receptive manner. An interactive curriculum design will go along way in answering these challenges (for examples of this type of curriculum, see Blaz 1999, 2002).

The Final Goal: Well-Rounded People

Lastly, the American educational system seeks to turn out "well-rounded people" (Larabee 2004). Such people might have specialized knowledge in some areas, but they are all expected to have a general acquaintance with many disciplines. Having passed through a system that requires them to study some mathematics, English, humanities, science, social science and a little foreign language, the average American student presumably has an array of interests. Thus, again, specialization in the American system comes later than it does in many other educational systems. Students are required to take courses that they might not be particularly interested in and that may appear to have little relationship to their career aspirations.

WHAT DOES THIS MEAN FOR THE CHINESE TEACHER?

Being well rounded also means participating in non-academic "extracurricular" activities in and out of school. Young people are continuously reminded that they will be more attractive to college and graduate admissions officers and to prospective employers if they participate in school clubs, sports, or community activities. So the learning of Chinese must include this concept of being well rounded. Isolating the Chinese language learning from the overall intent of the American educational system will not allow it to grow and flourish in the schools; however, encompassing the process of learning Chinese within the final educational assumption of well roundedness will help it grow in the schools (see Blaz 2002 for examples).

Current Issues Facing American schools

In America, when a problem is too hard for adults, we pass it on to the schools
Patricia Graham, 1996.

Because of the open nature of schooling and the fact that public schools are supported by citizens' tax dollars, and because schools and their curricula are social institutions, there are continuing controversies about one issue or another. Some of these issues discussed in the press confront only primary or secondary schools; some confront only postsecondary institutions. Some touch institutions at all levels. Collated below are summary statements of recurrent controversial issues that the schools are generally facing:

- Should primary and secondary schools allow students to pray to a Supreme Being during the school day?
- Should particular books (usually famous novels) that contain profane or sex-related language, "adult themes," or violence be assigned in classes or be available in school libraries?
- Can religious symbols be used in school activities related to holidays, especially Christmas and Easter, which have religious origins?
- What should students be taught about the origin of humankind; specifically, should they be taught the theory that humankind evolved from "lower animals" or the theory that a Supreme Being created humankind?
- What should students be taught about American history; specifically, how should the place of non-whites and women be portrayed in the story of the country's past? This conflict comes under the rubric of multicultural education.
- What measures can appropriately be taken to assure that schools in poorer school districts offer facilities and opportunities reasonably similar to those offered in wealthier areas.
- What measures, if any, should be taken to accommodate students who are not native speakers of English and may not be able to use English well or not at all?
- What is the proper balance between general education and specialized training intended to prepare students to work in particular fields?
- Should female secondary school students be allowed to participate on athletic teams (such as football and wrestling) that are traditionally all male?
- What is the proper balance between providing special assistance for students with special needs (for example, students with learning disabilities, physical limitations, or English language limitations) and "mainstreaming" them (that is, incorporating them into regular classrooms and school activities)?
- Does sexual inclusion education privilege gay, lesbian, and transsexual political agendas?

Schools are blamed, at least by some people, for many of the problems or failures of society in general, and they are often called upon to add one concern or another to their curriculum in order to remedy perceived social problems. Thus, schools may be asked to address matters such as values and ethics, conflict resolution, racial integration, preserving the environment, world peace, sex education, and health and fitness. In most other countries issues such as these would be placed not so much in the domain of the schools as in those of the family, religious organizations, political parties, or some other social institution.

The American system's decentralization serves to insulate educational institutions from national political entanglements and to give citizens some voice in what happens in their local schools. Schools can modify their curricula to accommodate needs and conditions that pertain only to their own areas. On the other hand, this decentralization makes it relatively easy for an outspoken and committed minority in a given community to embroil local schools in controversy and also makes it possible for particular schools to maintain low standards if they wish or feel compelled to do so.

The American educational system, like any other, is integrally related to the values and assumptions of the society that surrounds it. American ideas about equality, individualism, and freedom underlie the US educational system. Whatever its advantages and disadvantages, the system will retain its current general characteristics as long as the values and assumptions that predominate in the surrounding society continue to hold sway.

Part II: Managing the Classroom: Achieving Success in the Chinese Language Teaching Experience

For all classroom teachers, no matter what the grade level, developing the skills to allow learning to take place in a positive instructional environment is often the most challenging aspect in the profession. In this section, suggestions will be offered to help novice Chinese language teachers understand the concept of managing their instructional environment. The ideas presented have been proven successful for the majority of language teachers in a variety of instructional settings; however, there are a few common keys to success in working with American students and developing a successful foreign language program (e.g. Emmer et al. 2002). These axioms have been previously mentioned; nevertheless, it is necessary to repeat them because they are crucial in developing a successful program.

- Know the culture of the school and its students.
- Be very familiar with school building policies related to academic policies and disciplinary procedures.
- Develop a realistic language-learning curriculum.

Previously, it has been explained that having knowledge of what is commonly expected for a foreign language teacher in the school is crucial for the success of the

Chinese language program, and establishing a curriculum which reflects common language learning goals as well as reasonable learning outcomes will help 90 percent of the time in developing a good language learning atmosphere. The lack of clear expectations on the part of both the teacher and students will lead to frustration with learning, and frustration is often the number one cause of class disruptions. It is imperative for Chinese teachers to establish clear and reasonable goals for language learning as well as a very clear code of conduct for the students in their classroom. Most importantly, like everything else in American schooling, every school district and every school building has its own unique set expectations, and the novice teacher should become very familiar with these policies. In Appendix A, there is an example of a school building policy. Using this building policy as a model the following guidelines are presented and exemplified to help the novice teacher create the best classroom environment for Chinese language learning.

Establish Classroom Rules

GENERAL STUDENT EXPECTATIONS

Teachers will communicate their specific classroom expectations to students at the start of the school year/trimesters. The student will be expected to exhibit appropriate classroom behaviors as outlined by each classroom teacher. All students are expected to….(See Appendix A for complete example.)

As shown in Appendix A, most school building policies expect the classroom teacher to have from the very first day of school a list of expectations for student conduct and responsibilities that are unique to the teacher, the physical classroom, and the subject matter taught; yet this list must be in concert with the overall school policy. In order to have classroom rules be informed by practice, it is very important for the novice teachers to have a firm idea of how they wish to see their classroom develop into a positive learning experience. To accomplish this, it is crucial for novice teachers to create opportunities for observation of different Chinese language classrooms; however, if it is impossible to observe actual K–12 Chinese language teaching environments, make an opportunity to visit other foreign language classrooms. These informed observations are vital for understanding the organization and management issues central to teaching in American schools.

In Appendix B there is an example of one preservice teacher's reflections after spending 10 weeks observing and co-teaching in two different Chinese language classrooms[3]. In this reflection, the novice teacher was able to demonstrate how essential it is to conceptualize how she wanted the atmosphere of her classes to positively affect the learning of Chinese. It is not the purpose of this section to

---

[3]Names of schools, instructors and preservice teachers have been changed to ensure anonymity.

present a set list of classroom rules, because every situation is unique and every teacher is different, but what can be given is these four general guides to help the novice teachers establish their own list. Please understand the teacher MUST establish a list BEFORE beginning the first day of instruction.

GUIDELINES FOR DEVELOPING YOUR LIST

1. How do you want me to treat you?
2. How do you want to treat one another?
3. How do you think I want to be treated?
4. How should we treat one another when there's a conflict? (See Appendix B for example)

When the teacher has established the list of rules, remember it is necessary for the teacher to be consistent in enforcing the rules; inconsistency leads to problems.

Be Friendly but Firm. Act Confident!

The importance of developing a curriculum for Chinese instruction that is age appropriate and engaging for the students cannot be underestimated. When the teacher has spent the time developing a good pedagogical curriculum, it should be executed with confidence and enthusiasm: additionally it should demand equal enthusiasm from the students.

The teacher should start the class by beginning the instruction promptly at the sound of the bell, have a common greeting such as 上課 or 早 which signals to all of the students to stop personal conversations, pay attention to the teacher, and begin Chinese language instruction. Remember to approach all instruction with enthusiasm and vigor. Good-spirited teaching is infectious, and the teacher should want the students to be inspired to learn Chinese. If the teacher is ill tempered, how could it be expected that the students will be good learners? It is up to the teacher to model a positive attitude towards learning by exhibiting a true enthusiasm for teaching.

Be prepared to teach the lesson, and then the students will be prepared. Know the material before attempting to teach it. Present what is expected for the day's lesson on the chalkboard, webpage, or LCD screen in advance of the class. This is a form of accountability for the teacher as well as the students. The teacher should have lesson plans prepared in advance of the class and have all the teaching supplies ready. Classroom disruptions occur when the teacher has to search for materials. The teacher must not give the class the opportunity to let students' attention drift. Being on task and engaged in the learning process gives the students little opportunity to misbehave; so as the teacher, it is necessary to be on task and prepared as well. Be a model for the students.

With the mental preparation for class accomplished, there is also the physical side of teaching that requires mastering. Teaching is physically exhausting, especially if it is done well, so be physically fit. First, if the physical classroom setup allows, always move around the room because this motion keeps the students responsible for their own physical actions. It is very hard, for example to pass a note, eat potato chips, or text message, when the teacher might be looking over the students' shoulder at any moment.

If the teacher must stand in front of the classroom, learn "to ride the class" with your eyes. This technique takes practice; think of the class as a road on which you are driving your car and in order to pay attention to the road and traffic you need to constantly move your eyes. To ride a classroom with your eyes, teachers need to develop very good peripheral vision, because a good teachers should be able to see all the students all of the time, without moving their head! If you can't see all of the students, either move them or move yourself. Keeping eye contact with the students is very important as it lets them know you expect them to pay attention to the lesson and to you: further, it lets the class feel that the teacher knows what she is doing. It inspires confidence. Constantly looking down at notes or at the textbook will not create the confident atmosphere that is necessary while, projecting poise as a teacher helps to keep the pace moving in the lesson. To help accomplish this atmosphere, rarely sit during a lesson; if the teacher must sit down, she should sit amongst the students as it keeps them on their best behavior.

Additionally, the teacher's voice quality is important for effective classroom management. When you speak, speak to all of the students, not just one student, and if asking for an individual student to answer a question, ask the student to address his or her response to the entire class. The teacher must make sure that his or her voice is measured in volume; make sure it is loud enough for the entire class to hear and yet not too loud to be offensive to neighboring classrooms. If the teacher's voice is too soft, the class will lose interest in the lesson. However, never yell at the class. If the teacher must exhibit anger or frustration with class behavior, speak quietly and with much control; this tends to draw attention to the speaker in a more positive way. Again this technique takes practice.

How teachers call on students to participate is important, as are their physical movements. Ask the question before calling on the student. If a student appears to be losing interest in a lesson, ask the question and then call on the drifting student. Remember that teachers want students to experience success in the classroom and not be embarrassed; this is why it is important to ask the question before you call on the student. For example:

Teacher: Class, where is Hong Kong located? (Out of the corner of your eye you see Suzie starting to do her Algebra assignment.)

> Teacher: Suzie, please come to the map and point out to the class where Hong Kong is located.

Encourage the class to attempt to answer questions silently whether they have been called on or not. This technique holds all students responsible for what takes place during the class period. If in the above example, Suzie does not know where Hong Kong is, then handle it in this manner.

> Teacher: Wayne, will you show Suzie where Hong Kong is?

> Wayne accompanies Suzie to the map and points out the correct location of the former British colony.

By giving students multiple opportunities to "help" another student learn, it creates a collective community of learners, which encourages participation and does not privilege those students who learn easily. It is also important to call on students in a random manner rather than by rows. This really demands that all students be prepared to answer all questions at a given time.

Most importantly, novice teachers need to learn to feel the pulse of the class. By the fifth week of teaching, a teacher should be able to feel when changes need to be made to a lesson. For example, there is no need to spend ten minutes on an activity if the students obviously do not need the practice. At other times, however, a teacher may need to spend ten extra minutes on an exercise that he or she expected to do move more quickly. Be flexible and have a variety of activities to teach the same concept. It is important to understand that all students and classes learn differently.

Learn to Control the Classroom

A language teacher needs to develop a set of "influence techniques" which are sometimes paralinguistic and are used within teaching a lesson and must be developed in advance of actual need. These influence techniques are imbedded in skillful teaching so an uninformed observer would never be overtly aware that the teacher is controlling an individual student or a group of students who might be on the verge of misbehaving. The first technique is vocal and physical, but it is really a paralinguistic clue that lets an individual know that the teacher is aware of potential misbehavior. For example, the teacher notices a student is trying to unwrap a piece of candy underneath the desk (you notice this because you are moving around during the lesson- good for you!). So as not to draw too much attention to the potential breaking of a classroom rule, you shake your head and clear your throat "ahum!" at the same time. The clever teacher can execute this influence on the student without drawing the entire class's attention to the potential misdeed.

If the throat clearing and head shaking action does not have a deterring affect, stare at the culprit. It is really paramount for a teacher to develop a stare, and this is a technique you need to practice in front of the mirror. My favorite teacher in high school had the capacity to just stare at a student to command respect and get cooperation. This is again a technique that you need to develop; it does not necessarily come naturally. Scowling in front of the mirror may not be good for wrinkle prevention, but it is highly recommended to prevent potential miscreants from dominating the class.

If the above signals do not work, try what is called proximity control. An effective teacher can continue with a lesson and walk over and stand near the misbehaving student. Usually the proximity of the teacher to the student makes the student uncomfortable enough to stop the misbehavior or lessen the effect of potential misdeeds. If further action is necessary, take an interest in what the distraction is; if the student is secretly showing off a new cell phone, for example, go over to the student and ask to see it, admire the phone and then ask if you can call their parents on it to explain to them how their son or daughter is being distracted from learning by using the new phone. Do this with a smile and good humor, and this technique will keep the student guessing as to whether or not you are serious; it will also give them the opportunity to right their action without further interference, hopefully. If influence techniques do not stop the misbehavior, it is time to take assertive action, and this is usually most effective between student and teacher on a one-to-one basis.

How to Confront Misbehavior

Unfortunately there are students for whom the influence techniques described above have little to no effect. It becomes necessary to be assertive with chronic rule breakers. Try a two-step approach with these students. First, speak with the students outside of class; it is always best to confront the student(s) who misbehaves away from the entire class. It allows them to save face. So isolate the student(s) by asking them to talk with you either immediately after the class, before or after school or during a free period. Whichever works, it is important to speak with the culprits away from the rest of the class.

Imagine this scenario: After the first two weeks of school it is evident that there is a group of girls who just cannot stop talking amongst themselves when you are trying to teach. You have tried a variety of influence techniques in class. They work for a short while, but inevitably the girls resume their chatter. Ask the girls to come to your classroom after school.

Group the girls together in their usual seats in the classroom and speak to them very directly about why you have asked them to your classroom. For example: "I have asked you to stay after school today because I'm very concerned with the behavior in the 5th period class. I had to stop class three times today because of your loud talking. Your classmates cannot learn, and I cannot teach when noise interferes with students listening to Chinese. Your constant talking without permission breaks our classroom rules, and it cannot go on anymore. I would like us to work out a solution to this problem. Do you think we can?"

The above scenario is very constructive in nature, but it is assertive. The teacher describes her concerns clearly, insisting that misbehavior be corrected, and ends with an effort to engage both the teacher and the students to problem-solve together to reach a satisfactory conclusion. The first step to problem solve in this situation is to change where the girls sit. Hopefully the lack of proximity will inhibit their need to constantly talk without permission.

Remember when you must deal harshly with a student make an effort to reestablish rapport. Always keep in mind that you are the adult, the teacher, the individual who is responsible to create an atmosphere that encourages learning and your students are young, and in their youth they will test your limits and respond to firmness that is fair, not arbitrary nor mean spirited. Your students will make mistakes and so will you, but the teacher is the adult and has a very powerful responsibility to guide positively towards developing self-discipline in adolescents. Remember even though you are teaching Chinese, a subject, most importantly you are teaching young people, and remember they are young and require guidance and not unreasoned punishment. Be prompt with your disciplinary actions, be consistent and reasonable, and you will have little problems with classroom management.

Working with Parents

More and more frequently, an additional challenge in teaching is also working with your students' parents or caregivers. It is important to set the right tone with your students' parents from the first day of classes. I have included a sample letter that you could modify for your teaching situation and send to your students' parents (see Appendix C). As you can see from this letter, it allows the teacher to inform the parents how they can work in concert with him or her to set a positive atmosphere for learning. Especially given the fact that the majority of parents want the absolute best for their child, they want to know how they can help as well as what your expectations are for their children. Moreover, if it is necessary to contact the parent about a concern, approach parents as team members, especially since you have set the tone by sending the letter to them at the beginning of school. Then if there is an academic or behavioral concern that is serious enough for the parents to be informed, approach the situation in the following manner.

Work with the assumption that both you and the parents want what's best for the child; the point of the meeting is to find ways to work together and positively solve the problem. Remember that you need to set the tone for the meeting by being respectful of the parents' knowledge of their children and show your appreciation for the parents' efforts to rearrange work schedules to meet with you. Use the time wisely by being prepared and organized. Be aware, however, that teachers may intimidate parents who had difficulty themselves in school. This can be demonstrated by avoidance (parent constantly cancels the meeting), anger (parent is resentful of being called by a teacher), or by being defensive (parent makes unreasonable excuses for the student). When discussing a behavioral problem, stick to descriptions of behavior rather than characterizations of students. For example, "Mike calls other children names," rather than "Mike is mean". If the issue is academic, always document your concerns. For example, if the student has not been completing his or her homework, have the assignment book and worksheets samples available to show the parents.

Always assume that you and the parents can work together to problem solve the situation. Here is a scenario and a solution for working with a parent to help a student be a better and more responsible learner.

> Suzie Smith is a bright student but often turns in work late, and frequently it is incomplete. She is able to pass your tests, however, she could easily be a top student if she were prompt and better organized. Recently you sent her parents a progress report because of missing assignments, and Suzie and her mother have come in for a conference to discuss the situation. As things now stand, Suzie will fail your course this grading period. Her mother wonders whether you will allow Suzie to make up the missing work in order to avoid the failing mark.

The teacher, Ms. Lee, illustrates Suzie's problem with examples of her incomplete work and exams and has identified the problem and its consequences clearly to the girl's mother. Mrs. Smith shares with Ms. Lee that Suzie is in the school play and the practice schedule frequently goes late in the evening, which hasn't allowed Suzie time at home to do homework before she falls asleep. Both Mrs. Smith and Ms. Lee have identified the problem and select a solution. If school policy allows, perhaps Ms. Lee can allow Suzie to make-up or re-do her assignments but not the exams. Ms. Lee does have the option of assigning Suzie to an extra study hall to see that she completes her homework before play practice. Mrs. Smith, Ms. Lee and Suzie then talk together and obtain a commitment from Suzie to work harder in study hall and see if this changes her academic performance for the better.

Conclusion

Researchers have found that successful Chinese language programs in the schools encompass knowledge of the community and cultures of the schools in which they are housed (Moore, Walton & Lambert 1992; Schrier & Everson1999). If the novice Chinese language teachers take the time to familiarize themselves with local conditions of schooling and academic expectations of the student body, it will go a long way to insure the success of Chinese language teaching. Teachers should always remember that they are teachers not only of the Chinese language but first and foremost of students who are young impressionable adolescents. If they remember this, then success will follow.

Questions for Discussion

The following questions are designed for groups of two or three students. Participants are encouraged to share responses and experiences and if possible include in the discussion groups native speakers, non-native speakers and Heritage Speakers of Chinese.

1. Review the 6 premises of American schooling. Divide a paper into two columns and create a compare and contrast list of the goals of American schooling and those in China. What type of students do these goals of education create? How will it affect their ability to learn foreign languages?
2. Are you familiar with the variety of standardized tests found in the America schools? What do the initials NCLB stand for? What are the ACT and SAT exams? Did you know that the AP exam is not related to college admittance? What does the Advanced Placement exam allow the successful Chinese student to do? Can you name the tests American college graduates take to gain entrance to graduate schools?
3. As a novice teacher in a school, where would you find the local goals for foreign language instruction? The state standards for foreign language instruction? How will you incorporate them into your teaching?
4. When you have your first "back to school night"how would you discover which parents or caregivers have Chinese language backgrounds? Create a list of 5 ways to involve Chinese-speaking parents in your program.
5. Controlling a classroom of adolescents is always a challenge. List the rules you need to be familiar with before you begin your class. For example, where are you to find what the school building policy is on student behavior? How will you find out which administrator is in charge of student discipline?
6. For the final activity, create a set of classroom rules modeled on those of Yunghung Hsiao's classroom. Making sure that your rules reflect the values you have for Chinese learning and most importantly for the students you will teach.

References

Blaz, D. 1999. *Foreign language teacher's guide to active learning.* Larchmont, NY: Eye on Education.

Blaz, D. 2002. *Bringing the standards for foreign language learning to life.* Larchmont, NY: Eye on Education.

Emmer, E., C. M. Evertson, B. S. Clements, and M. E. Worsham. 2002. *Classroom manage-ment for secondary teachers.* 6th ed. Boston: Allyn & Bacon.

Graham, Patricia A. 1996. *S.O.S.: Sustain our schools.* New York: Hill & Wang.

Hochschild, J. L., and N. Scovronick. 2003. *The American dream and the public schools.* New York: Oxford UP.

Kohls, L. R. 2001 *Survival kit for overseas living for Americans planning to live and work abroad.* Boston: Intercultural Press.

Kohls, L. R., and J. M. Knight. 1994. *Developing intercultural awareness.* Intercultural Press: Boston.

Kliebard, H. M. 1986. *The struggle for the American curriculum 1893–1958.* Boston: Routledge.

Labaree, D. 2004 *The trouble with ed schools.* New Haven: Yale UP.

Moore, S. J., A. R. Walton, and R. D. Lambert. 1992. *Introducing Chinese into High Schools: The Dodge Initiative.* Washington DC: NFLC.

National Center for Educational Statistics. 2000. School level correlates with educational achievement. Washington DC: U.S. Department of Education.

Schrier, L. L., and M. E. Everson. 1999. From the margins to the new millennium: Preparing teachers of critical languages. In *Reflecting on the past to shape the future,* ed. D. Birckbichler and R. Terry, 125–161. Lincolnwood, IL: National Textbook.

Shimahara, Nobuo K., and Akira Sakai. 1995. *Learning to teach in two cultures: Japan and the United States.* Garland Publishing: New York.

UNESCO educational survey (n.d.) Retrieved August 8, 2007 from www.unesco.org/academia/schooling.

Appendix A: General Student Expectations[2]

Teachers will communicate their specific classroom expectations to students at the start of the school year/trimester. The student will be expected to exhibit appropriate classroom behaviors as outlined by each classroom teacher. All students are expected to:

1. Make school attendance a priority. Consistent and prompt attendance in every class is critical for successful academic performance.
    a. An unexcused absence will result in no credit for class work that day.
    b. For pre-excused/school-related absences students should have work for the day completed prior to being excused. The student should be prepared to take a quiz, test, or submit an assignment should it fall on the day of his/her return to school.
    c. The tardy policy will be enforced by each classroom teacher.

---

[2]These student expectations are an example of many found in school district handbooks and websites across the United States, This particular example is from the Iowa City Community School District, West High School, http://www.iccsd.k12.ia.us/Schools/West/handbook/studentexpectations.html.

2. Be prepared for and participate in class.
    a. Report to class prior to the tardy bell with pen/pencil, paper, text, notebook/folder, and other materials related to the class.
    b. Complete homework in a neat and legible manner.
    c. Achieve maximum performance in class through effort, attitude, and daily attendance. Sleeping is not permitted in any classroom. Items which inhibit maximum academic effort will not be allowed.
    d. Items which inhibit maximum academic effort will not be allowed. CD or MP3 players may not be turned on nor headsets worn during class. Pagers, beepers, portable/cellular telephones, and other similar communication devices are prohibited during school hours and may be confiscated. Cell phones may be used in the main or west wing office for emergency calls.
3. Respect other people and their property.
    a. At all times the student should act with courtesy toward teachers, staff members, and students. Both their actions and words should reflect such courtesy.
    b. The student is responsible for keeping all school property (books, classroom materials) in good condition.
4. Carry a student ID card.
    a. All students will be required to carry a West High ID card with them while in school and at school events. The ID card must be presented to check out books and to use computer resources.
    b. The ID also doubles as an activity card for students who purchase an activity pass.
    c. Replacement cards cost $5.00

This page was last updated on August 11, 2007.

Appendix B: Classroom Management

CLASSROOM MANAGEMENT FOR HIGH SCHOOL STUDENTS[4]

I have finished my practicum in two different high schools, Central High School, in a large city in Iowa and New Money High School, North Shore, Illinois. In these places I observed not only my cooperating teachers' vivid Chinese-language teaching strategies, but also their effective ways of managing classrooms.

---

[4]Many thanks to Yunghung Hsiao (Sandra) of Indian Trail Academy, Kenosha, Wisconsin, for allowing the use of her materials.

I discovered that the two teachers focus on encouraging students rather than pushing the students too hard while learning Chinese. Also, the two teachers think that high school students are able to control their behaviors. However, in my view, although high school students are not children any more, they still need to have clear behavioral principles to help them get more involved in their classrooms. Therefore, I decided to write some classroom guidelines for my future high school students.

Rule/Practice	Rationale
Prepare well before and after class.	Students should pay attention and take notes during each Chinese class period. Also, students should go over class materials at home before the instructor teaches new lessons.
Participate in class.	Students should participate in class, such as reading texts with peers.
Ask questions!	The teacher encourages students to ask questions. Therefore, if students have difficulties in understanding the language of Chinese, they should not hesitate or feel shy to ask the questions in or after class.
Work on self-confidence and self-esteem.	In this Chinese class, the teacher encourages each student to work on self-confidence and self-esteem while speaking Chinese.
Hand in assignments on time.	During each class the teacher will assign take-home studies for each student, and everyone should hand it in by the due date.
No other subjects!	Students might be busy with other subjects, but they cannot read other subjects in this Chinese-language class.
Focus on films.	In this Chinese class, the teacher will show Chinese movies to make the class more interesting. While watching the films, students should remain silent; in other words, students cannot chat with their classmates.
Use computers in the school lab.	The teacher will adopt computer programs in class in order to show Chinese characters, and students are very welcome to use these programs to do their assignments or group projects. In addition, the instructor encourages students to use CD-ROMs in the school computer lab to improve their Chinese pronunciation.
Get permission.	Students should get permission from the Chinese-language teacher when they need to leave their classroom or to do something else during the class periods.
No food in class periods.	Perhaps some students are used to eating snacks in other classes. However, in this Chinese class, students are not allowed to eat.
No passing notes in class.	Students cannot pass notes to each other during the Chinese class periods.
Apply the knowledge of Chinese to daily situations.	Students should try to apply the knowledge of Chinese to their actual life situations, such as making a short conversation in Chinese among peers or establishing a Chinese club at school

GENERAL CLASSROOM RULES FOR ELEMENTARY SCHOOL STUDENTS[5]

According to many studies, students can learn better within a quiet classroom atmosphere, perhaps because students stay more focused on class materials. In a noisy classroom students might be distracted while learning because of the environment. Therefore, how to properly manage a classroom is crucial for each teacher.

I currently teach students to speak Chinese every Saturday morning. The age levels of my students range from kindergarten through fifth grade. Perhaps because of such young age levels, my students often misbehave in class; for example, they are overly talkative. Also, because of diverse backgrounds among my students, I have to manage my classroom very carefully in order to avoid hurting a student's feelings or causing an unfair situation to occur for him/her.

Recently I held a parent-teacher conference in which the parents and I talked about not only the students' progress in Chinese language learning, but also their classroom behavior. The following rules were discussed and agreed upon among the parents and me in our meeting. I think that most of the following rules might be applied to a general Chinese-language classroom in a public elementary school as well.

Rule/Practice	Rationale
Pay Attention!	In class, students should pay attention to the Chinese-language teacher and focus on their texts, so they will learn best.
Watch Chinese Movies.	The teacher hopes to establish a fun and interesting Chinese-language learning environment in which students will watch Chinese movies or other visual aid programs. For this reason, students should keep quiet while enjoying these programs.
Sing Chinese songs	In order to enhance students' interest in learning Chinese, the instructor will teach the students to sing Chinese songs, which have the same tunes as American ones. Each student should sing the songs aloud in class.
Prepare Arts and Crafts	Because many Chinese characters are pictographic, the instructor will teach students to recognize Chinese characters by paper cutting. Or, the instructor will teach students to do some paper crafts in order to help students better memorize Chinese characters or phrases. Therefore, students are responsible for bringing their own art materials to class, if the teacher has earlier informed them to do so.
Turn in Homework	Each week the teacher will assign a bit of homework for practice, and students should turn in their homework on time. In addition, students should be honest with the teacher, if they did not finish their homework.
Ask Questions!	Chinese is a foreign language, so students should try to ask questions in class, when they do not understand class materials. Moreover, students should raise their hands before asking questions.

---

[5]Based on Yunghung Hsiao's current teaching experience, these guidelines are specifically for K–5.

Rule/Practice	Rationale
Keep a Sense of Humor!	Chinese might be hard for some students because of its non-alphabetic writing system and special pronunciation. For this reason, students should try to keep a sense of humor when they mispronounce a Chinese word or phrase, instead of being embarrassed.
Respect Each Other	Everyone is an individual, so students should be nice and respect each other. Moreover, students should accept different cultures among classmates. They should be aware that there will be no tolerance for aggression toward a culture in class.
Appreciate Different Opinions	Students are very welcome to express their own opinions. When a student gives an answer in class, the rest of the class should appreciate this student's answer, even though this student's opinions might be quite different from others. Furthermore, students cannot make fun of their classmates' answers.
No Name-Calling	Everyone has his/her own name in English and Chinese. Therefore, students should call their classmates by their Chinese or English names properly and politely. Students cannot tease any of their classmates in class; there will be no name-calling.
Put away toys.	During each class period, students cannot play with their own toys, such as *Pokemon* or Lego. Besides, students should be responsible for their own toys and their other property such as money as well.
Play Nicely	During recess, students should play with each other nicely. Also, students cannot go out to play until they get permission from the Chinese-language teacher.
Parental Involvement Welcome!	Parents are very welcome to participate in each meeting at school. Also, if possible, parents might spend some time working on Chinese with their children.

Appendix C: Letter to Parents

(This letter should be on school letterhead if possible)
September 4, 2007
Concerned Parent
101 Richardson Street
Caucus, IA 50000

Dear Parent or Guardian:

Thanks for trusting me with your student in Chinese I. I look forward to an exciting and valuable year in this class and I hope that your student does too.

As you know, proficiency in foreign languages is a valuable asset in today's world. That is why this year in Chinese I, we will focus on: *(list three or four areas of focus in the class)*

In order to accomplish those goals, I have established a set of guidelines concerning my expectations for homework, grading, and classroom behavior.

Please ask your child to review those expectations with you so that you may be aware of them as well.

You may be wondering what you can do to ensure your child's success, even if you have never studied a language other than English. Here are a few pointers that you can use at home with your student:

1. Ask your student what he or she remembers about the day's lesson. Have him or her explain the highlights.
2. Quiz your student. You can always give the English for a word and ask for its equivalent in Chinese.
3. Ask your student to teach you what he or she is learning. Teaching others is often an excellent way to learn.
4. Ask to see your student's quizzes, homework, and tests to note his or her progress. Don't expect perfection; mistakes are a necessary part of learning another language.
5. Compliment your student's progress in the language.

If you would like other hints and or suggestions on how to help your student learn Chinese, or if you notice that your student is struggling, please do not hesitate to contact me by phone (*give number*), e-mail, or in writing.

Remember that we both have your student's achievement as our priority.

In fact, you can help your student earn his or her first "A" in this class by writing and signing a short note to me that states that you have read this letter. It is the first homework assignment in Chinese I.

Thanks again for sending me your student. I look forward to our time together and to meeting you during the course of the school year.

Sincerely,

Ms. Ruby Lee
Upper Skunk River High School
Caucus, IA 50000

Notes on Contributors

T. Richard Chi is Professor of Chinese Language and Linguistics in the Department of Languages and Literature at the University of Utah. He does research in second language acquisition, teaching Chinese as a second language, curriculum model development, and instructional and assessment strategies. Professor Chi served as Department Chair from 1998 to 2004 and as Director of the Chinese School at Middlebury College from 1993 to 2002. He has conducted numerous workshops on the OPI and proficiency-based language instruction and assessment. He has also participated in research and material development projects for ACTFL, the Center for Applied Linguistics, the U.S. Department of Education, the Army Defense Language Institute, the National Foreign Language Center at the University of Maryland, and the College Board. Currently, he is College Board Advisor for AP Chinese and has served on the AP Chinese Development Committee since 2006.

Matthew B. Christensen is an Associate Professor of Chinese at Brigham Young University in Provo, Utah, where he has been teaching since 1995. His primary research is in Chinese language pedagogy. He is co-author of the books *Performed Culture: An Approach to East Asian Language Pedagogy,* with J Paul Warnick, and *A Performance-based Pedagogy for Communicating in Cultures: Training Teachers for East Asian Languages,* with Mari Noda. Other research interests include curriculum development, second language acquisition, and Chinese discourse analysis and pragmatics. Christensen has been involved with teaching training through regular courses he teachers, on-going TA training, and summer intensive teacher training programs at The Ohio State University and Brigham Young University. He is also the Associate Director of BYU's Chinese Flagship Center.

Michael E. Everson is an Associate Professor of Foreign Language Education at the University of Iowa. As such, he oversees undergraduate- and graduate-level programs in foreign language education, supervising one of the few K–12 Chinese teacher certification programs in the United States. He taught Chinese for ten years at the U.S. Air Force Academy and has published widely about how American students learn to read in Chinese. A two-time member of the Board of Directors of the Chinese Language Teachers Association, Professor Everson has presented workshops on a variety of topics involving Chinese language research and pedagogy and is active in a variety of strategic initiatives designed to expand K–12 Chinese language education in the United States.

Cynthia Ning is Associate Director of the Center for Chinese Studies at the University of Hawaii, as well as co-director of its Confucius Institute. She is also currently executive director of the U.S.-based international Chinese Language Teachers Association. She has written two sets of materials for Chinese language learning: *Communicating in Chinese* (beginning level) and *Exploring in Chinese* (intermediate level), both published by Yale University Press, and is working with the Press on a major new project to produce media-driven materials for learning Chinese. Her research interests and occasional teaching assignments focus on Chinese language pedagogy, Chinese film, and cross-cultural humor.

Leslie L. Schrier is an associate professor of foreign language and ESL education at the University of Iowa, where she works with pre-service foreign language and ESL teachers and teaches graduate courses in second language curriculum design and research methodologies used in teacher education. From 1990-1998, she was the Teacher Education Director for the Iowa Critical Languages Program. She is the founding president of the ACTFL special interest group on Teacher Development and is a member of the MLA Committee on Honors and Awards. From 2007–2008, she was the guest editor for *Hispania*, the journal of the American Association of Teachers of Spanish and Portuguese. She is currently principal investigator for Project RELEVANCE, a professional development project meeting the needs of in-service teachers working with English language learners. Her research interests are policy, planning, and procedures related to second language teacher development.

Madeline K. Spring (Ph.D., University of Washington) is Professor of Chinese at Arizona State University, where she serves as Director of the ASU Chinese Language Flagship Partner Program, Director of the ASU Confucius Institute, Co-Director of the Linguistics and Language Programs, and Director of the Chinese Language Program in the School of International Letters and Cultures. From January 2006 to August 2007 she was Academic Director of the Chinese K–16 Language Flagship Program at the University of Oregon. Her research interests lie in two main areas: Chinese language pedagogy (specifically, second language acquisition, teacher training, and literacy development) and medieval Chinese literature. Author of the multi-level textbook entitled *Making Connections: Improve Your Listening Comprehension in Chinese*, she has offered workshops nationwide on K–16 curricular articulation, technology-enhanced language learning, learning strategies, and issues in assessment.

Xiaohong Sharon Wen is an Associate Professor of Chinese. Her research interests include second language acquisition and Chinese language education. She has published more than 20 articles in refereed journals and books in the United States, Europe, and Asia. Her most recent book is *Studies of Chinese Language Acquisition by English Speakers: from Theories to Practice,* published by Peking University Press in 2008. As the Director of the Chinese program at the University of Houston, she has established the B.A. degree and the Minor in Chinese Studies, as well as a study abroad program that takes student to study in China every year. She is on the Boards of Directors of the Association of International Chinese Language Education (世界汉语教学学会), Chinese Language Teachers Association (CLTA), and CLTA-TX.

Yun Xiao is Associate Professor and Chair of the Modern Languages Department at Bryant University. Her research interests are second language acquisition and pedagogy, heritage language learning, and Chinese teacher education. Her recent publications include more than twenty articles and book chapters. She is the Primary author of *Readings in Chinese Literature Series* (Volume 1, 2007; Volume 2, forthcoming); co-author/co-editor of *Chinese as a Heritage Language: Fostering Rooted World Citizenry* (2008), (with Weiyun He), Honolulu, HI: University of Hawaii, National Foreign Language Resource Center.

Tianwei Tim Xie, Ph.D. in Foreign Language Education from the University of Pittsburgh (1992), has taught Chinese at the University of Pittsburgh, UC Davis, and University of San Francisco, and he is currently the Associate Professor at the Department of Asian and Asian American Studies at California State University, Long Beach. He has served on the Board of the Directors of the Chinese Language Teachers Association, Chinese SAT Committee and he is currently the CLTA Newsletter editor. His publications include books and papers on socio-linguistics, second language acquisition and his special interest:using computers for teaching and learning Chinese. His web site "Learning Chinese Online" http://learningchineseonline.net is one of the most popular web sites among Chinese teachers and learners.

Tao-chung Ted Yao is Professor of Chinese in the Department of East Asian Languages and Literatures at the University of Hawaii. He has a Ph.D. in Chinese Language and Culture from the University of Arizona. He is co-director of the Confucius Institute at the University of Hawaii. He is also a Vice President of the International Society for Chinese Language Teaching (世界汉语教学学会), and Chief Reader for AP Chinese.